100 Habits

OF SUCCESSFUL PUBLICATION DESIGNERS

Insider Secrets for **Working Smart** and **Staying Creative**

LAUREL SAVILLE

To the Little Falls Library
October 2009
L A Sa

ROCKPORT PUBLISHERS
BEVERLY MASSACHUSETTS

First published in the United States of America by
Rockport Publishers, a member of
Quayside Publishing Group
100 Cummings Center
Suite 406-L
Beverly, Massachusetts 01915-6101
Telephone: (978) 282-9590
Fax: (978) 283-2742
www.rockpub.com

Library of Congress Cataloging-in-Publication Data
Saville, Laurel.
100 habits of successful publication designers : insider secrets for working smart and staying creative / Laurel Saville.
p. cm.
ISBN 1-59253-444-9
1. Graphic design (Typography) I. Title. II. Title: One hundred habits of successful publication designers.

Z246.S25 2008
686.2'2–dc22

2008005808
CIP

ISBN-13: 978-1-59253-444-9
ISBN-10: 1-59253-444-9

10 9 8 7 6 5 4 3 2 1

Design: Kathie Alexander

Printed in Singapore

***Pol Oxygen*, designed by Marcus Piper**

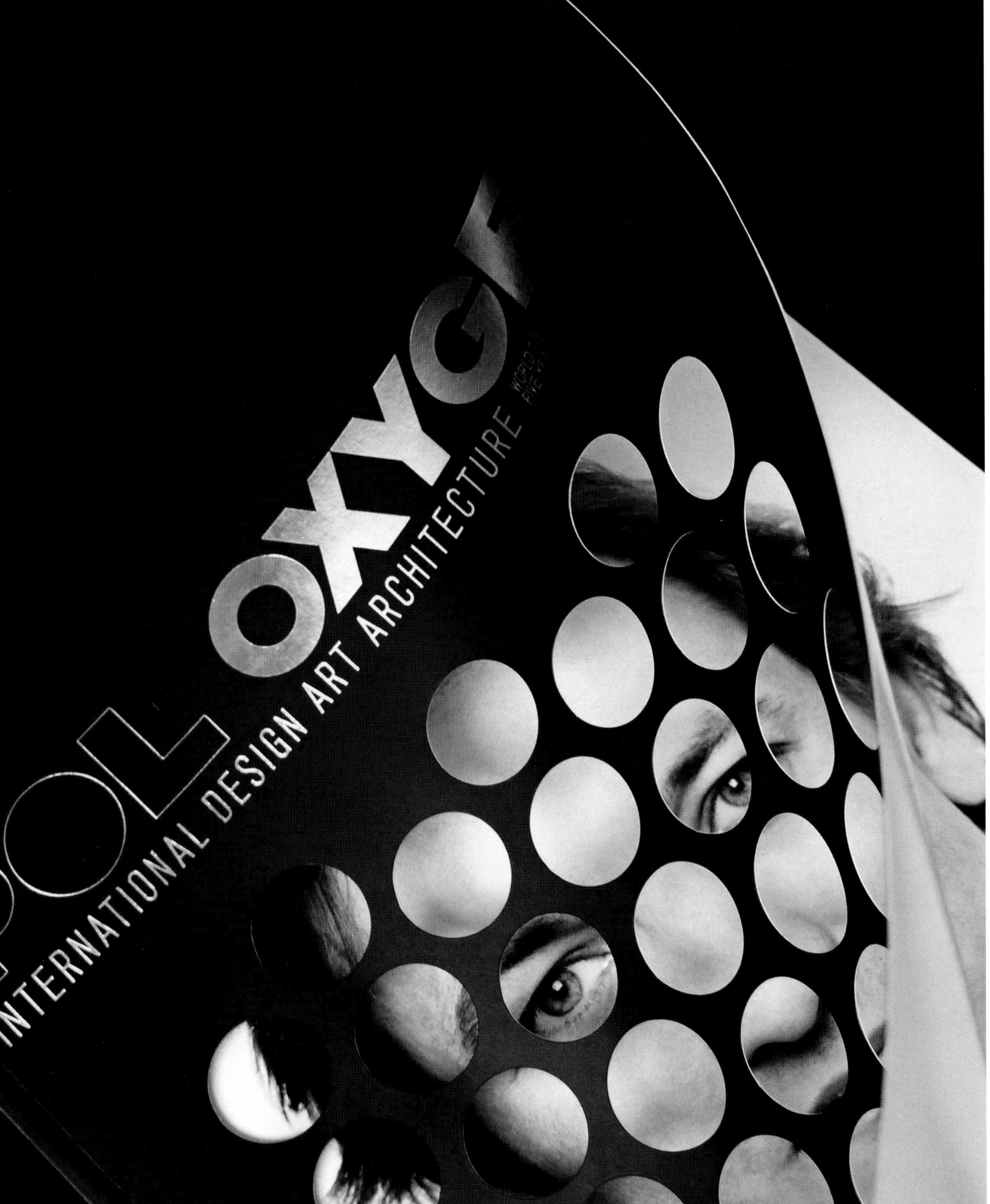
OXYGEN
INTERNATIONAL DESIGN ART ARCHITECTURE

Glenn Scott Photography

CONTENTS

INTRODUCTION

Like all graphic designers, publication designers love wrangling type and image into something engaging, pleasing, and aesthetically coherent on the page. But designers who devote much of their professional life to books, magazines, and newspapers take this interest one step further—they are fascinated by what the words and images actually say. Publication designers are committed to reading what they're given to design and turning it into something that will entice other people to read it as well. They are enchanted with the process of making something that has dimension and weight, and they enjoy imagining the commuter on the train, the couple on vacation, the visitor at the museum, the person relaxing with a cup of coffee on a Sunday morning picking up what they've made, turning the pages, engaging intellectually with what's in their hands, and, after a few minutes or hours, finding himself a better informed, perhaps even more interesting person for having done so.

Those most successful in this endeavor, whether they're making a little literary journal or a mainstream, wide-circulation magazine, see themselves as custodians of the work that writers, editors, illustrators, photographers, and artists have entrusted to their care. They express a remarkable degree of humility and deference in the face of what someone else has made and spend much of their day using their creative skills in service to the output of other creative minds. In the following pages, more than thirty designers, illustrators, editors, and writers freely share their insights, ideas, lessons learned, and satisfactions achieved while making reading material for a voracious world. Each expert brings a unique perspective to what makes a publication designer successful.

avant garb
ONE OF FASHION'S QUIETEST ACHIEVERS, LONDON DESIGNER HUSSEIN CHALAYAN CREATES CLOTHING
WITH A SCULPTURAL AESTHETIC, DRAWING FROM ARCHITECTURE, ENGINEERING AND EVEN POLITICS.
37 // SOCIAL FABRIC
WORDS // CAIA HAGEL
PORTRAIT // JULIAN ANDERSON
industrial
AT THE KORTRIJK INTERIEUR BIEN
VISITORS HAD TO PEER THROUGH
TO SEE KONSTANTIN GRCI

Pol Oxygen **is an Australian-based international magazine of design, art, and architecture. As art directed by Marcus Piper, its pages reveal the designer's appreciation for the form, function, and dimensionality of publications.**

THE EXPERTS

Make magazine, designed by Albertson Design

DAVID **ALBERTSON**, WWW.ALBERTSONDESIGN.COM

David Albertson founded Albertson Design in 1995. There he leads a diverse range of projects from new magazine launches to large-scale identity and brand communications efforts. Albertson Design developed the launch of *Make* and *Craft* magazines as well as created the identity for the Aspen Art Museum and an annual report for HP.

JAMES **BENNET**, WWW.THEATLANTIC.COM

Before joining the *Atlantic* staff, James Bennet was the Jerusalem bureau chief for the *New York Times*. During his three years in Israel, his coverage of the Middle East conflict was widely acclaimed for its balance and sensitivity. Bennet, a graduate of Yale University, began his journalism career at the *Washington Monthly*. Prior to his work in Jerusalem, he served as the *Times'* White House correspondent.

VICTOR **BURTON**, VICTOR@VICTORBURTON.COM.BR

Victor Burton is director of Victor Burton Design Gráfico Ltda, in Rio de Janeiro, Brazil, which principally is involved in editorial and environmental design. He began his career working for the Franco Maria Ricci publishing house in Milan, Italy, where he created his first book covers. He has completed more than 2,500 book covers and 180 luxury book projects. He was twice awarded by the Bienal de Design Gráfico and won the National Book Chamber of Brazil Prize for best book cover eight times.

CASEY **CAPLOWE**, WWW.GOODMAGAZINE.COM

Casey Caplowe is the creative director and cofounder of *GOOD*, a magazine about the people, ideas, and institutions driving change in the world. *GOOD* was named one of the hottest magazine launches of 2006 by Media Industry Newsletter and Mr. Magazine. *GOOD* is expanding its coverage of the Web, video, live events, and feature and documentary films. Caplowe was instrumental in developing the editorial vision as well as the look and feel of the *GOOD* brand, and he helped create the Choose *GOOD* Campaign, which donates every $20 (US) subscription fee to a nonprofit organization of the subscriber's choice.

ROBERTO **DE VICQ DE CUMPTICH**, WWW.DEVICQ.COM

Roberto de Vicq de Cumptich is from Rio de Janeiro, Brazil. He received his MFA from the Pratt Institute and, after ten years in branding, Web, and magazine design, he began working primarily with publishing houses in New York, first as creative director for Random House and then HarperCollins. He now has his own design studio where he develops an array of projects, from branding to typeface design. He has received numerous design awards, and his book, *Bembo's Zoo*, written for his daughter, was a finalist for the Newbery Award. He lectures and speaks frequently on design topics.

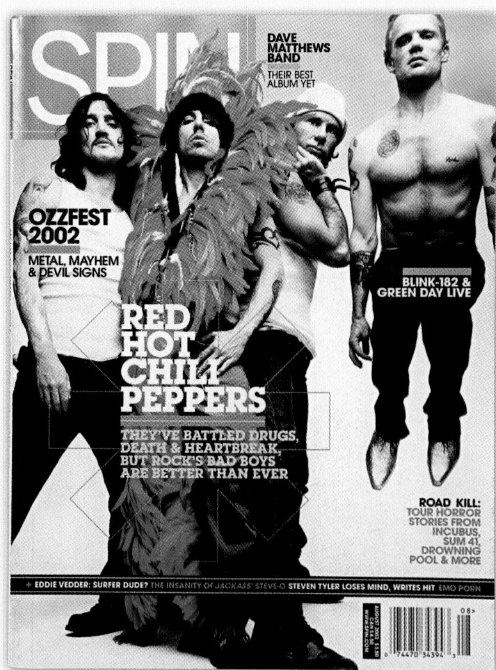

Spin magazine, art directed by Arem Duplessis

MAYA **DROZDZ**, WWW.VISUALINGUAL.ORG

Maya Drozdz received her BA in philosophy and critical theory from Cornell University and her MFA in 2-D design from Cranbrook Academy of Art. Her interests center on graphic design theory, particularly its intersection with popular culture and the urban environment. Her professional experience includes identity, print, interaction, and environmental design, as well as teaching, lecturing, writing, and curating design exhibits worldwide. She is a partner at the all-media design consultancy VisuaLingual.

NICOLE **DUDKA**, WWW.TRIBUNE.COM

Nicole Dudka joined the *Chicago Tribune* as an art director in 2006 after working at the *Hartford Courant*, where her work was honored by the Society for News Design and *Print* magazine. A graduate of Ball State University, she has a fondness for white space and insists that everyone looks better in high contrast.

ROB **DUNLAVEY**, WWW.ROBD.COM

Rob Dunlavey's editorial illustrations have appeared in many magazines and newspapers, from the *Wall Street Journal* and the *Los Angeles Times* to *Business Week* and *Better Homes & Gardens*. He also created illustrations for children's museums and has collaborated with Motion Theory on television commercials for HP. Dunlavey attended art classes at the Art Institute of Chicago and Southern Illinois University and received a master's degree in sculpture from Claremont Graduate University.

AREM **DUPLESSIS**, WWW.NYTIMES.COM

Arem Duplessis is the art director of the *New York Times Magazine*. He has held design director and art director positions at various magazines including *Spin*, *GQ* and *Blaze*. He has received numerous awards for his editorial design work and was nominated for a National Magazine Award in Design from the American Society of Magazine Editors in 2004. Duplessis has also judged and captained many design competitions.

JESSICA **FLEISHMANN**, WWW.STILL-ROOM.COM

After working as a chef and arts administrator, Jessica Fleischmann got an MFA in graphic design at California Institute of the Arts. She founded her own studio, still room, in the front room of her Echo Park home in 2006. Previously, she was design associate with Lorraine Wild and art director of *Western Interiors and Design* magazine.

VINCE **FROST**, WWW.FROSTDESIGN.COM.AU

Formerly an associate director at Pentagram's London office, Frost started his own design firm in 1994 and eventually moved it to Sydney, Australia. He has worked for a wide variety of clients, including the Sydney Opera House, Rizzoli Books, Tourism NT, Deutsche Bank, Mushroom Records, and various publications.

JASON **GODFREY**, WWW.GODFREYDESIGN.CO.UK

Jason Godfrey started Godfrey Design in 2002 in London. He has designed books for publishers Laurence King, Dorling Kindersley, and Pavilion as well as artists' catalogs and other handmade books. He has also designed stamps for the Royal Mail and the literary magazine *Beat*. He also worked at Pentagram in London and Eric Baker Design Associates in New York.

CARIN **GOLDBERG**, WWW.CARINGOLDBERG.COM

Carin Goldberg studied at the Cooper Union School of Art. She began her career as a staff designer at CBS Television, CBS Records, and Atlantic Records before establishing her own firm, Carin Goldberg Design, in 1982. Goldberg has designed hundreds of book jackets for all the major American publishing houses, as well as dozens of album covers for leading record labels. In recent years, her image-making expertise has expanded to publication design and brand consulting for clients including AR and Martha Stewart Living Omnimedia. From 2003 to 2004, she was also creative director at Time Inc. Custom Publishing.

LUKE **HAYMAN**, WWW.PENTAGRAM.COM

Luke Hayman studied graphic design at Central/St. Martin's School of Art in London. He has been design director of *New York* magazine, creative director of *Travel + Leisure* magazine, design director for *I.D.*, and the creative director of Media Central and Brill Media Holdings. In addition, he was senior partner and associate creative director in the Brand Integration Group in the New York office of Ogilvy & Mather. Hayman's editorial design work has been given highest honors by every major design association in the United States and in England. He joined Pentagram's New York office as partner in December 2006.

STEVEN **HELLER**, WWW.HELLERBOOKS.COM

Steven Heller is a designer, educator, and writer. The author, coauthor, or editor of more than 100 books on design and popular culture, Heller was an art director at the *New York Times* for more than thirty years, where he also writes reviews and obituaries. He is the founder and cochair of the MFA Designer as Author program at the School of Visual Arts, where he lectures on the history of graphic design. He is a contributing editor to *Print*, *Eye*, *Baseline*, and *I.D.* magazines, and editor at the *AIGA Journal of Graphic Design* and *AIGA VOICE: Online Journal of Design*.

ARTHUR **HOCHSTEIN**, WWW.TIME.COM

Arthur Hochstein is the art director at *Time* magazine. After studying journalism at the University of Missouri, Hochstein held a number of editing and design jobs at small publications. He began at *Time* as a freelancer and worked in a variety of roles prior to being named art director in January 1994. His work has been honored by the Society of Publications Designers, the Art Directors Club of New York and other organizations.

NICKI **KALISH**, WWW.NYTIMES.COM

Nicki Kalish is art director of the dining section of the *New York Times*, where she has been a designer since 1974. Kalish graduated from the Connecticut College for Women and received a BFA and a MFA in graphic design from Yale University.

ANITA **KUNZ**, WWW.ANITAKUNZ.COM

Anita Kunz has spent the last three decades making pictures for publishers in many countries. Predominately an editorial illustrator for the *New Yorker*, *Rolling Stone*, *Fortune*, *Time*, and many others, she also teaches, lectures, and has been involved with various advocacy organizations. Her paintings and sculptures have appeared in a number of solo shows in the United States and abroad, and she has won many awards. She was named one of the fifty most influential women in Canada by the *National Post*, Ontario, Canada.

Illustration for *Time* magazine, by Anita Kunz

KALLE **LASN**, WWW.ADBUSTERS.ORG

Kalle Lasn was born in Estonia during the middle of World War II. He and his family lived in a displaced persons' camp for five years before immigrating to Australia, where he received a B.S. in pure and applied mathematics. He worked in a variety of fields, including computer-simulated war games, market research, and documentary filmmaking. When mainstream media refused to run his spots about the disappearing old-growth forests of the Pacific Northwest, he launched *Adbusters* magazine, which was eventually followed by the Powershift Advertising Agency, and social marketing campaigns such as Buy Nothing Day and TV Turnoff Week.

JEREMY **LESLIE**, WWW.JOHNBROWNGROUP.CO.UK

Jeremy Leslie is executive creative director at John Brown Publishing in London. Previously, he ran his own studio, working for clients including *Blitz* magazine and *The Guardian*. Jeremy also spent three years as group art director at *Time Out*. He is a passionate advocate of editorial design, regularly contributing to the creative press and to design conferences on the subject. He is one of the three founders of the biannual independent magazine conference, Colophon—which launched in 2007 in Luxembourg—and has written two books on magazine design: *Issues* and *magCulture*. His blog can be read at www.magculture.com.

IdN magazine, published by Laurence Ng

ADAM **MACHACEK**, WWW.WELCOMETO.AS

Adam Machacek and Sebastien Bohner met while working as design interns at Studio Dumbar in The Hague, The Netherlands. They established their design firm, Welcometo.as in 2004 in Lausanne, Switzerland, and have worked on a variety of publications including magazines, exhibition catalogs, and theater programs. Machacek has an MA from the Academy of Arts in Prague and was the recipient of a design fellowship at Chronicle Books.

BRETT **MACFADDEN**, WWW.BRETTMACFADDEN.COM

Brett MacFadden first worked for Chronicle Books in San Francisco as an intern in 1999 and in 2002 joined the in-house team, acquiring a wife, many good friends, and no small number of book projects as designer and art director. In 2008, he opened his own design studio, also in San Francisco. He holds an MFA from the Cranbrook Academy of Art.

LAURENCE **NG**, WWW.IDNWORLD.COM

Laurence Ng began his career in the graphic arts industry by providing color separations and color correcting services. He founded *IdN* magazine in 1992 and was a pioneer in using desktop publishing technologies in a commercially viable manner. Today, *IdN* is an "international publication for creative people, devoted to bringing designers from around the globe together to communicate with, learn from, and inspire one another."

ARJEN **NOORDEMAN**, WWW.ELASTICBRAND.NET

Arjen Noordeman was born and raised in The Netherlands and studied graphic design at the Hogeschool voor de Kunsten in Arnhem. He received his MFA in 2-D design from Cranbrook Academy of Art, where he met his wife, Christie Wright. After working in various arenas of design, Nooredman and Wright founded the New York–based multidisciplinary studio, Elasticbrand, in 2006.

MARCUS **PIPER**, WWW.MARCUSPIPER.COM

Marcus Piper studied product design and then brought this functional, 3-D approach to the printed page, focusing on the interaction between the user and the product. This approach is evident in his work for *Pol Oxygen* magazine and *Crafts* (the British Crafts Council Magazine), which incorporate tactility and handcrafted elements. Under his art direction, *Pol Oxygen* has been awarded five consecutive Golds for best magazine by the Folio awards, and was named Magazine of the Year—the first Australian magazine to receive this honor—from the Society of Publication Designers.

Morf magazine, designed by Office of CC

MICHAEL **RAY**, WWW.ALL-STORY.COM

Michael Ray is the editor of *Zoetrope: All-Story*, a literary and art quarterly published by Francis Ford Coppola, as well as a screenwriter. Ray's film, *The Princess of Nebraska*, debuted at the 2007 Toronto Film Festival and is being distributed by Magnolia Pictures.

GRIM **REAPER**, WWW.MAGAZINEDEATHPOOL.COM

Grim Reaper is the hooded and scythe-bearing keeper of the blog *Magazine Death Pool*, which tracks the demise of "the golden age of magazines" and is dedicated to "those magazines that look like they may be joining that Great Trashbin in the Sky, polybagged onto the River Styx, with blow-in cards a one-way ticket to oblivion."

MARTHA **RICH**, WWW.MARTHARICH.COM

Martha Rich lived the typical suburban life until, just short of a picket fence and 2.5 children, her average American life unraveled. To cope with divorce, fate led her to an illustration class taught by the Clayton brothers. They persuaded her to ditch the pantyhose, quit her human resources job, and join the world of art. She has since created illustrations for *Rolling Stone*, *Entertainment Weekly*, *The Village Voice*, *Jane*, and many others. She graduated from Art Center College of Design, where she also teaches, and is currently based in Pasadena, obsessively painting underwear, wigs, lobsters, and Loretta Lynn.

EDEL **RODRIGUEZ**, WWW.EDELRODRIGUEZ.COM

Edel Rodriguez was born in Havana, Cuba. He received a BFA in painting from Pratt Institute and an MFA from Hunter College. He utilizes a variety of materials to create work that ranges from conceptual to portraiture and landscape. In addition to editorial work for numerous publications, including the *New Yorker*, *Time*, *Rolling Stone*, *Texas Monthly*, *Playboy*, *National Geographic Traveler*, the *New York Times*, *Fortune*, *The Nation*, and *Vibe*, he has also illustrated three children's books and created a stamp for the U.S. Postal Service. His illustrations have been widely recognized and received many awards.

JANDOS **ROTHSTEIN**, WWW.JANDOS.COM

Jandos Rothstein is an assistant professor at George Mason University and design director of *Governing* magazine. He has redesigned or helped launch more than twelve magazines and newspapers and writes regularly about design and social issues for a number of publications, including *Print* magazine, *The Design Journal*, *Voice: The AIGA Journal of Design*, and the *Washington City Paper*. He is the author of the magazine design blog www.designingmagazines.com and the book *Designing Magazines*.

INA **SALTZ**, WWW.BODYTYPEBOOK.COM

Ina Saltz is an art director, designer, writer, photographer, and associate professor of art at the City College of New York in the Electronic Design and Multimedia Program. Her areas of expertise are typography and magazine design. She's also a regular columnist for *STEP Inside Design* and writes for other design magazines, including *Graphis* and *How*. For more than twenty years, she was an editorial design director at *Time*, *Worth*, *Golf*, and other publications. Ina also lectures at Stanford University's Publishing Course and wrote a book, *Body Type: Intimate Messages Etched in Flesh*, documenting typographic tattoos.

TODD **SIMMONS**, WWW.WOLVERINEFARMPUBLISHING.ORG

Todd Simmons lives in Fort Collins, Colorado, where he runs Wolverine Farm Publishing, a nonprofit, volunteer bookstore, literary magazine, publishing house, and special events organization. He and his wife and son "are trying to find a run-down house that can easily be converted into a large book, one to read the rest of their lives." Todd is also working on a book about bicycles.

Red magazine, designed by Agnes Zeilstra

SCOTT **STOWELL**, WWW.NOTCLOSED.COM

Proprietor of the design studio Open, Scott Stowell was formerly art director at Benneton's *Colors* magazine in Rome, Italy, and a senior designer at M&Co. He has a BFA in graphic design from the Rhode Island School of Design and teaches at Yale University and the School of Visual Arts.

JASON **TREAT**, WWW.THEATLANTIC.COM

Jason Treat has been the art director for the *Atlantic* since December 2005. He previously served as the art director for Atlantic Media Company's creative services, designing in-house creative for the *Atlantic*, *National Journal*, *Government Executive*, *Hotline*, and other publications.

CHRIS **VERMAAS**, VER@XS4ALL.NL

After traveling for many years around the world, Chin-Lien Chen from Taiwan and Chris H. Vermaas from The Netherlands founded their own design studio, Office of CC, in Amsterdam, where they specialize in identities, infographics, signage systems, and books. In addition, Office of CC has written many articles on design issues, and Vermaas has taught at several schools around the world. He is currently head of the graduate program of MaHKU's Editorial Design, lectures at the AKI-academy, and is a visiting professor at the University of Twente and the Plantin Institute in Antwerp. Chen and Vermass "have two kids, who do not have the intention of becoming designers."

MICHAEL **WORTHINGTON**, WWW.COUNTERSPACE.NET

Michael Worthington has taught in the graphic design program at the California Institute of the Arts since 1995. He is the founder of Counterspace, a Los Angeles design studio specializing in editorial and identity projects for cultural clients.

AGNES **ZEILSTRA**, WWW.REDMAGAZINE.CO.UK

Agnes Zeilstra lives in Monnickendam, The Netherlands. She graduated from the Arnhem Academy in graphic design and worked as a graphic designer for a Dutch fashion brand in Amsterdam before joining the staff of *Red*, a woman's fashion magazine that is part of Hachette Filipacchi media.

Chapter One:

UNDERSTANDING PUBLICATIONS

According to Chris Vermaas the client for the secondhand-car journal, *AutoPrijswijzer*, told him, "'Leave the fashionable typographic tricks at home in your drawers.' He didn't want to win design awards, he didn't want to end up in the museum—these were his own words—he wanted to make a graphic tool that serves a need, reaches an audience, and generates a lot of money." All of which this publication did.

1

READ THE CONTENT

JEREMY **LESLIE**

STEVEN **HELLER**

INA **SALTZ**

The fundamental difference between publication design and other forms of graphic design is the primacy of content. Sure, if you're designing a brochure you have to understand the company you're working for, or if you're doing an album cover you should listen to the music. But most publications live, die, and are driven by words—lots of words—and a publication designer's audience is first and foremost a reader. So the designer must be as well.

Successful publication designers say familiarizing themselves with content is the most important activity they do. Jeremy Leslie, creative director at John Brown Publishing in London and author of the *MagCulture* blog, says, "The first thing is to read the stuff you're laying out. It sounds natural, but there are people who don't." Designer, educator, and writer Steven Heller echoes this exhortation. "There's a whole generation that's not reading anymore, not just designers," he says. "But it's really simple: If you get a manuscript, you should read it. If you don't read the whole thing, you won't know what's going on, you won't get the nuances, and it will come back to bite you. There are times when you read something and it's boring, but even that is something you have to know if you're a designer."

And when reading, don't just look for word count or line length. "There are people who just flow in the words," says Leslie. "That's not design, that's filling up space." It's important to absorb, understand, and respect the work of the author. As Ina Saltz, an educator and designer, notes, "What differentiates editorial designers from others is that they care deeply about the content. Otherwise, they should go work someplace else where images drive things."

Left and opposite: When Virgin Atlantic Airlines developed an on-board magazine, *Carlos*, they needed a publication that reflected the hipness of their brand. John Brown Publishing and creative director Jeremy Leslie developed a magazine that was full of style and substance, with features about celebrities appearing alongside reports from around the globe.

2

CONTENT INFORMS DESIGN; DESIGN YIELDS TO CONTENT

LUKE **HAYMAN**

INA **SALTZ**

STEVEN **HELLER**

KALLE **LASN**

JEREMY **LESLIE**

Experienced and effective publication designers try to enhance what's being communicated by the editorial mission of the magazine and what's being written in each specific article. Luke Hayman, partner at Pentagram and designer of such iconic magazines as *New York*, says it most simply: "Always defer to the content to drive the design." This doesn't mean that design is any less important to the overall, finished piece, but that design performs a slightly different function in publications than in, say, packaging. "Visuals are important," notes Ina Saltz, "but they are less important than the marriage of visuals and content. Being a magazine art director is all about enhancing the content and becoming a visual journalist."

Taking on this role is anything but a passive stance. In fact, the best designs come from using the content to inspire, inform, and improve design. "The thing that sparks my imagination is the content," says Saltz. Steven Heller agrees. "Let your mind make connections as you read," he suggests. "It's kind of a mystery where the inspiration will crop up. But you know when you look at a design that really works, that the designer really understood the concept and the content. And, likewise, you can tell when they were just following the template." Jeremy Leslie suggests thinking of design as one member of a three-part team: "The big difference in magazine design is that you are working with content. You have the images and the words, and the designer is the third element on the page, who has to work with everything there. Even if the reader is not design-savvy, he should subconsciously know that the design has added something to the page and to the understanding of the content."

This is no small responsibility. Kalle Lasn, founder of *Adbusters* magazine, feels that designers need to recognize and then embrace the impact their work can have. "I think that designers are some of the most powerful people in the world, if only they'd wake up to that fact," he says. "They don't create the content, write the words, or come up with the concepts, but they are the people who take those concepts, words, ideas, and shape them, give a tone to them, create an aesthetic around them, and decide what's important. Designers set the mood and the tone of our culture."

COVER STAR

NICOLE KIDMAN

AN APPRECIATION

BY

RYAN GILBEY

12

WHEN SHE ARRIVED IN HOLLYWOOD, NICOLE KIDMAN WAS JUST MRS TOM CRUISE. NOW – AFTER THE DIVORCE, THE OSCAR AND ALL THE RUMOURS – SHE'S ABOUT TO STAR AS A CLONED HOUSEWIFE IN 'THE STEPFORD WIVES', SHE'S THE MOST POWERFUL ACTRESS IN THE INDUSTRY, AND SHE'S THE FACE OF CHANEL. SO JUST HOW DID SHE PULL IT OFF?

ILLUSTRATED BY

JO RATCLIFFE

CITY STORIES

Local news from our global correspondents

ILLUSTRATED BY
JONATHAN SCHOFIELD

06

JOHANNESBURG

STARS IN STRIPES – THE SWANKA SHOWDOWN

As a chilly Highveld darkness settles over Johannesburg, a group of Zulu men congregate outside Jeppe Men's Hostel. Some sing traditional Zulu gospel songs in harmony. Others exchange conversation. They call themselves Swankas.

Every Saturday night, these poor, migrant workers come here to compete against each other for an unusual honour: that of best-dressed man. Dingaan Zulu is one of them. During the week, he wears dusty blue overalls and a hard hat when he works a jackhammer on Johannesburg's demolition sites. But on Saturdays he swanks, transforming himself into a dandyish city gentleman.

"Altogether I have about 13 suits, but there are only nine that I am entirely confident about," he says proudly. Tonight he is wearing a pin-striped, tailor-made suit. On his feet are shiny black and white brogues. Expertly knotted around his neck is a pink tie. With matching socks. It's an ensemble that he hopes will win him the weekly prize of R100 (about £7). It is not the money that keeps the Swankas coming here each week. Instead, they say they are after far greater riches: honour and pride.

Dingaan Zulu and his fellow Swankas move into the ramshackle hostel basement, which houses a makeshift catwalk. Audience members are trickling in, taking their seats to watch the weekly swank-off. The men make sure to avoid the piles of rubbish and junk lying scattered across the hostel floor. They don't want to dirty their Italian leather shoes or soil the hems of their carefully chosen suits. In the harsh, bright light of the hostel basement, these men resemble preening peacocks, shiny, colourful and proud. They are here to show off. "You need to make sure others see you looking good," Dingaan says, smoothing his tie.

"When we speak of Swankas we speak of those who dress well, who wear the latest suits and model before the judges. These are gentlemen who are well dressed in the Western way and like to show off their attire," says one regular audience member. Judging a winner is serious business. To ensure impartiality and objectivity, organisers pluck a stranger from the dark Johannesburg streets. Once the rules are explained, he sits down with a pen and paper, and spends the rest of the night judging.

One after the other, Dingaan and his fellow competitors swank before the judge, who quickly learns to take this as seriously as the Swankas take it. No mirth allowed. Sartorial honour is at stake. The men perform elaborate modelling moves before him with presentation, style and detail all important. They tip their trilbies. Smooth their silk ties. Twang their braces. Finger their buttons. Flick their cuffs. Twirl around on their walking sticks. Flourish patterned silk handkerchiefs from finely stitched pockets. It is an astounding and mesmerising show.

Swanking has been going on nearly every Saturday in Johannesburg since the Fifties. It began when migrant workers, who mostly lived in single-sex hostels, returned home for their annual Christmas visit. They would parade in their best clothes to the villagers to measure their success, having practised and performed beforehand in the hostels. More than half a century later, the tradition still lives on in Johannesburg's migrant community.

Dingaan Zulu has been swanking for years now, spending much of his meagre income on clothes and accessories. He sends what is left back home to his family in rural Zululand. "The most expensive suit I've bought was R1500 (£105). On that day, when I left the store, tears came to my eyes. I thought, 'How can I spend so much on something I can't even eat?'"

But he does not regret his fashion extravagances because he has often won the weekly competitions. Swanking makes him feel like a man amongst men – migrant men who, for one evening a week, can forget about the harsh realities of modern city life.

ROBYN CURNOW

LONDON

SLEAZE: STYLE BITES BACK

Sleazenation is dead. Long live *Sleaze*. From the years 1995 to 2003, *Sleazenation* was a feisty, independently-published style magazine that took a side-on look at popular culture while flying the flag for the cutting-edge music, style, asymmetric haircuts and electroclash bootlegs generated in the clubs and bars of Shoreditch. That was until newly appointed editor Neil Boorman pulled the plug with a December 2003 issue bearing the letters RIP on an all-black cover. Rumours of its death proved exaggerated, however. A month later Boorman relaunched the magazine with a shortened name – just *Sleaze* – and a sharper attitude. The cover of the first issue showed a photo of Victoria Beckham in flames, reflecting Boorman's intention to abandon coverage of celebrity and "retail therapy" in favour of something angrier, edgier and paradoxically, more optimistic. "It's clear that we're heading towards a sterile monoculture but there's no point moaning on about it," he writes in his editorial. "We need to rebuild

07

***Make*, as designed by Albertson Design, has become more than a magazine. By tapping into the growing D.I.Y. culture, the brand has grown from a quarterly publication to include books, products, events, and a comprehensive website.**

3

DAVID **ALBERTSON**

ENJOY THE CONTENT

When comparing publication design to other forms of graphic design, David Albertson of San Francisco–based Albertson Design points to the profound impact working with interesting content makes. "Publications are deeper, richer pieces of communication, and in that sense, it's more fulfilling than, say, doing marketing communications materials," he explains. "The work derives from a personal vision as opposed to a business objective. Artistically it can be more rewarding because you're working with stories about people and current events, for instance. They're more rooted in the reality of what's actually going on, what's happening culturally, and it can be very rewarding to be involved with that kind of rich content." With the reward comes a responsibility to ensure the design lives up to the level of work that some other creative, engaged, dedicated person created. "Good graphic design," Alberston says, "makes a publication something that you don't want to get rid of. It gives it a kind of staying power. You can see where somebody has put a lot of effort into design, and that makes you want to buy the magazine and keep it. And really good graphic design can elevate content—can make great content even greater—if it's done in an ingenious and creative way that makes everybody, including the publisher, editor, writer, designer, and photographer look really smart." Design should have a multiplier effect, making everything it touches more than it would be standing on its own.

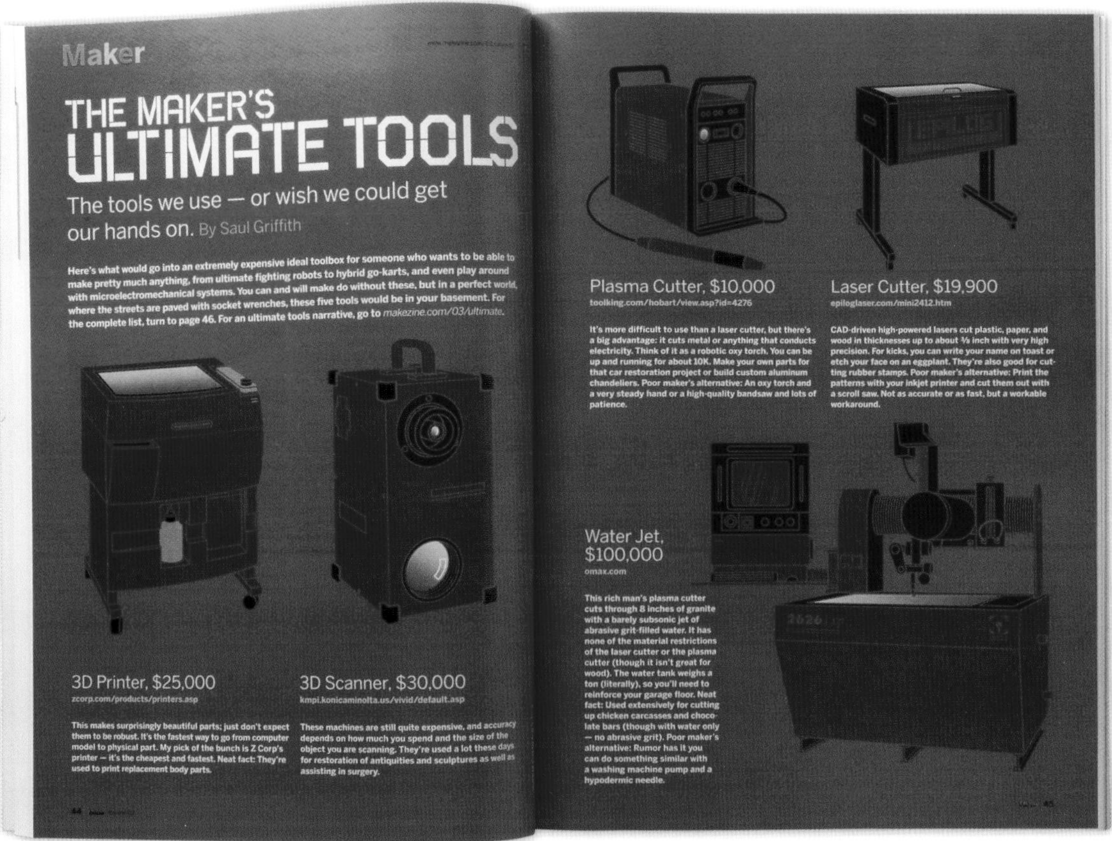

Maker

THE MAKER'S ULTIMATE TOOLS

The tools we use — or wish we could get our hands on. By Saul Griffith

Here's what would go into an extremely expensive ideal toolbox for someone who wants to be able to make pretty much anything, from ultimate fighting robots to hybrid go-karts, and even play around with microelectromechanical systems. You can and will make do without these, but in a perfect world, where the streets are paved with socket wrenches, these five tools would be in your basement. For the complete list, turn to page 46. For an ultimate tools narrative, go to *makezine.com/03/ultimate*.

3D Printer, $25,000
zcorp.com/products/printers.asp

This makes surprisingly beautiful parts; just don't expect them to be robust. It's the fastest way to go from computer model to physical part. My pick of the bunch is Z Corp's printer — it's the cheapest and fastest. Neat fact: They're used to print replacement body parts.

3D Scanner, $30,000
kmpi.konicaminolta.us/vivid/default.asp

These machines are still quite expensive, and accuracy depends on how much you spend and the size of the object you are scanning. They're used a lot these days for restoration of antiquities and sculptures as well as assisting in surgery.

Plasma Cutter, $10,000
toolking.com/hobart/view.asp?id=4276

It's more difficult to use than a laser cutter, but there's a big advantage: it cuts metal or anything that conducts electricity. Think of it as a robotic oxy torch. You can be up and running for about 10K. Make your own parts for that car restoration project or build custom aluminum chandeliers. Poor maker's alternative: An oxy torch and a very steady hand or a high-quality bandsaw and lots of patience.

Laser Cutter, $19,900
epiloglaser.com/mini2412.htm

CAD-driven high-powered lasers cut plastic, paper, and wood in thicknesses up to about ⅓ inch with very high precision. For kicks, you can write your name on toast or etch your face on an eggplant. They're also good for cutting rubber stamps. Poor maker's alternative: Print the patterns with your inkjet printer and cut them out with a scroll saw. Not as accurate or as fast, but a workable workaround.

Water Jet, $100,000
omax.com

This rich man's plasma cutter cuts through 8 inches of granite with a barely subsonic jet of abrasive grit-filled water. It has none of the material restrictions of the laser cutter or the plasma cutter (though it isn't great for wood). The water tank weighs a ton (literally), so you'll need to reinforce your garage floor. Neat fact: Used extensively for cutting up chicken carcasses and chocolate bars (though with water only — no abrasive grit). Poor maker's alternative: Rumor has it you can do something similar with a washing machine pump and a hypodermic needle.

4

ACCEPT THAT DESIGN CAN ONLY DO SO MUCH

AGNES **ZEILSTRA**

CASEY **CAPLOWE**

While design is powerful, magazines are—usually and primarily—meant to be read. And designers have little or no say over what's being written. When asked how she keeps the Dutch women's magazine *Red* interesting, designer Agnes Zeilstra says, "That question is more for the ones that write, and especially for the fashion people." She limits her responsibility to what she, as a designer, can control. "For me, it's important that we're up to date."

Because publication designers defer to content, they also have to make the best of what's provided. As Casey Caplowe, a founding editor for *GOOD* magazine, points out, "Good design is not going to save bad content." But design can certainly make bad content more interesting to look at and the overall experience of paging through a magazine much more pleasurable. Focus on what design can do, and do it well.

5

NICOLE **DUDKA**

INTERN, INTERN, INTERN

Nicole Dudka, art director at the Chicago Tribune, has a simple piece of advice for aspiring publication designers: "Intern, intern, intern." And she adds, do it while you're young, unattached, and can check out newsrooms in different parts of the country, where the vibe—and the opportunities—will be different.

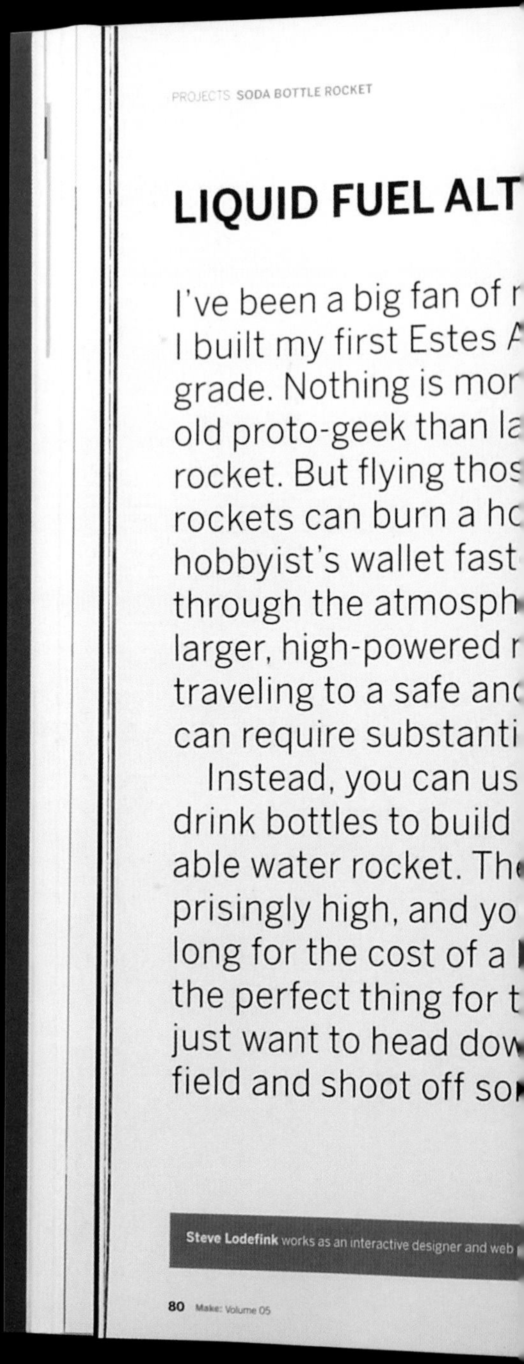

***Make* magazine, designed by Albertson Design**

www.makezine.com/05/rocket

RNATIVE

del rocketry since
na back in third
xciting to a 9-year-
ching a homemade
one-shot solid-fuel
through a young
than they burn
e, and with today's
kets, locating and
uitable launch site
planning and effort.
2-liter carbonated
inexpensive, reus-
hrill factor is sur-
can fly them all day
le air and water. It's
se times when you
to the local soccer
e rockets!

er for The Walt Disney Internet Group in Seattle.

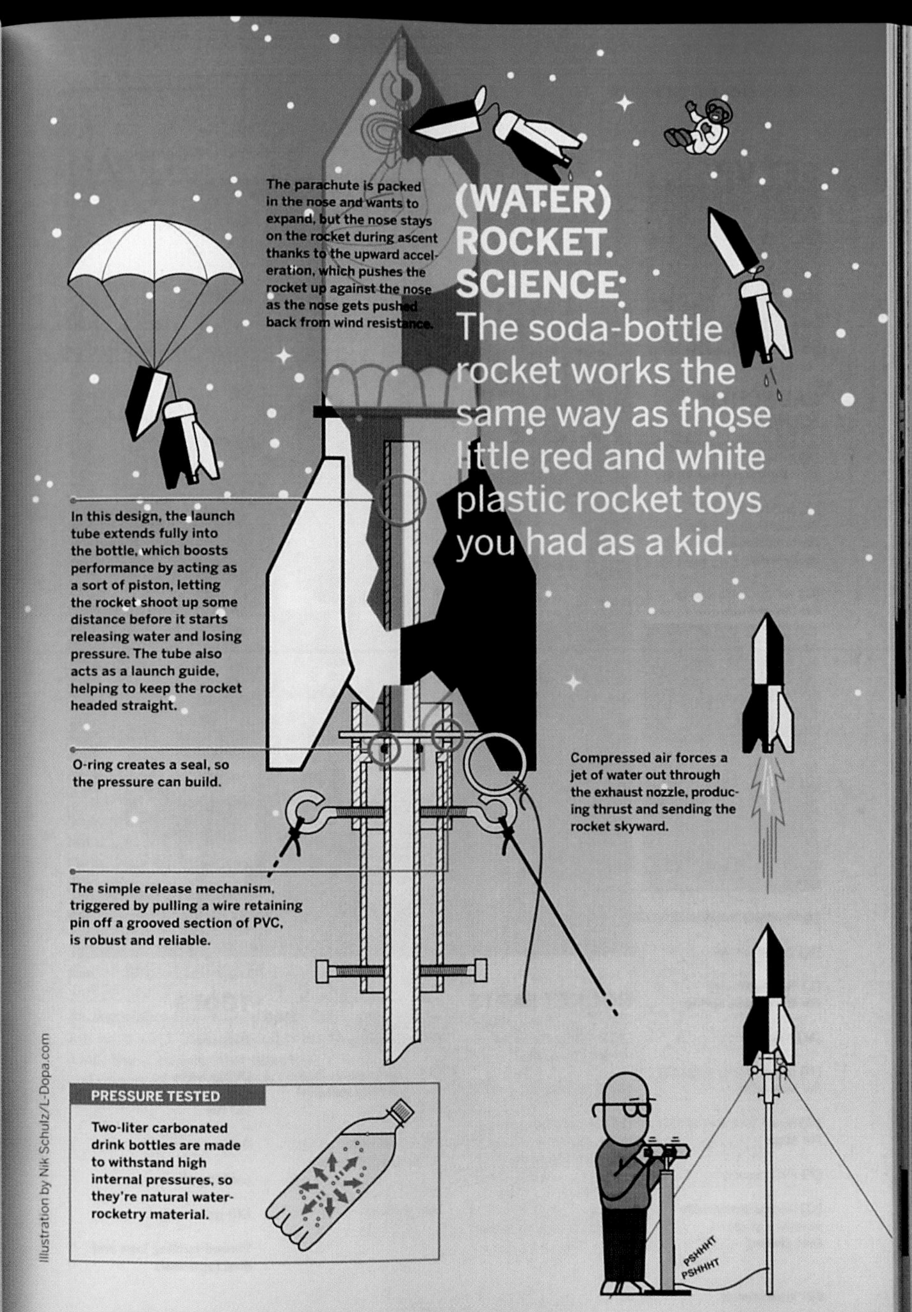

(WATER) ROCKET SCIENCE
The soda-bottle rocket works the same way as those little red and white plastic rocket toys you had as a kid.
The parachute is packed in the nose and wants to expand, but the nose stays on the rocket during ascent thanks to the upward acceleration, which pushes the rocket up against the nose as the nose gets pushed back from wind resistance.
In this design, the launch tube extends fully into the bottle, which boosts performance by acting as a sort of piston, letting the rocket shoot up some distance before it starts releasing water and losing pressure. The tube also acts as a launch guide, helping to keep the rocket headed straight.
O-ring creates a seal, so the pressure can build.
The simple release mechanism, triggered by pulling a wire retaining pin off a grooved section of PVC, is robust and reliable.
Compressed air forces a jet of water out through the exhaust nozzle, producing thrust and sending the rocket skyward.
PRESSURE TESTED
Two-liter carbonated drink bottles are made to withstand high internal pressures, so they're natural water-rocketry material.
PSHHHT
PSHHHT
Illustration by Nik Schulz/L-Dopa.com

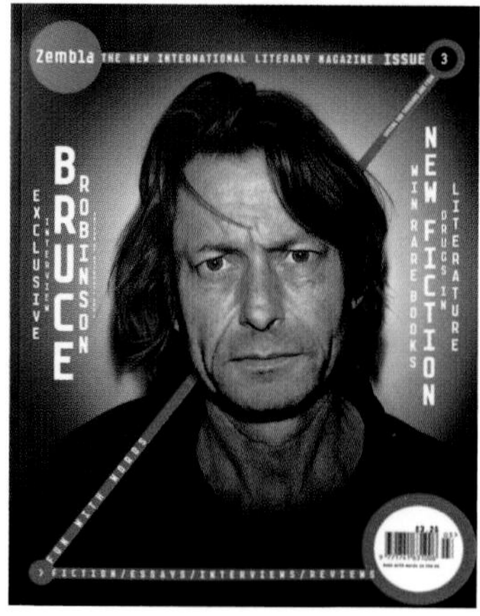

6

VINCE **FROST**

JEREMY **LESLIE**

CARIN **GOLDBERG**

KALLE **LASN**

NICOLE **DUDKA**

LISTEN, LEARN, STUDY

"There's nothing worse than a young designer who thinks they know everything," says Australia-based designer Vince Frost. After designing for decades and working with dozens of fresh-out-of-school designers, "I'm always surprised at how little experience people have when they come out of college," he says. "But the most important thing is to be enthusiastic and want to learn and grow. The best designers are those that listen and learn." In publication design, the lessons are many. There are the basics of type families and grids and editorial wells. But there is also adopting the right state of mind. "We've set ourselves up as experts," Jeremy Leslie notes, "and you can't be an expert without questioning, because that's how we learn. Children question everything. We have to behave like children."

Designer and educator Carin Goldberg says that one of the most useful things is to learn the history of publication design itself. "You have to study magazine design," she says. "A magazine's voice is the sum total of many parts, and it takes planning and organization. The process is less intuitive than other design media." She's suggesting an effort that should take designers far beyond the classroom. "Magazine design is one of the hardest things to teach because there are so many elements. It's a complex project. You can't look at a magazine through a keyhole, one page at a time," she says. "You have to look at it as a complete thing that moves and undulates. I suggest to my students that they deconstruct and analyze the structure and voice of other successful magazines that work in order to understand how to organize a good one." She recommends, for example, the work of Alexey Brodovitch, Ruth Ansel, Bea Feitler, and Fabian Baron of *Harper's Bazaar* and other magazines; Cipe Pineles of *Seventeen*; Fred Woodward of *Rolling Stone*; M&Co. of *Colors* and *Interview*; Robert Priest and John Korpics of *Esquire*.

For his part, Kalle Lasn emphasizes that it's just as important to look into the hearts as well as the portfolios of legendary designers. "When I look back on the history of design," he says, "it's filled with wild, passionate, crazy people who changed the aesthetic of their times and were involved in the big debates of their times." He's hopeful that the most recent generation of designers is ready and willing to do the same.

Above and opposite: *Zembla*, designed by Frost Design, takes some standard magazine cover motifs, from the necessity of barcodes to the branding elements of titles and taglines, and combines them with type and image in inventive ways that will get noticed on a newsstand.

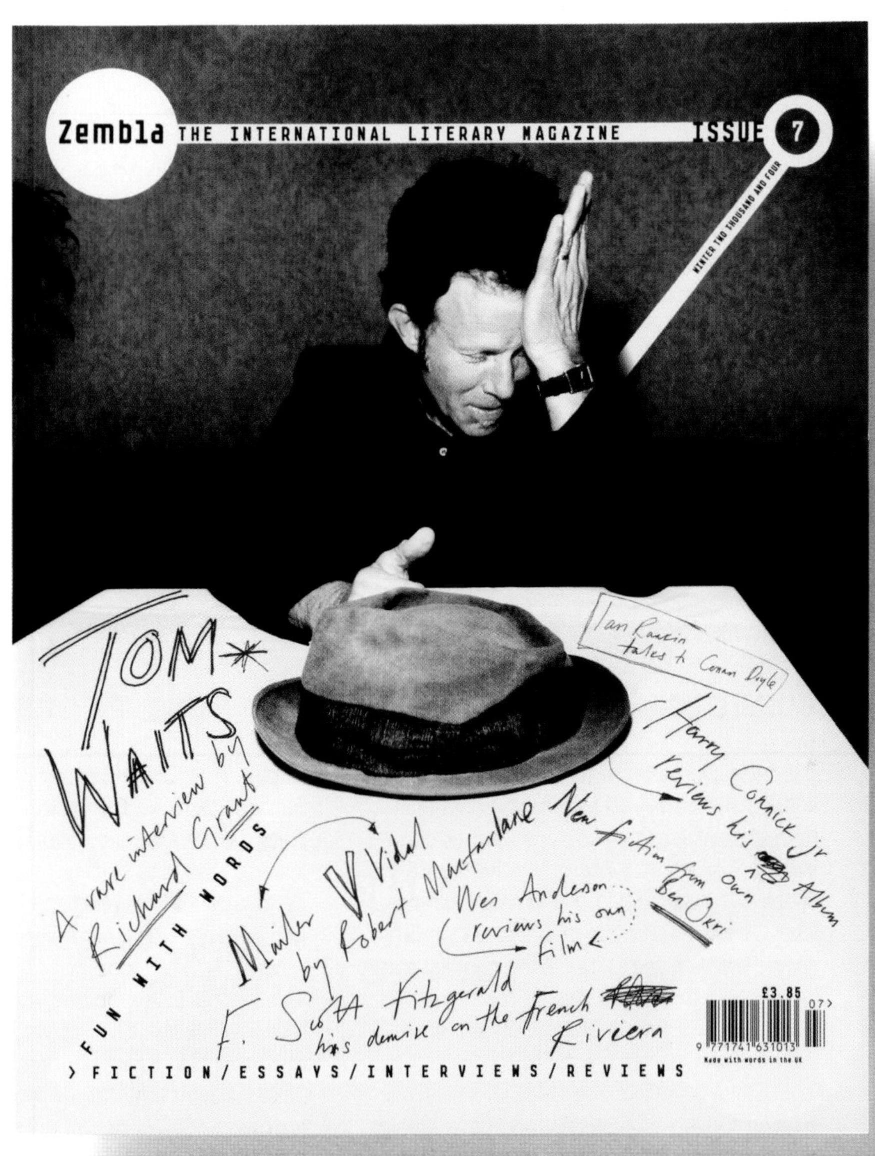
Zembla
THE INTERNATIONAL LITERARY MAGAZINE
ISSUE 7
WINTER TWO THOUSAND AND FOUR
Ian Rankin talks to Conan Doyle
TOM WAITS
A rare interview by Richard Grant
Harry Connick Jr reviews his own Album
FUN WITH WORDS
Mailer V Vidal by Robert Macfarlane
New fiction from Ben Okri
Wes Anderson reviews his own film
F. Scott Fitzgerald his demise on the French Riviera
£3.85
> FICTION/ESSAYS/INTERVIEWS/REVIEWS
Made with words in the UK

7 IT'S NOT ABOUT YOU

MARCUS **PIPER**

ARJEN **NOORDEMAN**

"A magazine is for the reader, not the art director," notes Marcus Piper, who is the art director of *Pol Oxygen* magazine and also runs his own design studio in Sydney, Australia. "Graphic statements have their place, and in that place, make great pieces of work, but we are not designing magazines so people can see how incredibly creative we are." Publication designers consistently point out that whatever flexing of creative muscles they do is always in service to showing off the content. As Piper says, "Content is king. If the magazine were about me, it would be a different thing. Of course, there are some magazines you buy because of the person who designed it, but you may only buy it once. You have to be mature enough in your self to know when to be expressive and when to let the content do the work." Having said that, this focus on content is no excuse to shirk design duties. As Arjen Noordeman, partner at Elasticbrand in New York, notes, "It should never be about the designer. But you can add to the experience in a positive way."

8 SURROUND YOURSELF WITH THE BEST PEOPLE

CARIN **GOLDBERG**

CASEY **CAPLOWE**

AREM **DUPLESSIS**

The best way to learn the design restraint and humility necessary to publication design is through a process of soaking up, not showing off. As Carin Goldberg tells her students, "Seek out publications and creative directors who are the best in the business. No matter what the magazine is, what the subject matter is—it could be *Peanut Butter Today*—it's whom you're working with that's important. Work with the best and learn from them."

Beyond the team of editors and other designers, magazine art directors must also consider—and respect—the community of writers, illustrators, photographers, artists, and readers essential to a publication's success. As Casey Caplowe explains, "We really wanted to create a platform rather than a megaphone for ourselves. It's about creating spaces and then inviting really interesting people to play in those spaces. We want design to solve problems. We don't want to do design for design's sake."

This cooperative effort of magazine making leads to pretty deep gratifications, as noted by Arem Duplessis, art director for the *New York Times Magazine*. "The most satisfying thing for me is helping one of my designers get to a good place with their story. I love collaboration, and when everything is clicking, it's a wonderful thing."

The Interventionists **is a book featuring the work of forty artists. According to Noordeman, "A lot of these people were already nonconformists, so they appreciated that the graphic design was out there, with loud graphic elements and loud colors. They got a kick out of it because that's the way they made their art."**

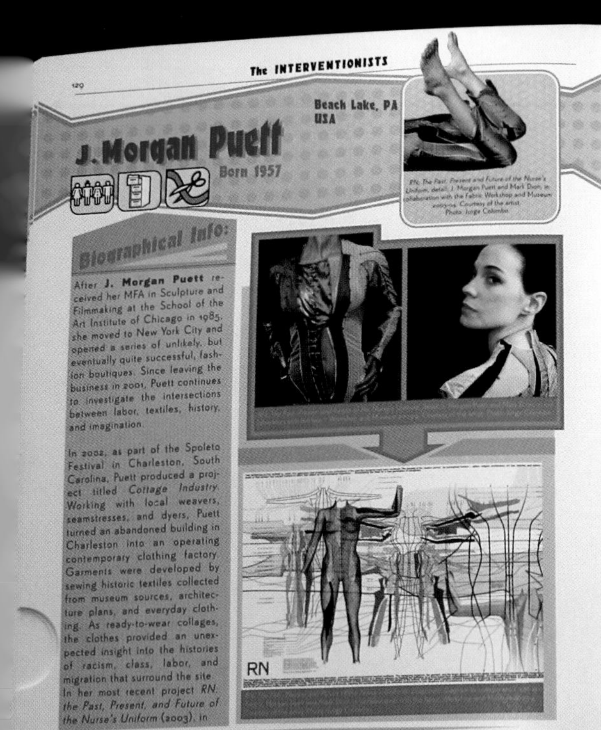
129

The INTERVENTIONISTS

J. Morgan Puett

Beach Lake, PA
USA

Born 1957

Biographical Info:

After **J. Morgan Puett** received her MFA in Sculpture and Filmmaking at the School of the Art Institute of Chicago in 1985, she moved to New York City and opened a series of unlikely, but eventually quite successful, fashion boutiques. Since leaving the business in 2001, Puett continues to investigate the intersections between labor, textiles, history, and imagination.

In 2002, as part of the Spoleto Festival in Charleston, South Carolina, Puett produced a project titled *Cottage Industry*. Working with local weavers, seamstresses, and dyers, Puett turned an abandoned building in Charleston into an operating contemporary clothing factory. Garments were developed by sewing historic textiles collected from museum sources, architecture plans, and everyday clothing. As ready-to-wear collages, the clothes provided an unexpected insight into the histories of racism, class, labor, and migration that surround the site. In her most recent project *RN: the Past, Present, and Future of the Nurse's Uniform* (2003), in

RN

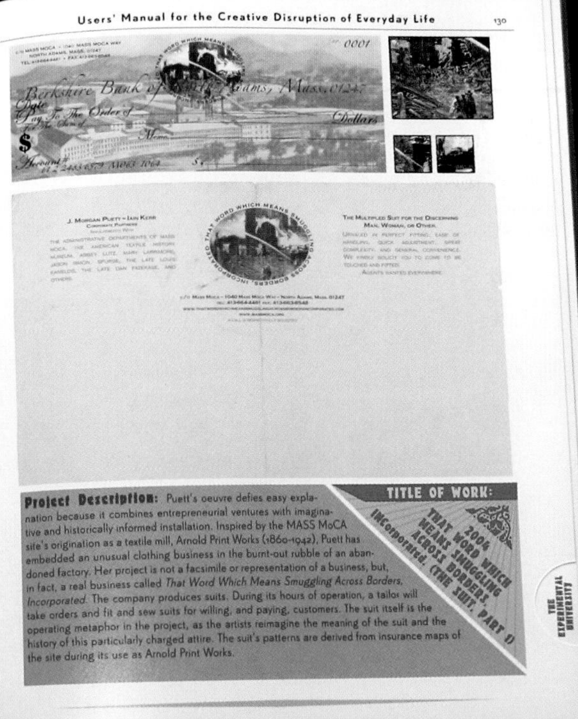
Users' Manual for the Creative Disruption of Everyday Life 130

Project Description: Puett's oeuvre defies easy explanation because it combines entrepreneurial ventures with imaginative and historically informed installation. Inspired by the MASS MoCA site's origination as a textile mill, Arnold Print Works (1860–1942), Puett has embedded an unusual clothing business in the burnt-out rubble of an abandoned factory. Her project is not a facsimile or representation of a business, but, in fact, a real business called *That Word Which Means Smuggling Across Borders, Incorporated*. The company produces suits. During its hours of operation, a tailor will take orders and fit and sew suits for willing, and paying, customers. The suit itself is the operating metaphor in the project, as the artists reimagine the meaning of the suit and the history of this particularly charged attire. The suit's patterns are derived from insurance maps of the site during its use as Arnold Print Works.

TITLE OF WORK:
2006
THAT WORD WHICH MEANS SMUGGLING ACROSS BORDERS, INCorporated. (THE SUIT, PART I)

THE EXPERIMENTAL UNIVERSITY

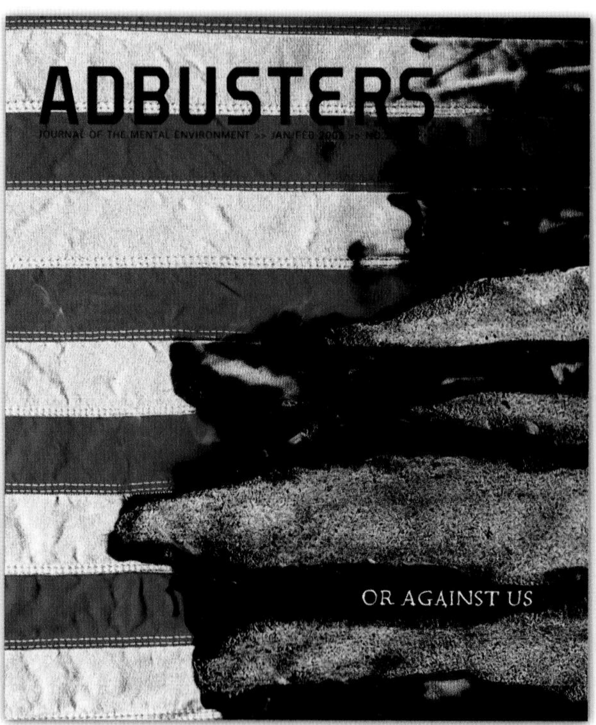

KALLE **LASN**

BE BRAVE, BOLD, PASSIONATE

"I think a magazine is supposed to engage in some kind of public discourse in an interesting way, a profound way, a provocative way," Kalle Lasn states. While he accepts that some mass-consumption publications are necessary, he laments that there are so few willing to take big risks. "The commercialization of magazines means that too many of them are playing a marketing game instead of giving their readers stuff that comes from their guts and is meant to provoke," he says. "The passion isn't there. Instead we have a passion to satisfy advertisers or a marketing idea. The soul of magazines has been lost. The whole idea of a designer as an author, a communicator, has been lost."

His answer? Designers need to reconnect to the primal source of their work. "Good design emanates from passion," he says, "from the very guts of the designer. The designer must take all their yearnings and passions and political views and anger and all the things that make up life and have it pouring into the design." However, even Lasn has a pragmatic side. "Of course the job of design is to learn how to channel all this emotion—to take the things that are closest to the designer and learn how to channel it. The important thing is not to turn design into a profession that is only serving the needs of clients. I realize you have to do this, but designers have taken it too far."

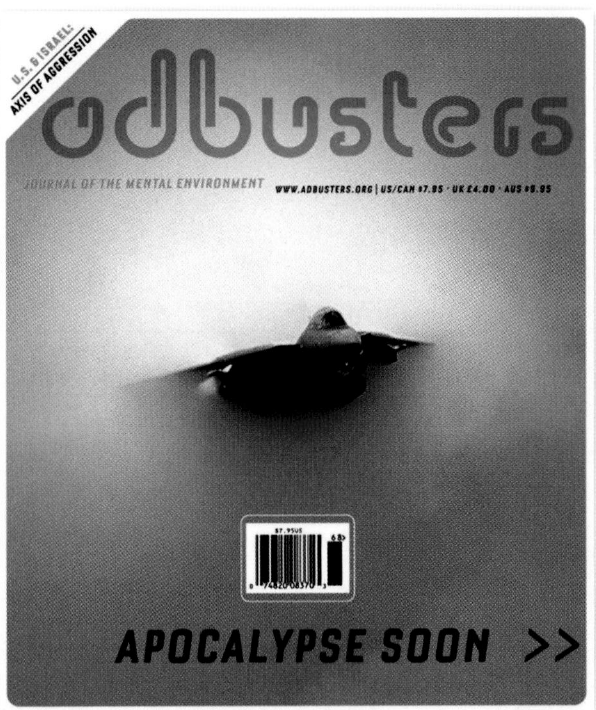

10

CARIN **GOLDBERG**

MARCUS **PIPER**

ADAM **MACHACEK**

BEGIN BY ASKING A LOT OF QUESTIONS

"There are all kinds of questions you always ask yourself no matter what you're designing," notes Carin Goldberg. "You have to look at what the publication is about, what the content is, who is the reader and where do they live, what is the mood, the agenda," she continues. "You have to think of the project holistically because you're solving several problems within one issue. Hierarchy and voice are priorities. Whether it's a book, or a magazine, or a poster, or book jacket, you always begin with the boilerplate questions and allow the answers to evolve as you begin to put pen to paper."

Every experienced editorial designer has his own set of questions, but they all reflect the effort of trying to understand what the publication is about. As Marcus Piper says, "I guess it's like knowing where the project is coming from and where it is going. The trick is to find the most appropriate and creative approach between those two points." In some cases, these queries can and should lead to a certain level of subject immersion. Adam Machacek, cofounder of Welcometo.as in Switzerland, says, "The first thing is, of course, the research, when the topic is becoming part of your daily thinking." For example, he designed a book for an exhibit on rock music and its impact on the visual culture of the 1960s. He says, "We spent hours with the curator of the exhibition, touching, smelling, and selecting all the exhibits to be reproduced in the catalog. Being in his house, surrounded by his never-ending collection felt like being in a magic library." As they were designing, even the studio playlist changed to reflect the music of the exhibit and served to inspire the designers as they worked.

Opposite and above: After finding himself shut out by the mainstream media, Kalle Lasn launched *Adbusters* as a soapbox for the causes he believes in. The magazine design reinvents itself in every issue to reflect the challenging issues presented.

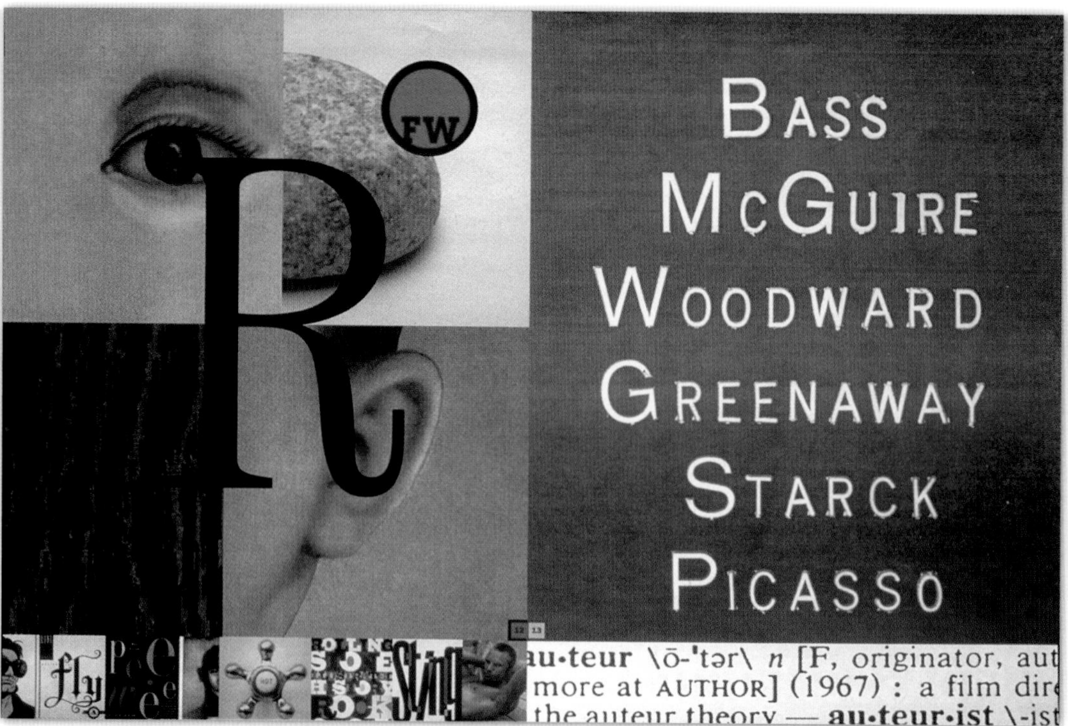

11

THINK ABOUT THE FUTURE

VINCE **FROST**

Publications provide a unique opportunity for a designer. In most graphic design projects, you design it, print it, and then it's over. A publication is more of a living, growing, evolving organism that blooms again and again in response to the environment in which it's created and the content that it presents. Therefore, it's important for the designer to be forward-looking. "In the beginning, especially on a start-up publication," says Vince Frost, "there may be no history. So we talk to the person about the future, not the past. They have goals and we want to understand their long-term objectives and create solutions that are about the future, not where they are today." This clarifies another interesting point about publications: Instead of trying to achieve multiple, sometimes competing objectives in a single, one-time piece, an editorial designer can use several issues of a publication to fully realize the multifaceted vision of its editors and contributors.

Above and opposite: In *U&LC*, as designed by Carin Goldberg, type and image are not used in service to the design; they *are* the design.

12

INA **SALTZ**

ASK YOURSELF HOW YOU CAN MAKE A DIFFERENCE

This basic question is what Ina Saltz asks herself before approaching a publication design project, especially if it's a redesign. As with any project, the designer is there to solve problems, make improvements, and express a vision, within the constraints of time and budget. In determining how she can have the most positive impact, Saltz asks herself a series of defining questions: "Does the magazine already look great, or are they looking for something different? Is this something where I can make it ten times better or just take it up a notch? How much can I do, how much will I be allowed to do, how much will the budget allow me to do, what is the editorial mission of this product, and can I fulfill that mission in a better way?" While asking herself these things, Saltz keeps in mind the fundamental nature of a publication: "A magazine is a product serving a need like any other product, but its purpose is to communicate, impart information, and inspire, so I ask myself how I can make that happen in a better way than it's happening now," she says.

13

LUKE **HAYMAN**

AREM **DUPLESSIS**

START WITH SOMETHING SIMPLE

Publications are complex projects with many disparate components to consider and integrate. So, especially when starting from scratch, sometimes the best way to ground the project is to start with the most basic component. "I try to start with something simple, first," Luke Hayman says, describing his process for designing a new magazine. "Mostly, I start with type, like for a column. I try to get the fonts working, get the basic grid and text font down first, and then build from there. I don't start with the features or the cover; I start with the nitty-gritty stuff first."

When the design is already established, some art directors, like Arem Duplessis, put pictures before fonts. "I start by conceptualizing ideas for the imagery," he says. "When the design process begins, the designers will create something specific to the content and imagery of their stories." These layouts are posted on a display wall so Duplessis can "check for an even flow." The rest of the design is filled in from there.

The Making, and Unmaking, of a

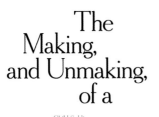

Child Soldier

One boy's tortuous entanglement in an African civil war.

By Ishmael Beah

38

Illustrations by Brian Rea

to follow the path until we received instructions on what to do next. We walked for long hours and stopped only to eat sardines and corned beef with gari, sniff brown brown and take more white capsules. The combination of these drugs made us fierce. The idea of death didn't cross my mind, and killing had become as easy as drinking water. After that first killing, my mind had stopped making remorseful records, or so it seemed.

Before we got to a rebel camp, we would deviate from the path and walk in the forest. Once the camp was in sight, we would surround it and wait for the lieutenant's command. The rebels roamed about; some sat against walls, dozing off, and others, boys as young as we, stood at guard posts passing around marijuana. Whenever I looked at rebels during raids, my entire body shook with fury; they were the people who had shot my friends and family. So when the lieutenant gave orders, I shot as many as I could, but I didn't feel better. After every gunfight, we would enter the rebel camp, killing those we had wounded. We would then search the houses and gather gallons of gasoline, enormous amounts of marijuana and cocaine, bales of clothes, watches, rice, salt, gari and many other things. We rounded up any civilians — men, women, boys and young girls — hiding in the huts and houses and made them carry our loot back to the base. We shot them if they tried to run away.

On one of these raids, we captured a few rebels after a long gunfight and a lot of civilian casualties. We undressed the prisoners and tied their arms behind their backs until their chests were tight as drums. "Where did you get all this ammunition from?" the corporal asked one of the prisoners, a man with an almost dreadlocked beard. He spat in the corporal's face, and the corporal immediately shot him in the head at close range. He fell to the ground, and blood slowly leaked out of his head. We cheered in admiration of the corporal's action and saluted him as he walked by. Suddenly, a rebel hiding in the bushes shot one of our boys. We dispersed around the village in search of the shooter. When the young muscular rebel was captured, the lieutenant slit his neck with his bayonet. The rebel ran before he fell to the ground and stopped moving. We cheered again, raising our guns in the air, shouting and whistling.

During that time, a lot of things were done with no reason or explanation. Sometimes we were asked to leave for war in the middle of a movie. We would come back hours later after killing many people and continue the movie as if we had just returned from intermission. We were always either on the front lines, watching a war movie or doing drugs. There was no time to be alone or to think. When we conversed with one another, we talked only about the movies and how impressed we were with the way either the lieutenant, the corporal or one of us had killed someone. It was as if nothing else existed.

The villages that we captured and turned into our bases as we went along and the forests that we slept in became my home. My squad was my family, my gun was my provider and protector and my rule was to kill or be killed. The extent of my thoughts didn't go much beyond that. We had been fighting for more than two years, and killing had become a daily activity. I felt no pity for anyone. My childhood had gone by without my knowing, and it seemed as if my heart had frozen. I knew that day and night came and went because of the presence of the moon and the sun, but I had no idea whether it was a Sunday or a Friday.

Taken From the Front

In my head my life was normal. But everything began to change in January 1996. I was 15.

One morning that month, a truck came to the village where we were based. Four men dressed in clean blue jeans and white T-shirts that said "Unicef" in big blue letters jumped out. They were shown to the lieutenant's house. It seemed as if he had been expecting them. As they sat talking on the veranda, we watched them from under the mango tree, where we sat cleaning our guns. Soon all the boys were told to line up for the lieutenant who selected a few of us and asked the adult soldiers to take away our guns and ammunition. A bunch of boys, including my friend Alhaji and me, were ushered to the truck. I stared back at the veranda where the lieutenant now stood, looking in the other direction, toward the forest, his hands crossed behind his back. I still didn't know exactly what was going on, but I was beginning to get angry and anxious. Why had the lieutenant decided to give us up to these civilians? We thought that we were part of the war until the end.

We were on the road for hours. I had gotten used to always moving and hadn't sat in one place idly for a long time. It was night when the truck stopped at a center, where there were other boys whose appearances, red eyes and somber faces resembled ours. Alhaji and I looked at this group, and he asked the boys who they were. A boy who was sitting on the stoop angrily said: "We fought for the R.U.F.; the army is the enemy. We fought for freedom, and the army killed my family and destroyed my village. I will kill any of those army bastards every time I get a chance to do so." The boy took off his shirt to fight, and on his arm was the R.U.F. brand. Mambu, one of the boys on our side, shouted, "They are rebels," and reached for his bayonet, which he had hidden in his army shorts; most of us had hidden either a knife or a grenade before our guns were taken from us. Before Mambu could grab his weapon, the R.U.F. boy punched him in the face. He fell, and when he got up, his nose was bleeding. The rebel boys drew out the few bayonets they had in their shorts and rushed toward us. It was war all over again. Perhaps the naïve men who had taken us to the center thought that removing us from the war would lessen our hatred for the R.U.F. It hadn't crossed their minds that a change of environment wouldn't immediately make us normal boys; we were dangerous, brainwashed to kill.

One boy grabbed my neck from behind. He was squeezing for the kill, and I couldn't use my bayonet effectively, so I elbowed him with all my

40

ILLUSTRATION BY BRIAN REA

THE NEW YORK TIMES MAGAZINE / JANUARY 14, 2007 41

Sometimes images are so powerful in their stark simplicity, they are better left unadorned by design techniques, as in this article in the *New York Times Magazine*.

THE HARTFORD COURANT

ARTS

WWW.CTNOW.COM SUNDAY, MARCH 5, 2006 SECTION G

Bloody Sunday

The Dark World Of Tony Soprano & Co. Dawns For Final Time

A Lot Of Love In New HBO Series About Family

14

VINCE **FROST**

AREM **DUPLESSIS**

NICOLE **DUDKA**

WORK QUICKLY

"I enjoy doing things quickly," says Vince Frost. "Getting the energy up, being excited, just blitzing the project. The quicker you do it, the better it is for everyone. If you spend too much time analyzing it, it loses impact and passion." Sometimes working quickly is a necessity as well as a choice. Arem Duplessis points out, "We do not have the luxury of time working on a weekly. You have to be a quick thinker, and you have to know when to release the mouse." Nicole Dudka was drawn to newspapers specifically because of the speed in which she is forced to work. "I fell in love with the deadlines," she says. "It's a faster turnaround, allows you to be creative really fast, forces you to think on your feet, and for better or worse, you start again the next week." Her technique for compressing her design process involves sketching at both ends of the spectrum. "I work in versions. I start by sketching a busy, mostly cluttered, energetic version, and then go the opposite direction and come up with the most minimal version. Sometimes you find something in between, and sometimes people fall in love with the thing that only took two minutes. It's a process of elimination."

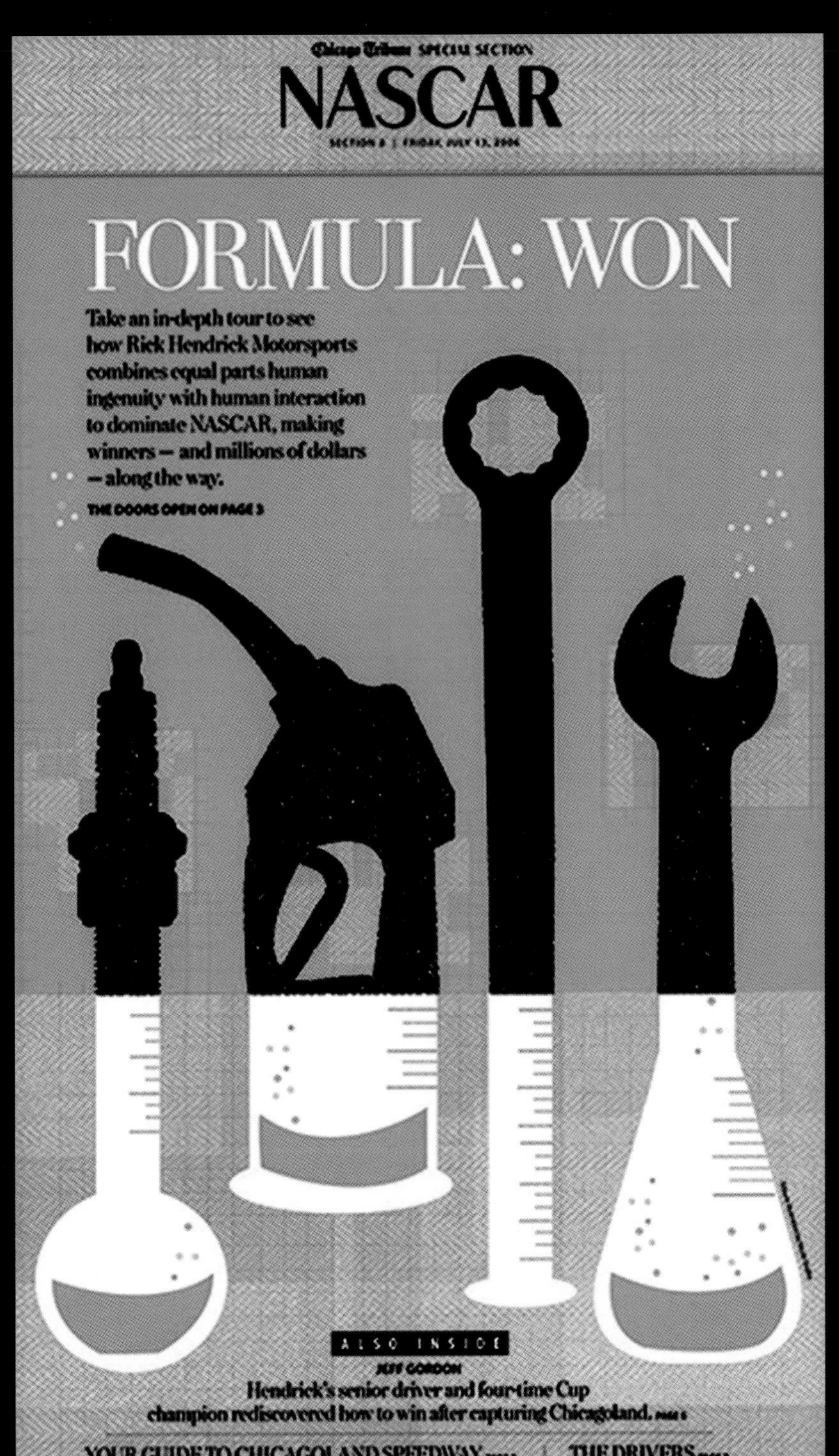

Chicago Tribune SPECIAL SECTION

NASCAR

FORMULA: WON

Take an in-depth tour to see how Rick Hendrick Motorsports combines equal parts human ingenuity with human interaction to dominate NASCAR, making winners — and millions of dollars — along the way.

THE DOORS OPEN ON PAGE 3

ALSO INSIDE

JEFF GORDON

Hendrick's senior driver and four-time Cup champion rediscovered how to win after capturing Chicagoland.

YOUR GUIDE TO CHICAGOLAND SPEEDWAY | THE DRIVERS

Opposite and above: In the *Chicago Tribune*, Dudka illustrates articles on common topics by creating images other than "those things that immediately come to mind and every other publication would use."

Left and opposite: *33 Thoughts* magazine was developed for an accounting firm willing to take some risks. "It's purely an experience for customers of that consultancy to show they're in touch with the concerns of that group," says Leslie. "They're also trying to position themselves as the outsider. So the magazine looks different from what you'd expect, but the content is very practical to its audience."

15

CONSIDER THE CONTEXT OF THE CONTENT

JEREMY **LESLIE**

As you get into actual page design and laying out specific pieces of writing, you must begin to consider not just what's being said, but how it's being said. "You need to understand not just the nature of the piece but also the angle of the piece," says Jeremy Leslie. "Is it a puff piece, a diss of a celebrity, a harrowing news piece, or an upbeat news piece? Once you figure that out, you have to look at the article in the context of the whole magazine as well as the history of the magazine." It's important that these considerations, which will not appear overtly to the reader, are implicit in the design. This gives a reader clues as to the nature of the magazine, the content of what they might be reading, and creates cohesion from one issue to another so readers can navigate and bond with the publication.

BAROMETER

40 Paying attention?

How multimedia communications give us self-inflicted attention deficit disorder (ADD).

VOCAB FOR A WIRED ERA
Screen-sucking: wasting time stuck online when you could be working.
EMV or email voice: the ghostly phone voice that people assume when they are talking to you yet reading their email.
Gemmelsmerch: the ubiquitous force that distracts us from whatever we are doing.
Source: CrazyBusy: Overstretched, Overbooked and About to Snap! Strategies for Coping in a World Gone ADD, by Dr Edward Hallowell

It was only a matter of time before the frenzied pace of wired life began to draw serious attention from the medics. Constant demand via email, mobile and BlackBerry has long been seen as a cause of stress. But now psychiatrist Dr Edward Hallowell, a former practitioner at Harvard Business School, has come up with a still more worrying diagnosis. Society is suffering, he says, from an epidemic of self-inflicted ADD.

Sounds alarmist? Well, check out the symptoms: struggling to focus, restless, impatient, frustrated; juggling multiple projects but getting none done. "In general, feeling busy beyond belief, but not all that productive."

The upshot is that the multi-tasker can't take in the whole picture or think in depth – zapping instead from one superficial thought to another. The implications for business are clear. Instead of concentrating on one task and doing it well, people end up doing two or more below their true ability. As for creativity, forget it. The problem has become so bad, says Hallowell, that it is even prompting people to report what they fear is early Alzheimer's. "But it's not that people's memories are deteriorating; it's just that they cannot absorb all the information being thrown at them."

Short of doctoring the water cooler with Ritalin, or imposing a multimedia blackout, what's to be done? The answer lies in self-discipline. "Business people are suckers for this idea that you have to work harder all the time. But to manage in this environment, you have to exercise restraint." Above all, keep this as your mantra: "The harder work is the thinking, not the collecting of information."

10

BROUGHT TO YOU BY BOO STOY HAYWARD

BAROMETER

Signs of the times

Given the new phase of volatility in the markets, we need every bit of help we can get second-guessing the future. Try the following alternative market indicators...

SKIRTS. Attention has always focused on hemlines – the longer they go, the worse the outlook. But don't disregard shape. Connoisseurs of past investment manias may well find themselves troubled by this year's Tulip styles. The concurrent revival of that 1980s standard, the Bubble, gives even more cause for concern.
SKIPS. The prevalence of builders' accoutrements – scaffolding, battered white vans and so on – has long been a favoured informal indicator of rosy times. Economist David Smith prefers the skip index: proliferating numbers on the streets are "normally the first cuckoo of economic spring".
LADY IN RED. During the 1990s boom, the Wall Street day traders learnt to pay close attention to business channel CNBC's anchorwoman, Maria 'Money Honey' Bartiromo. Whole web sites were devoted simply to discussing the nuances of every change of hairdo – and when Money Honey wore red, it was taken as a sure 'buy' signal.
BOY RACERS. US economists have established a link between the number of speeding tickets traders clock up and the turnover in their portfolio – a useful way of gauging market volatility. Trades increased by an average of almost 10 per cent for each speeding ticket received.
SLAP AND TICKLE. Strong cosmetics sales are a warning that the all-important female consumer is tightening her belt. Lipstick is a cheap fix if you can't afford a new outfit.
HIP-HOP LYRICS. For an insight into future consumer trends, pay close attention to what da crew have to say about luxury brands. Market research outfit Brandstand has a Billboard Charts Index that tots up the references in rap songs, such as Busta Rhymes and P Diddy's *Pass the Courvoisier.*
NORTHAMPTON. This seemingly uninspiring Midlands town apparently tracks the rise and fall of the national economy perfectly...
TOWER BRIDGE. The number of times the bridge is raised is no longer a useful indicator of UK import/export activity, just of the traffic in cocktail cruisers.

When Money Honey wore red, it was taken as a sure 'buy' signal

11

BROUGHT TO YOU BY BOO STOY HAYWARD

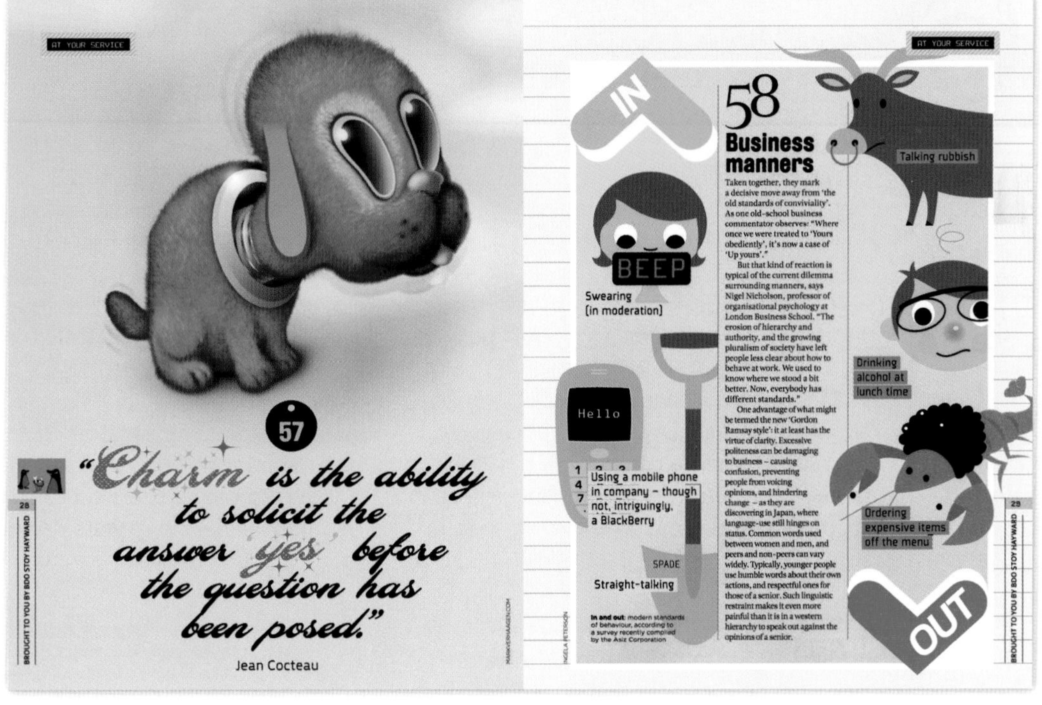

AT YOUR SERVICE

57

"Charm is the ability to solicit the answer 'yes' before the question has been posed."

Jean Cocteau

28

BROUGHT TO YOU BY BOO STOY HAYWARD

AT YOUR SERVICE

58 Business manners

Taken together, they mark a decisive move away from 'the old standards of conviviality'. As one old-school business commentator observes: "Where once we were treated to 'Yours obediently', it's now a case of 'Up yours'."

But that kind of reaction is typical of the current dilemma surrounding manners, says Nigel Nicholson, professor of organisational psychology at London Business School. "The erosion of hierarchy and authority, and the growing pluralism of society have left people less clear about how to behave at work. We used to know where we stood a bit better. Now, everybody has different standards."

One advantage of what might be termed the new 'Gordon Ramsay style': it at least has the virtue of clarity. Excessive politeness can be damaging to business – causing confusion, preventing people from voicing opinions, and hindering change – as they are discovering in Japan, where language-use still hinges on status. Common words used between women and men, and peers and non-peers can vary widely. Typically, younger people use humble words about their own actions, and respectful ones for those of a senior. Such linguistic restraint makes it even more painful than it is in a western hierarchy to speak out against the opinions of a senior.

In and out: modern standards of behaviour, according to a survey recently compiled by the Asiz Corporation

29

BROUGHT TO YOU BY BOO STOY HAYWARD

16

BE WILLING TO BE SMART INSTEAD OF BEAUTIFUL

VINCE **FROST**

STEVEN **HELLER**

ARTHUR **HOCHSTEIN**

AREM **DUPLESSIS**

Great design almost always serves the project at hand rather than itself, and this is especially critical for content-driven projects like publication design. The designer's role is to enhance the subject matter provided, make it more intriguing, engaging, and edifying for the reader, and to never upstage what's happening on the page. Designers should always be looking for the best means to visually communicate what's being written. "It's not about making it look cool, or finding a cool font," says Vince Frost. "It's really about finding the best approach for that particular opportunity. You don't want to inflict your style on a project." Or, as Steven Heller suggests, "Try not to impose your signature on something that shouldn't be signed."

This willingness to stay behind the scenes is perhaps nowhere as important as at a news magazine. Arthur Hochstein, art director at *Time*, says that brains must come before beauty. "We take a restrained approach," he explains. "Being part of the news process is as important as good design. You have to throw a lot of work out, you have to change things all the time, and you have to be someone who can roll with things. You have to understand that it's a collective pursuit, and design is one aspect, but it's not the final determining factor. Sometimes you want to be the smartest girl in the class instead of the best looking."

Arem Duplessis concurs. "You can't just design to make something beautiful. Read the stories and understand what the editorial mission is. You should know the magazine's demographics and who the core audience is before you even touch a sketch pad."

Above and opposite: & is a magazine from D&AD, a U.K.–based "educational charity that represents the global creative, design, and advertising communities" by "setting industry standards, educating and inspiring the next generation, and demonstrating the impact of creativity and innovation on enhancing business performance."

Ampersand
Issue 1
Volume 1

obsession *n* 1. an idea or feeling that completely occupies the mind

Editor
Lakshmi Bhaskaran
lakshmi@dandad.co.uk
Design & Art Direction
Vince Frost & Anthony Donovan
Frost Design, Sydney
www.frostdesign.com.au
Advertising
Katherine Howells
katherine@dandad.co.uk
'&', D&AD
9 Graphite Square,
Vauxhall Walk
London SE11 5EE
T: +44 (207) 840 1111
E: ampersand@dandad.co.uk
W: www.dandad.co.uk
Printed by Beacon Press using *pure***print**® environmental print technology
'&' is printed on 100% Recycled Paper
Cover Photography
Ben Stockley

Welcome to this, the first issue of our new look members' magazine, '&'. As longstanding members will recall, '&' has existed before in a number of different formats. In 2003, D&AD spent a year experimenting with its design, before taking respite to carry out a major review and consider the magazine's future. In an age fuelled by digital communication we even found ourselves asking the question, 'do we actually need a traditional magazine?' The answer was a resounding Yes and the feedback unequivocal: that our members value, not only the tactility of a traditional publication but also its content – from the latest D&AD news and views to industry-related features to profiles celebrating our most inspiring creatives. Our research also led us to the format you see before you as the most preferred by our members ● And so we are back, stronger than ever, with a new design, definitive format and updated content that we hope you will find as exciting and stimulating to read as we have to create. I am also absolutely delighted that the creative team who produced the last award-winning issue of '&', Lakshmi Bhaskaran as editor and Vince Frost as creative director, are back with us to take '&' forward as a permanent fixture here at D&AD ● D&AD members will receive four issues of the magazine a year from September 2006. And, as with all of our print material, '&' will adhere to D&AD's strict environmental policy, which we began to implement in mid-2005 ● We are re-launching '&' in the run up to Congress 2006 and will be using the magazine to keep you fully up to speed about this world-class event, as well as other activities here at D&AD ● This is your magazine and we would love to hear what you think. Get in touch by email to: ampersand@dandad.co.uk
Michael Hockney Chief Executive, D&AD

welcome

ALAN FLETCHER

Alan Fletcher, the most highly regarded graphic designer of his generation, died in September. Quentin Newark offers a personal recollection of an iconic figure

Alan Fletcher is dead. Suddenly, the whole world of design is so much smaller. There seem to be no figures of his grandeur and depth waiting in the wings. He was the last of his kind. Fletcher immediately takes his place in the pantheon of greats, many of whom he knew: Herbert Bayer, Saul Steinberg, Willi Fleckhaus, Josef Müller-Brockmann, Paul Rand, and two of his personal friends and mentors, Saul Bass and Robert Brownjohn.

Alan was there at the birth of British graphic design. With his partners Colin Forbes and Bob Gill, and a handful of others, he created a marriage of dry grid European modernism and sassy Madison Avenue 'Big Idea' advertising that most recognise as the best form of graphic design: structured, cool typography supporting a clever, simply executed concept.

He also co-founded D&AD, in emulation of the New York Art Directors' Club. From its inception, Alan and his friends ensured that it exceeded its model: D&AD admitted both art directors and designers. And, as we have seen, this fundamental principle of inclusion has seen the value of D&AD's pursuit of excellence expand far beyond any disciplinary or geographic border.

Alan went on to co-found Pentagram, which became one of the most influential and highly regarded design studios in the world. It remains the only true inter-disciplinary practice of any scale, combining architecture, graphic design, product design and interiors. Anyone who visited in its heyday, when its founding partners were still at the helm, could see that it was part workplace and part club. You ate lunch there, read the papers, gazed at Theo Crosby's mask collection and sat with Alan in the evening when he held court over a jug of iced Vermouth. Alan was always open to conversation, with anyone. He could appear fierce – he sported a four-inch scar on his cheek – but he was actually very warm and at ease in company. He always accepted people, was always attentive, always frank. He had countless friends.

Alan often talked of design as 'sensual pleasure', and the feel of a project that was going well as 'drunkenness'. He did his best to construct his life so he could be 'drunk' as much as possible. The world, he said, would be a better place 'if everyone concentrated on having a good time ... they wouldn't be arguing, or cutting each other dead in the street, or shooting each other, or whatever, because that is contrary to having a good time. What is the alternative? Having a boring or unpleasant time? Design is a style of living.' He talked of the integration of his life and work as 'seamless', and he took this literally. At his home, a big sliding door could be pulled open to join his white studio to his living room.

After 20 years at Pentagram, Alan left to work freelance, quickly landing a plum job as art director of Phaidon Press. In a typical understatement, he said he found dealing with art as a subject matter was 'more stimulating than dog food'. He played no small part in making Phaidon the great art publisher it is. Five years ago, he won Novartis as a client and worked with a small team on the regeneration of a campus occupying a huge part of the city of Basle. I know this project made him very happy, since it so completely fulfilled his mantra of being 'involved with intelligent people on stimulating projects'. As well as a logo, he designed fountains, street signs, an apiary, and the 'wonderwall' a long, painted steel fence skirting the site, elaborately cut through with hundreds of silhouettes of nearly every item on earth: jet fighters, yachts, snails, knights, elephants and artichokes.

Alan's productivity in his last years was astonishing. He exhibited an unforgettable set of bizarre papier-maché animals at the Royal Academy. His work expanded to include watercolours of flowers, drawings made while walking, collages involving sandpaper, sculptures made of pencils, and several drawers of alphabets cut from the crude lettering on cardboard boxes. I once sat with him and looked through a pile of 300 drawings of people's shadows he had made over the course of a month. While none of this is strictly 'design', the images and ideas were often used as the centrepiece of a poster, a logo or the cover of a book.

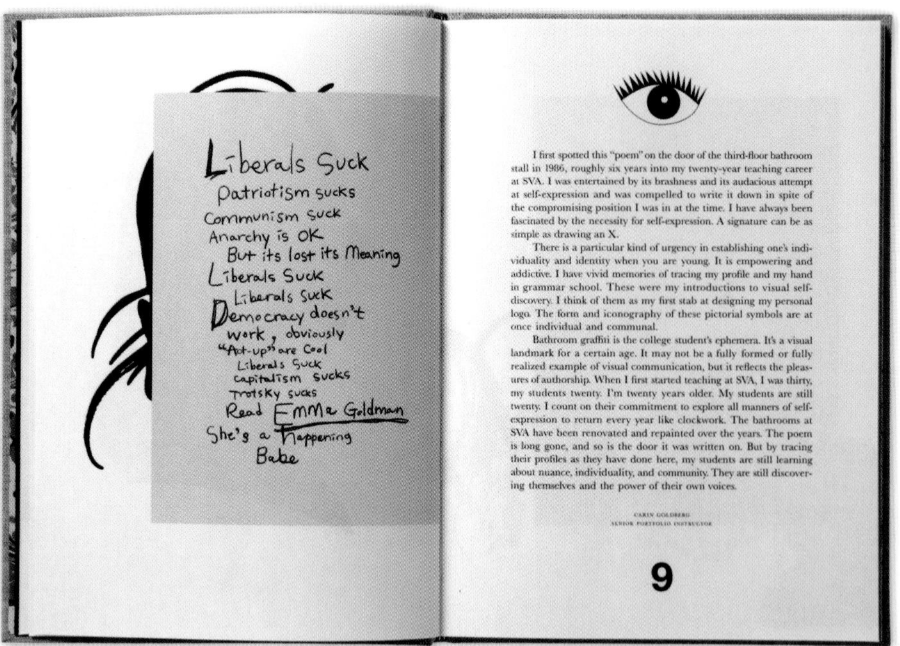

I first spotted this "poem" on the door of the third-floor bathroom stall in 1986, roughly six years into my twenty-year teaching career at SVA. I was entertained by its brashness and its audacious attempt at self-expression and was compelled to write it down in spite of the compromising position I was in at the time. I have always been fascinated by the necessity for self-expression. A signature can be as simple as drawing an X.

There is a particular kind of urgency in establishing one's individuality and identity when you are young. It is empowering and addictive. I have vivid memories of tracing my profile and my hand in grammar school. These were my introductions to visual self-discovery. I think of them as my first stab at designing my personal logo. The form and iconography of these pictorial symbols are at once individual and communal.

Bathroom graffiti is the college student's ephemera. It's a visual landmark for a certain age. It may not be a fully formed or fully realized example of visual communication, but it reflects the pleasures of authorship. When I first started teaching at SVA, I was thirty, my students twenty. I'm twenty years older. My students are still twenty. I count on their commitment to explore all manners of self-expression to return every year like clockwork. The bathrooms at SVA have been renovated and repainted over the years. The poem is long gone, and so is the door it was written on. But by tracing their profiles as they have done here, my students are still learning about nuance, individuality, and community. They are still discovering themselves and the power of their own voices.

CARIN GOLDBERG
SENIOR PORTFOLIO INSTRUCTOR

9

17

THINK OF DESIGN AS A COMPASS

STEVEN **HELLER**

ARTHUR **HOCHSTEIN**

CARIN **GOLDBERG**

"Great design," says Steven Heller, "creates an identity, a personality for a publication. And a personality helps because you know where you are. A magazine is a storehouse of very disparate stuff, but a good design will glue it together and give you a sense of place. It's like having a compass that tells you how to get where you're going." This is the primary role of publication designers: to create a way for readers to understand, access, and navigate the information being presented. Designers are notoriously interested in change, both creating it and following it, often simply for the sake of change. But in many cases, this inclination does nothing but cause confusion for the reader. "I try to distinguish between designer boredom and utility for the reader," Arthur Hochstein explains. "We might want to do something different just because we already did it last week, but in terms of what the reader is getting, this may be a problem."

Readers expect a certain comforting familiarity in a destination they return to weekly or monthly or even just a few times a year. Even if their expectation is to be surprised, they still don't want design to confound the habits they have formed when it comes to how they peruse their favorite publications. "There's a great deal of responsibility designing a magazine," Carin Goldberg notes. "A magazine is something that will, hopefully, be around for a long time. You want your readers to become loyal customers by meeting their expectations while continuing to surprise. For example, departments are the sections a reader looks forward to and anticipates. They give the magazine continuity and a foundation. A magazine must have a philosophy that cultivates followers. The designer has to approach this philosophy responsibly because it doesn't just happen once."

Carin Goldberg designed and edited this book for the School of Visual Arts, *Senior Library 2004*, which discusses art, design, and education, and also shows various artifacts from the process.

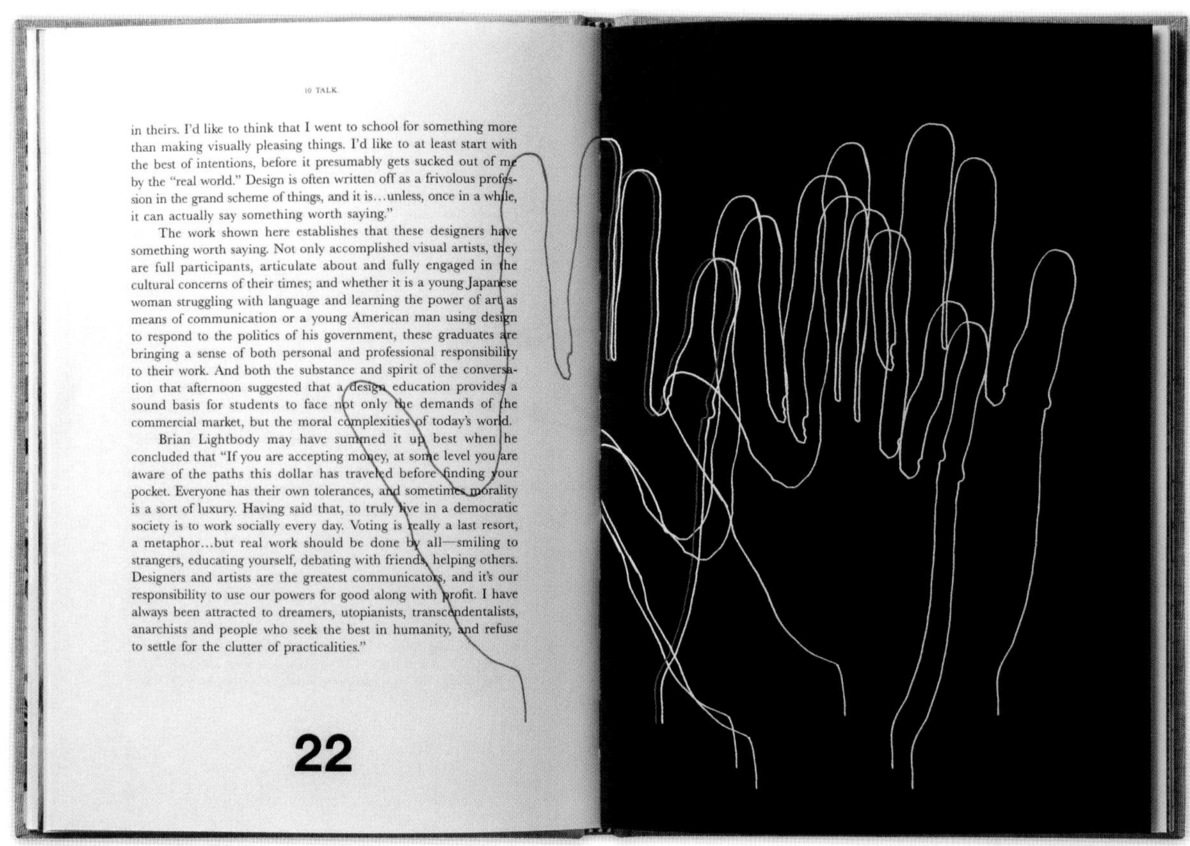

10 TALK.

in theirs. I'd like to think that I went to school for something more than making visually pleasing things. I'd like to at least start with the best of intentions, before it presumably gets sucked out of me by the "real world." Design is often written off as a frivolous profession in the grand scheme of things, and it is…unless, once in a while, it can actually say something worth saying."

The work shown here establishes that these designers have something worth saying. Not only accomplished visual artists, they are full participants, articulate about and fully engaged in the cultural concerns of their times; and whether it is a young Japanese woman struggling with language and learning the power of art as means of communication or a young American man using design to respond to the politics of his government, these graduates are bringing a sense of both personal and professional responsibility to their work. And both the substance and spirit of the conversation that afternoon suggested that a design education provides a sound basis for students to face not only the demands of the commercial market, but the moral complexities of today's world.

Brian Lightbody may have summed it up best when he concluded that "If you are accepting money, at some level you are aware of the paths this dollar has traveled before finding your pocket. Everyone has their own tolerances, and sometimes morality is a sort of luxury. Having said that, to truly live in a democratic society is to work socially every day. Voting is really a last resort, a metaphor…but real work should be done by all—smiling to strangers, educating yourself, debating with friends, helping others. Designers and artists are the greatest communicators, and it's our responsibility to use our powers for good along with profit. I have always been attracted to dreamers, utopianists, transcendentalists, anarchists and people who seek the best in humanity, and refuse to settle for the clutter of practicalities."

22

18 MAKE SURE YOUR MAGAZINE SPEAKS INTELLIGENTLY TO ITS AUDIENCE

JEREMY **LESLIE**

A magazine, unlike most other graphic design projects, is a kind of repeated, continuous conversation between audience and contributors. As with any conversation, it is respectful to keep in mind the background, interests, and opinions of those you are attempting to engage. "The first thing to consider is who the magazine is for," says Jeremy Leslie, "because there's nothing sadder than a magazine without readers." It is also vital to assume your readers are smart and paying attention. "People experience a magazine more than once," Leslie notes. "It's an ongoing relationship and you need to know that a fair amount of your readership will recall something that happened six months ago, and so you have to build a visual language that is both instantly recognizable and intelligent." After all, there are so many publications available that if readers don't like one, there's certainly another one close by on the newsstand that is bound to attract their interest. "Anyone can create a magazine and put it out there, but if no one buys it, it's a failed magazine no matter how great it looks or how well designed it is," he concludes.

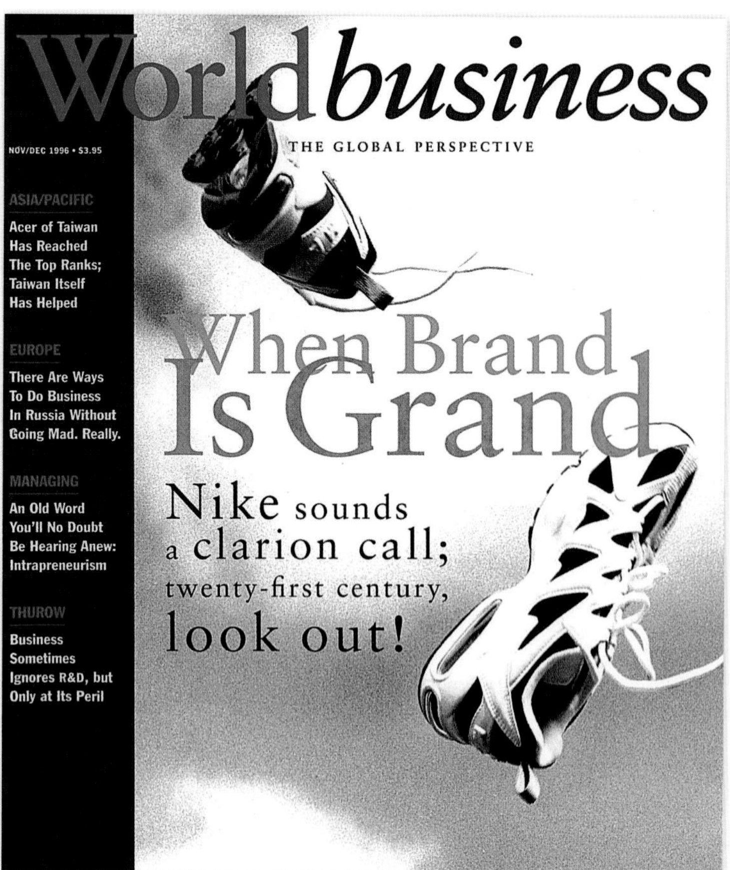

19

CHALLENGE YOUR READERS

KALLE **LASN**

If you assume the inherent intelligence of your audience, then you know they're not only going to be insulted by pandering and patronizing in any form, but they will probably enjoy the bracing effect of an occasional challenge. "If you start second-guessing your readership," says Kalle Lasn, "then you've lost your passion. If you think deeply about what readers really want, they don't necessarily want the same grid or familiarity; what they really want is to be surprised and delighted and to have an epiphany from you, something that knocks them for a loop. They want their comfort level broken rather than enhanced." After all, even someone simply looking for a bit of gossip while waiting in the doctor's office is still looking for the titillation of discovering something they didn't know. As Lasn says, "A really successful magazine is a surprise with every issue."

Above and opposite: *World Business* and *Worth* magazine covers, designed by Ina Saltz, are demonstrations of the balancing act a logo has to play with strong images and variety of typefaces in order to attract readers and potential readers.

20

CONSIDER THE BUSINESS SIDE

JEREMY **LESLIE**

VINCE **FROST**

A commercial publisher is a business, and magazines are its product. So drumming up sales—both from readers buying the magazine and advertisers paying for pages—should be every much a part of the design equation as font styles and column inches. "You have to consider things such as how the publisher is going to go about creating a strategy for distribution and such," notes Jeremy Leslie. "These are not just considerations for the business team, but for the designer as well, and if a brief comes out and it doesn't have that information, you must go and get it." By expanding your role beyond straightforward graphic design, you also have the added advantage of making yourself much more valuable to the client, whether that's your editor or a corporation. As Vince Frost says, "I take a very entrepreneurial approach and look at the whole business. There's so many ways we can help, such as creating better systems. To me, it's about giving design business advice."

21

ARJEN **NOORDEMAN**

EDIT YOURSELF

Designers seem naturally inclined to try new things. And sometimes, they try all of them at once. This approach may be extremely productive as part of initial explorations, but knowing what to take out of it is as important as knowing what to put in. "I like to be lavish and luxurious and add as many bells and whistles as possible," notes Arjen Noordeman, "But then I want to scale it back. That's often for the budget, but it's also good for the design. I have a tendency to want everything that's possible, but concepts often communicate more clearly when you bring it down to the essence, and when I'm forced to do that, I'm happier in the end."

Noordeman draws first on his design education and then on his design upbringing. "I come from the Dutch school of design," he explains, "where everything is very stark and minimal, where the teachers are always saying 'why is this here?' 'why is that there?' Dutch design whittles everything down to the bare essentials needed to get the message across. I was seduced by the Deconstructivism approach to design and I went to Cranbrook to see this other kind of design. I really expanded my vocabulary there, which was great, but then I was struggling with restraints and wanting to pull out all the stops and discovering that it's not always good to do that, either. So I've taught myself to pull out all the stops at first, and then edit, edit, edit down to the essence of the design."

Cyber-Neologoliferation

In the age of the Internet, the Oxford English Dictionary is coming face to face with the boundlessness of the English language.

By James Gleick

When I got to John Simpson and his band of lexicographers in Oxford earlier this fall, they were working on the P's. *Pletzel, plish, pod person, point-and-shoot, polyamorous* — these words were all new, one way or another. They had been plowing through the P's for two years but were almost done (except that they'll never be done), and the Q's will be "just a twinkle of an eye," Simpson said. He prizes patience and the long view. A pale, soft-spoken man of middle height and profound intellect, he is chief editor of the Oxford English Dictionary and sees himself as a steward of tradition dating back a century and a half. "Basically it's the same work as they used to do in the 19th century," he said. "When I started in 1976, we were still working very much on these index cards, everything was done on these index cards." He picked up a stack of 6-inch-by-4-inch slips and riffled through them. A thou-

Typography by Sam Winston

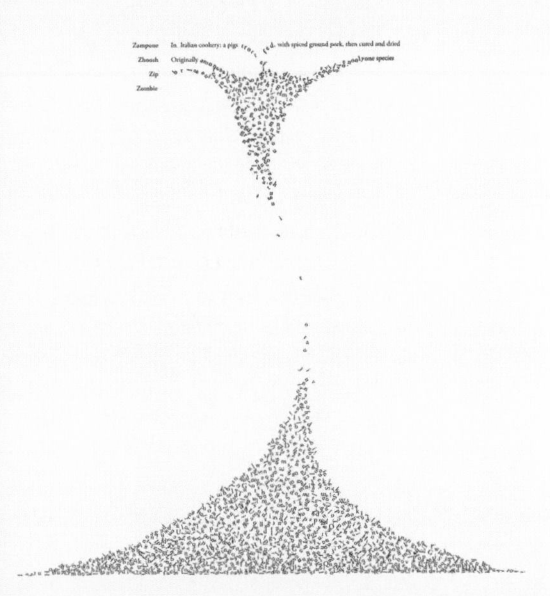

and radio transcripts. The corpus sends its home-built Web crawler out in search of text, raw material to show how the language is really used.

I'm too embarrassed to ask the lexicographers if they have a favorite word. They get that a lot. Peter Gilliver tells me his anyway: *twiffler.* A twiffler, in case you didn't know, is a plate intermediate in size between a dinner plate and a bread plate. "I love it because it fills a gap," Gilliver says. "I also love it because of its etymology. It comes from Dutch, like a lot of ceramics vocabulary. *Twijfelaar* means something intermediate in size, and it comes from *twijfelen*, which means to be unsure. It's a plate that can't make up its mind!"

Fiona McPherson gives me *mondegreen.* A mondegreen is a misheard lyric, as in, "Lead on, O kinky turtle." It is named after Lady Mondegreen. There was no Lady Mondegreen. The lines of a ballad, "They hae slain the Earl of Murray,/And laid him on the green" are misheard as "They hae slain the Earl of Murray and Lady Mondegreen."

"A lot of people are just really excited by that word because they think it's amazing that there is a word for that concept," McPherson says.

I have my own favorites among the newest entries in O.E.D.3. *Pixie dust* is, as any child knows, "an imaginary magical substance used by pixies." *Air kiss* is defined with careful anatomical instructions plus a note: "sometimes with the connotation that such a gesture implies insincerity or affectation." *Builder's bum* is reportedly Brit. and colloq., "with allusion to the perceived propensity of builders to expose inadvertently this part of the body."

It is clear that the English of the O.E.D. is no longer the purely written language, much less a formal or respectable English, the diction recommended by any authority. Gilliver, a longtime editor who also seems to be the O.E.D.'s resident historian, points out that the dictionary feels obliged to include words that many would regard simply as misspellings. No one is particularly proud of the new entry as of December 2003 for *nucular*, a word not associated with high standards of diction. "Bizarrely, I was amazed to find that the spelling n-u-c-u-l-a-r has decades of history," Gilliver says. "And that is not to be confused with the quite different word, *nucular,* meaning 'of or relating to a nucule.'" There is even a new entry for *miniscule*; it has citations going back more than 100 years.

Yet the very notion of correct and incorrect spelling seems under attack. In Shakespeare's day, there was no such thing: no right and wrong in spelling, no dictionaries to consult. The word *debt* could be spelled det, dete, dett, dette or dept, and no one would complain.

Then spelling crystallized, with the spread of printing. Now, with mass communication taking another leap forward, spelling may be diversifying again, spellcheckers notwithstanding. The O.E.D. so far does not recognize *straight-laced*, but the Oxford English Corpus finds it outnumbering *strait-laced*. Similarly for *just desserts.*

To explain why cyberspace is a challenge for the O.E.D. as well as a godsend, Gilliver uses the phrase "sensitive ears."

"You know we are listening to the language," he says. "When you are listening to the language by collecting pieces of paper, that's fine, but now it's as if we can hear everything said anywhere. Members of some tiny English-speaking community anywhere in the world just happen to commit their communications to the Web: there it is. You thought some word was obsolete? Actually, no, it still survives in a very small community of people who happen to use the Web — we can hear about it."

In part, it's just a problem of too much information: a small number of lexicographers with limited time. But it's also that the O.E.D. is coming face to face with the language's boundlessness.

The universe of human discourse always has backwaters. The language spoken in one valley was a little different from the language of the next valley and so on. There are more valleys now than ever, but they are not so isolated. They find one another in chat rooms and on blogs. When they coin a word, anyone may hear.

Neologisms can be formed by committee: *transistor,* Bell Laboratories, 1948. Or by wags: *booboisie,* H.L. Mencken, 1922. But most arise through spontaneous generation, organisms appearing in a petric dish, like *blog* (c. 1999). If there is an ultimate limit to the sensitivity of lexicographers' ears, no one has yet found it. The rate of change in the language itself — particularly the process of neologism — has surely shifted into a higher gear now, but away from dictionaries, scholars of language have no clear way to measure the process. When they need quantification, they look to the dictionaries.

"An awful lot of neologisms are spur-of-the-moment creations, whether it's literary effect or it's conversational effect," says Naomi S. Baron, a linguist at American University, who studies these issues. "I could probably count on the fingers of a hand and a half the serious linguists who know anything about the Internet. That hand and a half of us are fascinated to watch how the Internet makes it possible not just for new words to be coined but for neologisms to spread like wildfire."

It's partly a matter of sheer intensity. Cyberspace is an engine driving change in the language. "I think of it as a saucepan under which the temperature has been turned up," Gilliver says. "Any word, because of the interconnectedness of the English-speaking world, can spring from the backwater. And they are still backwaters, but they have this instant connection to ordinary, everyday discourse." Like the printing press, the telegraph and the telephone before it, the Internet is transforming the language simply by transmitting information differently. And what makes cyberspace different from all previous information technologies is its intermixing of scales from the largest to the smallest without prejudice, broadcasting to the millions, narrowcasting to groups, instant messaging one to one.

'When you are listening to the language by collecting pieces of paper, that's fine, but now it's as if we can hear everything said anywhere,' says one editor.

So anyone can be an O.E.D. author now. And, by the way, many try. "What people love to do is send us words they've invented," Bernadette Paton says, guiding me through a windowless room used for storage of old word slips. *Will you put the word I have invented into one of your dictionaries?* is a question in the AskOxford.com FAQ. All the submissions go into the files, and until there is evidence for some general usage, that's where the wannabes remain.

Don't bother sending in *FAQ.* Don't bother sending in *wannabes.*

They're not even particularly new. For that matter, don't bother sending in anything you find via Google. "Please note," the O.E.D.'s Web site warns solemnly, "it is generally safe to assume that examples found by searching the Web, using search engines such as Google, will have already been considered by O.E.D. editors." ■

TYPOGRAPHY BY SAM WINSTON

In the *New York Times Magazine*, Arem Duplessis and his team show how free and flexible a designer can be, while still maintaining the integrity of the brand and bringing dimension to information, text, and images.

22

JEREMY **LESLIE**

BE WILLING TO ASK, "WHAT IF?"

Publications are a group endeavor. Hopefully, your team is made up of really smart people who've given plenty of thought to what they're trying to create and how it will live in the world. Unfortunately, designers are often brought in toward the end of the planning phase and asked to tactically execute on a strategy they may not have participated in developing. But it's never too late to step back and challenge assumptions. "Never take stuff for granted," says Jeremy Leslie. "It comes down to teamwork. If you're sitting around with a group of colleagues trying to work out how something should be, I would hope that at least one person at the table would say, 'what if?' What if that really isn't good enough, what if we dropped the intro and went straight here, what if we chopped it up into pieces...." If your team is intelligent, courageous, and interested in making an impact with their publication, they'll certainly value the questions and explorations, even if, in the end, they serve to reinforce the original approach.

23

NICKI **KALISH**

AGNES **ZEILSTRA**

BALANCE THE FAMILIAR WITH THE UNEXPECTED

Magazine and newspaper readers tend to come back to the same publication over and over again. As creatures of habit, they also tend to develop a personal method for navigating the content, perhaps skimming everything before digging in, maybe going directly to a favorite section, or methodically moving from front to back. Publication designers respect reader expectations by maintaining consistency in familiar places even as they carve out areas where they can play with the element of surprise. "You want people to know where to look for things," notes Nicki Kalish, art director of the Dining Section of the *New York Times*. "There are always our regular columns, so there's continuity. The Minimalist and the restaurant review, for example, always fall on the same page." In Agnes Zeilstra's woman's magazine, *Red*, they regularly feature "articles about real people and famous people—and there's always one fashion production about clothes."

This consistency does not mean that publication designers lack issues to wrestle with. "We just changed a font and that made the magazine look fresh again. But it's also very important to be consistent," says Zeilstra. For Kalish, "The design challenge comes with the cover stories. There are usually three of them, and they all jump to their own space on the interior pages. Those need to be reinvented every week. There's consistency from week to week with the regular columns falling in the same place, so there's a certain amount of the new and a certain amount of the familiar. I strive to make each cover as distinct as possible from the last one, so there is variety."

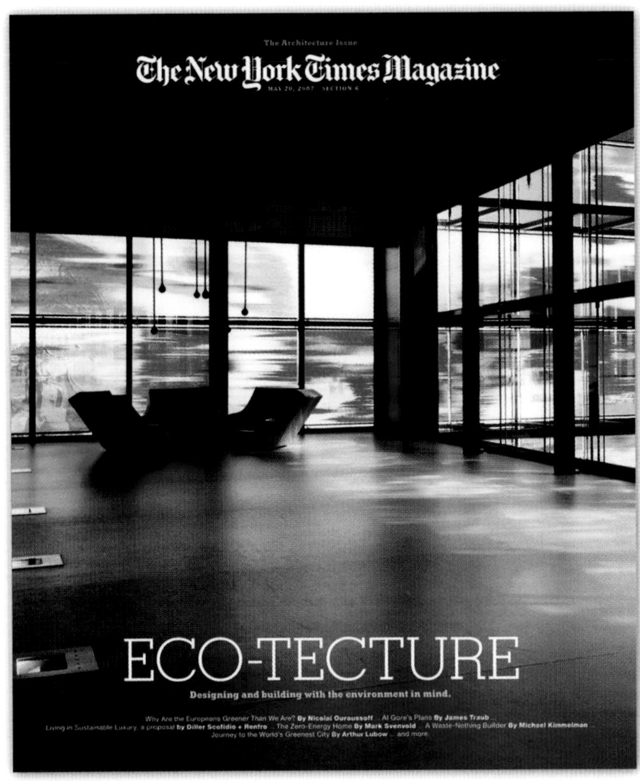

Because the *New York Times Magazine* does not have to compete on the newsstand, its designers have more freedom, especially with covers.

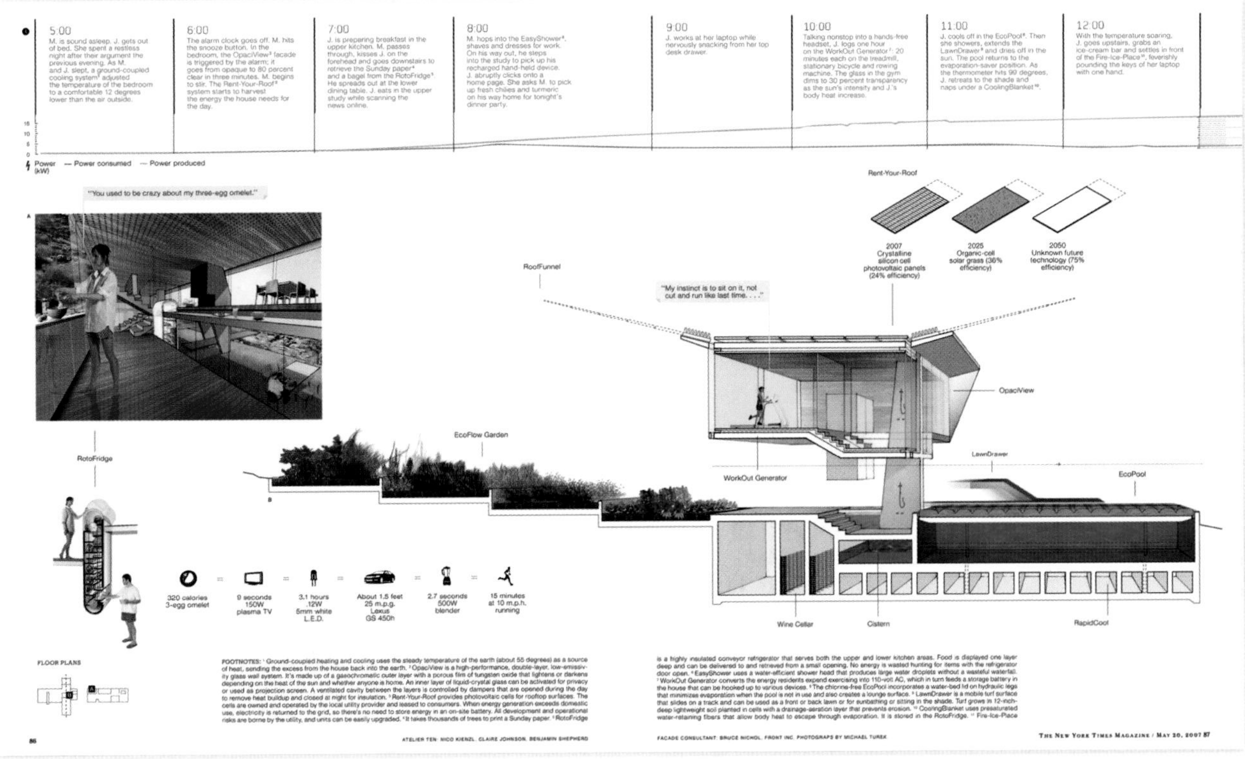

24

MAXIMIZE THE OPPORTUNITIES THAT PRINT MAKES POSSIBLE

LAURENCE **NG**

IdN, international designer's network magazine, is a showcase for design from all over the world. Each issue has a theme, planned as much as six months in advance, to which designers contribute, creating a publication that is chockablock with powerful images and artwork. Publisher Laurence Ng explains how his team uses the power of the printing press to make all this design shine individually and the magazine work as a whole: "Our job is to make the artwork more presentable and more visually impactful," he says. "Most of it has a lot of visual impact already, but because there are so many different articles, and we don't want them to crash, we have to package them individually. So, we use different page layouts, printing techniques and even, in some cases, different paper, to make them look different." This means magazines are printed in at least six colors, with sometimes up to six different papers, a few different varnishes, and even different-size sheets in a single issue.

One of the ways *IdN* keeps everything from becoming too crazy is by using a grid for individual articles, but no overall grid for the magazine as a whole. While Ng readily admits that this process—which requires them to do all prepress work in-house and sometimes work with several different printers in several different countries on a single issue—is a "nightmare," the results are spectacular. "A lot of designers out there still want to feel and touch. On the website, you don't feel the paper, the print quality, so we still want to produce quality magazines," he says.

Above and opposite: *IdN* magazine, produced in Asia, features the best in graphic design from around the world. The extreme visual impact of the content is showcased in pages that push printing capabilities by using multiple varnishes, extra colors, several kinds of paper, and even different sheet sizes in a single issue.

IdN
THE ART DIRECTORS ISSUE.
ERICANDMARIE FAGETA HI
LIEUXCOMMUNS NON-FORMAT
RGBSTUDIO RUMBERO DESIGN
SYLVIA TOURNERIE VISIONAIRE
The Power of Print
AND YOUR ALL-TIME FAVOURITE FREE DVD
UN HIVER A

НОЯБРЬ
1917
ИЗ ОГНЯ
РЕВОЛЮЦИИ
МИРОВОЙ БУРЖУАЗИИ
ARSEN MESHERYAKOV
ART DIRECTOR OF DESIGN STUDIO AGEY TOMESH AND PUBLISHING HOUSE WAM (WORLD ART MUSEUM)
ARSEN MESHE

***IdN* magazine, published by Laurence Ng**

CREATIVE COUNTRIES MEXICO
PRESENTS
JULIO CARRASCO P.76-78
CESAR MORENO P.74-75
LUIS TORRES P.79-81
COLOURFUL! PASSIONATE! SENSUAL!

JUST AS A HUMAN BIRTHMARK NEVER GOES AWAY, SO THE ARTISTIC IMPRINT OF A COUNTRY'S CULTURAL HERITAGE NEVER ENTIRELY DISAPPEARS.

就像一個人的胎記永遠不會消失，一個國家的文化傳承所留下的藝術印記，也從來不會全然消亡。

風格和技術可以改變，流行來了又去，但有些事物可以在世代間沿傳，經得起時間考驗。以墨西哥為例，活潑的色彩和充滿生氣的態度，可以說是他們基因的一部份，然而他們的藝術觀卻相當前衛。在上一期我們介紹了八位年輕墨西哥創意工作者的作品，經由他們在個別領域的努力，他們創造了新的浪潮。在這一期中，我們將繼續對當代墨西哥藝術場景的探索，引介更多不斷求新求變的設計師。

25

ENJOY THE END OF THE PROJECT AS MUCH AS THE START OF IT

JASON **GODFREY**

JEREMY **LESLIE**

Magazine work is cyclical. Whether it's a weekly or a monthly or quarterly, there is a rhythm of creating a structure, filling the structure, sending it off, and starting over again. Jason Godfrey, of Godfrey Design in England, fondly recalls his time working for Conde Nast in New York. "You design for a month, you get it out of the studio, and then you start again. I quite enjoyed it," he says. "And I think it's peculiar to the publication design process where every month you start with a completely clean slate. Other projects can tend to drag on, but with a magazine, you work for a month and then start over. You work toward the day you get it off to production, and there's this palpable sense of relief. And then you start on a new one."

Of course, that relief may be moderated by some degree of frustration over what you were not able to accomplish in the deadline allowed. "I think that picking up a magazine and checking it out is always a thrilling and nauseating experience," says Jeremy Leslie. "You put a lot of yourself into this thing, and it's exciting to see how some of it comes off, but also it never really fully works." Fortunately, there's always the next issue waiting for your attention, giving you the opportunity to improve on your own work. "I love working with magazines because they're still developing and moving on," Leslie explains. "There's a really gentle, pleasant cycle to seeing it come out, and it's never perfect, and you're always stretching for perfection."

CREATIVE COUNTRY - RUSSIA

Casting off thE shacklEs of socialist rEalism

拋開社會寫實主義的桎梏

text by Eva Rukhina

俄羅斯，建構主義發源地。但說到設計創作，在將近 100 年前，不幸地被刻板教條給牽制住了。1920 年代，當時的前衛藝術家如 Lissitsky 、 Malevich ，以及攝影師 Rodchenko 發明了現代印刷藝術的基本原則－圓、三角和四角的崇高性，留白的重要性，照片的蒙太奇效果，和戲劇性的透視效果。但是，他們明智的遠見，很快就被 1930 年代蘇聯的宣傳攻擊和社會寫實主義的陰影給淹沒了。

過去這 80 年來，俄羅斯可說是毫無「設計」可言。「設計」這個字只意味工業設計，由於蘇聯時期所製造的產品皆其貌不揚又呆板，甚至還有負面的意涵。對蘇聯的職業設計師來說，使用這些日常機械工具，可真不是什麼賞心悅目的事。而人們卻還得天天生活在沮喪糟糕的建築、大量製造的家具，和沒有美感的室內裝潢之中。

這樣的蘇維埃聯邦在 15 年前已經瓦解了，但可怕的後果仍是到處可見。儘管莫斯科改變迅速，很難再找到一家老式的咖啡館和商店，因為所有地面上的物件都被重新設計過和改建。但在嶄新的購物廣場和流行的餐廳中，總夾雜着廢棄工廠和醜陋的典型五層公寓。

這種對比令人沮喪，尤其對那些適應了新生活，而不願意認同過去的當代設計師們而言。只要開車稍微離開莫斯科，他們會覺得自己正經歷着過往的創傷。這樣令人灰心的文化傳承，是俄羅斯現代生活的背景。然而，每年的新觀念又一層一層往上加，希望盡快地將 20 世紀的恐懼淡忘。

1998 年的經濟危機，重大地改變了這個國家的視覺文化。新世代的設計師發展了新規則，一步一步改變着週遭的世界。所有東西，從電視台的識別，到紅酒的標籤，都變得雅致又簡約。俄羅斯人複製荷蘭最棒的印刷設計，並快速學到如何再製二流的西方編排，設計公司出產的作品平均水準快速提昇，但少有真正有趣的作品現身。

這篇文章報導的俄羅斯藝術家皆很獨特，各有其強烈的個人風格。有時他們隱藏自己俄羅斯的根源，有時又將俄羅斯民族的特色表露無遺。無論創作的方式是向主流的國際風格靠攏，或是回溯到民族根源的認同，他們的作品總是極為幽默，又不曲高和寡，令人耳目一新。

IdN magazine, published by Laurence Ng

MAGAZINE MAKEOVER

JASON **TREAT**, JAMES **BENNET**

The *Atlantic Monthly* has been, for 150 years, a magazine for readers. Dedicated to the long form of journalism and offering a range of in-depth investigative and analytical pieces about culture, politics, global issues, and more, it is a publication that people sit down with for some serious mental engagement. As such, a recent redesign could have been an exercise fraught with hazards. The design and editorial team had to tread lightly with the weight and wisdom of history as well as the habits, moods, and expectations of a loyal, intellectual, educated—and therefore, demanding—set of readers.

"Everything we knew about our readership is that people spend a lot of time with the magazine," notes art director Jason Treat. "The mandate was to create a magazine that celebrates this and is a pleasure to read." However, staff also recognized that even dedicated readers have their limits. "The goal was to make it easier to move through the magazine," says editor James Bennet, "and to make it less intimidating. The feeling and feedback from colleagues was that you were too often faced with dense pages of text, and that even among readers devoted to the long form, it was a little too much to ask."

In the redesigned *Atlantic Monthly*, an interior spread acts as a second cover, increasing opportunities to showcase stunning photography and to direct readers to feature pieces.

BEFORE

AFTER

Primary Sources

Tales from the couch in the Oval Office; the emerging Islamist majority in Palestine; the curious phenomenon of the "daughter gap"

HISTORY

The Presidential Mind

THE ATLANTIC

APRIL 2006 | VOLUME 297 | NUMBER 3

(Contents continued)

THE CRITICS BOOKS, MANNERS, MORES

PURSUITS & RETREATS

COVER PHOTOGRAPH

HEADING AND CALENDAR DRAWINGS

THIS MONTH ON THE ATLANTIC ONLINE: www.theatlantic.com

The Issue in Brief

The Atlantic

OCTOBER 2007 | VOLUME 300 | NUMBER 3

ON THE PREVIOUS PAGE

DIMINISHING RETURNS? A worker descends a staircase at an oil-production facility in Sudan. Controversial companies—such as those that do business with repressive regimes like Sudan's—create dilemmas for would-be socially responsible investors, as Henry Blodget details in "The Conscientious Investor."

PHOTO BY MICHAEL FREEMAN/CORBIS

THE AGENDA

FEATURES

POETRY

THE CRITICS

OTHER DEPARTMENTS

COVER *by Samantha Appleton*

HEADING DRAWINGS *by Istvan Banyai*

HIGHLIGHTS THIS MONTH ON **theAtlantic.com**

SLIDESHOW: A HAPPY PLACE Mark Jenkins, author of this month's Travels article, narrates photos from Bhutan, where the phallus is a celebrated symbol and the government monitors the Gross National Happiness.

INTERVIEW: SURVIVAL OF THE KINDEST Olivia Judson, author of "The Selfless Gene," discusses the evolutionary roots of altruism and fellow feeling.

INTERVIEW: THE PAKISTAN QUESTION Joshua Hammer, author of "After Musharraf," talks with *Atlantic* senior editor Joy de Menil about Pakistan's future and its implications for the United States.

PLUS: BLOG POSTS BY ANDREW SULLIVAN, JAMES FALLOWS, AND MORE

In before and after comparisons, both the *Atlantic Monthly*'s design problems and solutions became obvious. In redesign, the magazine maintained its commitment to the long form of journalism while making the extraordinary writing they're known for more accessible to readers.

30 THE AGENDA
THE ATLANTIC OCTOBER 2007

PRIMARY SOURCES

HOMELAND SECURITY

Money for Nothing

State governments are receiving homeland-security grants faster than they can spend them, according to the most recent figures from the Department of Homeland Security. Since 2002, the department has awarded $16 billion, but so far states have picked up only $11 billion; the remainder is sitting unspent in the nation's capital. Even attractive targets for terrorists, like the District of Columbia and New York state—both of which have complained about grant cuts—haven't been able to keep up with the federal government's largesse; New York has spent only 52 percent of its grants, the District 62 percent. New Mexico has been the stingiest (or the most prudent, depending on your point of view), spending only half of its grants to date, while South Dakota has burned through 86 percent of the $96.5 million earmarked to thwart threats in the Badlands. The states say that matching-fund requirements, bidding and contracting procedures, and back-ordered goods have kept much of the money on ice.

—"Agency Roll-up," Department of Homeland Security

Burning a Hole in Their Pocket

Total homeland-security money allocated and percent not spent, by state

Most Money Allocated …		
California	$1,609,729,984	34.8%
New York	$1,451,835,176	47.9%
Texas	$962,780,438	30.1%
Florida	$697,759,563	34.3%
Illinois	$686,090,209	31.6%
… Versus Least Money Allocated		
South Dakota	$96,549,974	14.3%
North Dakota	$92,039,799	15.7%
Delaware	$91,503,145	26.9%
Vermont	$90,966,144	19.6%
Wyoming	$79,829,261	16.2%

RELIGION

Mrs. Pascal's Wager?

Does a fear of hellfire make women more religious than men? "Risk preference theory"—which holds that because females are more risk-averse than males, they are, for example, more likely to attend church as a hedge against the possibility of spending eternity in hell—is the latest attempt to explain the piety gap between men and women. (Other proposed hypotheses suggest that women traditionally have had more time to attend church and that they've seen religion as a source of affirmation in male-dominated societies.) Now a study by two researchers at the University of Arizona aims to dispel the hellfire argument, noting that it presupposes that speculation about the afterlife determines people's religiosity. Researchers studied people who believed in an afterlife and people who didn't, and found not only that women who don't believe in life after death are more religious than men who don't expect an afterlife, but that the gap between the sexes was larger among those who don't anticipate an eternal reward or punishment. Women who don't believe in the afterlife are nearly twice as likely as men with similar beliefs to view the Bible as the literal word of God; women who do believe are only 1.27 times as likely to take the Bible literally. Similarly, women who don't believe in hell attend church more frequently than men who share their skepticism, but women who do believe in hell don't attend church much more often than their male counterparts.

—"Risky Business: Assessing Risk Preference Explanations for Gender Differences in Religiosity," Louise Marie Roth and Jeffrey C. Kroll, American Sociological Review

MAYBE SHE'S born with it

PUBLIC HEALTH

Big Government, Small Results

Turns out Uncle Sam hasn't done that much to stop teens from drinking and driving. The official story goes that the 1984 Federal Uniform Drinking Age Act, which threatened to withhold federal funds from states that didn't raise their drinking age to 21, ended the glory days of teens driving to another state to get drunk and then careening home. According to federal estimates, pushing a uniform minimum drinking age nationwide saved 21,887 lives through 2002. New research argues that it wasn't so: By studying state-by-state data, the authors found that most of the reduction in fatalities came from states that had raised the drinking age before the federal law went on the books; in states that raised the drinking age to comply with the federal pressure, there was little effect. Furthermore, fatalities in states that raised the age early dipped only briefly; in the other states, they either remained steady or increased after the age was changed. The authors conclude that the overall reduction in traffic deaths has had more to do with safer cars and better medical treatment for accident victims than with policies handed down from on high.

—"Does the Minimum Legal Drinking Age Save Lives?" Jeffrey A. Miron, Elina Tetelbaum, National Bureau of Economic Research

THE AGENDA 33
THE ATLANTIC

Random Justice

If you're a Chinese refugee seeking asylum in the United States, what's your best bet? First, move to San Francisco. Then try to find an immigration lawyer, prove that a dependent is counting on you, and pray for a female judge. According to a recent study by three law professors, factors like ethnicity, geography, and the gender of the judge—along with a healthy dose of luck—play a far bigger role than the merits of the case in determining whether a refugee is granted asylum in the United States. The authors analyzed hundreds of thousands of cases and found a huge geographic variance in the rates at which applicants prevailed. In 2005, for instance, the Houston field office granted asylum to only 17 percent of applicants; the Arlington, Virginia, office approved 52 percent. … asylum, whereas only 18 percent of their compatriots in Newark, New Jersey, did. Demographics may account for some of this variance, but they don't explain the discrepancies that the authors found in the judgments of officials in the same buildings: At the federal immigration court in Miami, one judge granted asylum to 88 percent of Colombian applicants, yet another ruled in favor of just 5 percent. The researchers also discovered that asylum seekers with lawyers were granted refuge far more often than those without, that those with dependents had slightly better odds, and that female judges granted asylum at a substantially higher rate than their male counterparts.

—"Refugee Roulette: Disparities in Asylum Adjudication," Jaya Ramji-Nogales, Andrew I. Schoenholtz, and Philip G. Schrag, Stanford Law Review

SOCIETY

Empty-Nesters, Unite!

The kids are, eh, all right. A new poll from the Pew Research Center shows that more people now consider adequate income and an equitable division of household labor more essential to a happy marriage than having children. Researchers asked more than 2,000 adults what they considered important for a successful union; having children ranked eighth out of nine choices, ahead of only "agreement on politics." Just 41 percent said that kids were "very important"—a plunge of 24 percentage points since the last such study, in 1990. ("Sharing household chores" shot up 15 percentage points over the same period, landing in third place.) The report attributes the shift in part to a change in moral thinking that has also led to greater social acceptance of cohabitation, premarital sex, and unwed childbearing. As a result, the authors say, "In the United States today, marriage exerts less influence over how adults organize their lives and how children are born and raised than at any time in the nation's history."

—"As Marriage and Parenthood Drift Apart, Public Is Concerned About Social Impact," Pew Research Center

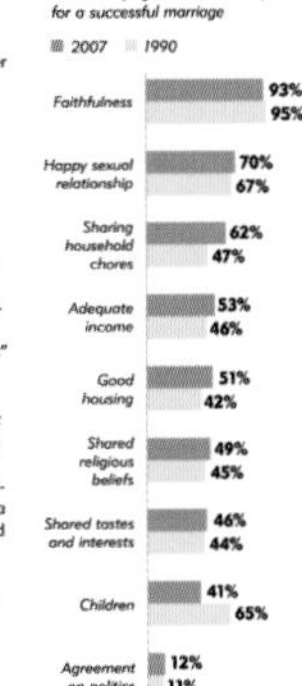

SLOUCHING to conquer

PSYCHOLOGY

Standing Tall

One hundred thirty-five years ago, Charles Darwin wondered whether pride led to good posture, or whether it was the other way around—that a ramrod back inspired self-confidence. A little of both, says a new study—but only for men. The authors asked participants to take a math test while sitting either slumped or upright; they found that men felt better about their performance on the test if they sat upright. Women, however, felt more confident about their performance if they slouched. The men who'd been sitting up straight went on to score better than their hunched counterparts; the women's scores showed no such disparity. The authors suggest that men rely more on internal cues when determining how they feel and that women rely more on external ones—an upright posture forces them to be more self-conscious, which previous studies have shown can hurt how well they do on math tests.

—"Not All Who Stand Tall Are Proud: Gender Differences in the Proprioceptive Effects of Upright Posture," Tomi-Ann Roberts and Yousef Arefi-Afshar, Cognition and Emotion

After months of experimentation, the redesign got a kick forward when Bennet came on as the new editor. "James took a couple of months to get acclimated and then came into my office and said, 'Let's redesign it,'" Treat recalls. This spirit of a joint venture between editor and designer was pervasive throughout the effort and was a cornerstone of its success. "The collaboration was great," says Bennet. "Jason cares a lot about the editorial fundamentals of the magazine. I've had other friends editing other magazines who have a designer with rigid notions of what the magazine should be, rather than what it is, and they're doing more design for design's sake, rather than design for the reader's sake." Treat returns the compliment. "The breakthrough for me was having editorial walking hand in hand with design," he says. "Designing in a vacuum is fun, but it's all theoretical until you have something you can actually use and implement."

The redesign of *Atlantic Monthly* involved a balancing act of respecting orthodoxy, even as the team sought to improve it. "We weren't going to start jumping stories," notes Bennet. "We weren't going to violate our traditions." But they did want to appeal to existing and new readers, as well as different reading styles. "We wanted to serve two types of audiences with one magazine," says Treat. "Those that spent sixty-five minutes with it, and those that skimmed it in the airport or during a subway ride, flagging stories they would come back to later." The design solutions involved a combination of bold additions and small touches that make the magazine more enticing, welcoming, and functional. To start with, the owner requested a table of contents that was only one page. "That idea originated from him as a reader," explains Bennet. "He feels readers want one place where they can go and learn everything about the magazine. The question was how to create an aesthetically pleasing version of that." By incorporating this mandate with another, to become a better showcase for photography, the challenge was resolved. The magazine now has, essentially, two covers: one in the usual place and another within the first few spreads that features a full-bleed photo with a description of the feature articles overlaid on the far right. A complete, single-page table of contents follows. Meanwhile, the full-bleed-photo-with-article-information treatment is also used on feature and section openers, signaling readers when they're coming to new or different sorts of articles.

BEFORE

AFTER

86

87

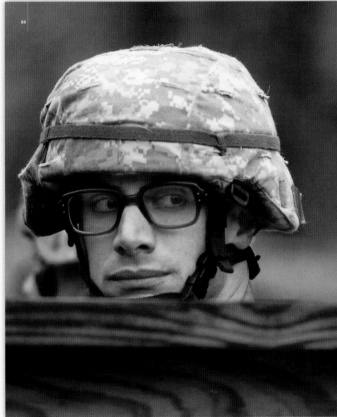

To fight today's wars with an all-volunteer force, the U.S. Army needs more quick-thinking, strong, highly disciplined soldiers. But creating warriors out of the softest, least-willing populace in generations has required sweeping changes in basic training.

BY BRIAN MOCKENHAUPT

Photographs by Mike Haskey

The Army We Have

Guns N' Roses' "Welcome to the Jungle" begins to blare through the trees behind us. "On your feet!" a drill sergeant shouts at the hundreds of men from Alpha and Charlie companies lining a street at Fort Benning. It's 4:30 a.m. Down the road, the first soldiers from Delta Company, 2nd Battalion, 58th Infantry Regiment bob into view. After marching through the sticky Georgia night »

AFTER

24 THE AGENDA
THE ATLANTIC JULY/AUGUST 2007

THE WORLD IN NUMBERS

Attacking cocaine at its source was meant to drive up prices, yet U.S. street dealers are selling it for less than ever.

Snow Fall

BY KEN DERMOTA

If the four-year slog in Iraq seems endless, consider this: The "war on drugs," begun by Richard Nixon, escalated under Ronald Reagan, and continued by every president since, is now in its 37th year. In this long struggle, the past few months have been especially fruitful. In March, the U.S. Coast Guard intercepted a freighter off Panama laden with 20 tons of cocaine, in the largest maritime bust ever. That was followed in April by Colombian authorities' seizure of a 15-ton cache most likely awaiting shipment to Mexico.

Of course, the good news is soured by the fact that cocaine production remains robust enough to allow shipment in 20-ton batches. The Coast Guard would need to repeat its recent haul about every two weeks to intercept all the cocaine that Colombia sends north, and there's no guarantee traffickers wouldn't just ship more to make up for the losses, as they have always done.

The map to the right tracks cocaine shipments from Bolivia and Peru, and from Colombia, which is the source of about 90 percent of the cocaine sold by U.S. dealers. As each kilo island-hops across the Caribbean or travels north through Central America and over the U.S.-Mexican border, its value increases. The rising price reflects cumulatively higher risk to distributors—mostly of shootings or arrests at international borders. Clearly, policing has a big impact on cocaine prices: On the streets of Bogotá, a *gramo* of cocaine can be had for under $2. Recreational users in America, on the other hand, typically pay upward of $50 a gram.

Yet over time, cocaine prices per pure gram in the United States have steadily fallen, from $600 in the early 1980s to less than $200 by the mid-1990s. In 2000, under Plan Colombia, the U.S. took the fight directly to the coca fields, spending nearly as much each year on aerial coca eradication and fighting cocaine-dealing rebels in Colombia as Ireland spends on its entire military. Plan Colombia has cost $4.7 billion since its inception, but cocaine on U.S. streets has only gotten cheaper, while American demand has remained steady.

Why the price decline? More-efficient distribution networks may be part of the answer. Some smugglers now bring "factory-to-you" prices to New York by picking up their dope in Colombia and eliminating middlemen. At the same time, a surge in trade between the U.S. and Mexico has made smuggling safer and cheaper by providing endless nooks and crannies among the billions of dollars' worth of legitimate goods flowing over the border each year.

Inside the United States, retailers have reduced prices by cutting the take of street-corner vendors, some of whom now make less than the minimum wage. Ironically, aggressive imprisonment of drug offenders may contribute to this phenomenon: When convicts rotate out of prison, stigmatized by felony convictions and possessing no licit skills, they are sometimes willing to sell dope for less than they were earning before they went in. Sellers up and down the food chain also appear willing to work for less because the risks involved in selling cocaine have declined: Violence has trailed off since the 1980s crack boom ended, and since 2001, federal drug prosecutions have fallen 25 percent, as agents have been reassigned to chase terrorists.

Many experts say that if we can't keep the price of cocaine out of reach for more people, some money would be better spent on rehabilitation of drug users, and on education. Sea changes in policy, such as decriminalization or legalization of drugs, look politically untenable. In fact, 37 years in, there is still little pressure to end the war on drugs, despite its high costs in blood and treasure: Since 1981, the United States has spent about as much on its "war" on all illicit drugs as it did on its real war in Vietnam—some $600 billion to $800 billion in today's dollars. So far, victory has proven just as elusive.

Ken Dermota is a journalist in the Washington bureau of Agence France-Presse.

THE AGENDA 25
JULY/AUGUST 2007 THE ATLANTIC

Border Traffic

In 2005, 5 million trucks and 92 million personal vehicles crossed the border from Mexico, as did about 90 percent of the cocaine used in the U.S. Before NAFTA, cocaine was carried in overloaded Cessnas across the Caribbean, a risky and expensive trip. Today, most cocaine goes by ship to Mexico; there, traffickers often "shotgun" the load, scattering it into single kilograms to cross the border and reducing overall risk.

'A Hell of a Lot of Coca'

Since 2000, American crop dusters have cumulatively sprayed an area the size of Delaware and Rhode Island to eradicate coca bushes in Colombia. But coca cultivation on small plots and in out-of-the-way places has made up for lost production. The State Department, after discovering thousands of hectares planted outside the areas it had been tracking, said last year it cannot reliably tally coca production. "It's all rather irrelevant," a State Department official who wished to remain anonymous said. "There's still a hell of a lot of coca out there."

The Brazilian Boom

Cocaine bound for Brazil mostly stays there: A recent boom in demand has made Brazil the No. 2 destination for cocaine, behind the U.S.; it has also fueled the growth of larger and more powerful gangs. In 2006, when wardens attempted to interfere with communications between the imprisoned leaders of São Paulo's fearsome First Capital Command gang and its foot soldiers, the latter went on a bombing and killing spree that left more than 150 people dead and halted commerce for days.

* All data from the DEA. 1999 prices come from cities and surrounding areas. 2005 prices come from regional DEA divisions.

68 CHINA MAKES, THE WORLD TAKES
THE ATLANTIC JULY/AUGUST 2007

the hinterland working in Shenzhen is arguably better off economically than an American in Chicago living on minimum wage. She can save most of what she makes and feel she is on the way up; the American can't and doesn't. Over the next two years, the minimum wage in the United States is expected to rise to $7.25 an hour. Assuming a 40-hour week, that's just under $1,200 per month, or about 10 times the Chinese factory wage. But that's before payroll deductions and the cost of food and housing, which are free or subsidized in China's factory towns.

Chinese spokesmen do make a different point about their economy, and they rattle it off so frequently that Western audiences are tempted to dismiss it. They say, "Whatever else we have done, we have brought hundreds of millions of people out of poverty." That is true, it is important, and the manufacturing export boom has been

CHIP RESISTORS displayed in martini glasses at a booth inside the SEG Electronics Market in Shenzhen

a significant part of how China has done it. This economic success obviously does not justify everything the regime has done, especially its crushing of any challenge to one-party rule. But the magnitude of the achievement can't be ignored. For all of the billions of dollars given in foreign aid and supervised by the World Bank, the greatest good for the greatest number of the world's previously impoverished people in at least the last half century has been achieved in China, thanks largely to the outsourcing boom.

Has the move to China been good for American companies? The answer would seemingly have to be yes—otherwise, why would they go there? It is conceivable that bad partnerships, stolen intellectual property, dilution of brand name, logistics nightmares, or other difficulties have given many companies a sour view of outsourcing; I have heard examples in each category from foreign executives. But the more interesting theme I have heard from them, which explains why they are willing to surmount the inconveniences, involves something called the "smiley curve."

The curve is named for the U-shaped arc of the 1970s-era smiley-face icon, and it runs from the beginning to the end of a product's creation and sale. At the beginning is the company's brand: HP, Siemens, Dell, Nokia, Apple. Next comes the idea for the product: an iPod, a new computer, a camera phone. After that is high-level industrial design—the conceiving of how the product will look and work. Then the detailed engineering design for how it will be made. Then the necessary components. Then the actual manufacture and assembly. Then the shipping and distribution. Then retail sales. And, finally, service contracts and sales of parts and accessories.

The significance is that China's activity is in the middle stages—manufacturing, plus some component supply and engineering design—but America's is at the two ends, and those are where the money is. The smiley curve, which shows the profitability or value added at each stage, starts high for branding and product concept, swoops down for manufacturing, and rises again in the retail and servicing stages. The simple way to put this—that the real money is in brand name, plus retail—may sound obvious, but its implications are illuminating.

At each factory I visited, I asked managers to estimate how much of a product's sales price ended up in whose hands. The strength of the brand name was the most important variable. If a product is unusual enough and its brand name attractive enough, it could command so high a price that the retailer might keep half the revenue. (Think: an Armani suit, a Starbucks latte.) Most electronics products are now subject to much fiercer price competition, since it is so easy for shoppers to find bargains on the Internet. Therefore the generic Windows-style laptops I saw in one modern factory might go for around $1,000 in the United States, with the retailer keeping less than $50.

Where does the rest of the money go? The manager of that factory guessed that Intel and Microsoft together

CHINA MAKES, THE WORLD TAKES 69
JULY/AUGUST 2007 THE ATLANTIC

would collect about $300, and that the makers of the display screen, the disk-storage devices, and other electronic components might get $150 or so apiece. The keyboard makers would get $15 or $20; FedEx or UPS would get slightly less. When all other costs were accounted for, perhaps $30 to $40—3 to 4 percent of the total—would stay in China with the factory owners and the young women on the assembly lines.

Other examples: A carrying case for an audio device from a big-name Western company retails for just under $30. That company pays the Chinese supplier $6 per case, of which about half goes for materials. The other $24 stays with the big-name company. An earphone-like accessory for another U.S.-brand audio device also retails for about $30. Of this, I was told, $3 stayed in China. I saw a set of high-end Ethernet connecting cables. The cables are sold, with identical specifications but in three different kinds of packaging, in three forms in the United States: as a specialty product, as a house brand in a nationwide office-supply store, and with no brand over eBay. The retail prices are $29.95 for the specialty brand, $19.95 in the chain store, and $15.95 on eBay. The Shenzhen-area company that makes them gets $2 apiece.

In case the point isn't clear: Chinese workers making $1,000 a year have been helping American designers, marketers, engineers, and retailers making $1,000 a week (and up) earn even more. Plus, they have helped shareholders of U.S.-based companies.

All this is apart from a phenomenon that will be the subject of a future article: China's conversion of its trade surpluses into a vast hoard of dollar-denominated reserves. Everyone understands that in the short run China's handling of its reserves has been a convenience to the United States. By placing more than $1 trillion in U.S. stock and bond markets, it has propped up the U.S. economy. Asset prices are higher than they would otherwise be; interest rates are lower, whether for American families taking out mortgages or for American taxpayers financing the ever-mounting federal debt. The dollar has also fallen less than it otherwise would have—which in the short run helps American consumers keep buying Chinese goods.

Everyone also understands that in the long run China must change this policy. Its own people need too many things—schools, hospitals, railroads—for it to keep sending its profits to America. It won't forever sink its savings into a currency, the dollar, virtually guaranteed to keep falling against the RMB. This year the central government created a commission to consider the right long-term use for China's reserves. No one expects the recommendation to be: Keep buying dollars. How and when the change will occur, what it will be, and what consequences it will have, is what everyone would like to know.

One other aspect of China's development to date has helped American companies in their dealings with it. This is the fact that China, so far, has been different in crucial ways from America's previous great Asian challenger: Japan. Americans have come to view the Japanese economy as a kind of joke, mainly because the Tokyo Stock Exchange has been in a slump for nearly 20 years. Nonetheless, Japan remains the world's second-largest economy. Toyota has overtaken General Motors to become the largest automaker; Japan's exporters have continually increased their sales of electronics and other high-value goods; and the long-standing logic of the Japanese system, in which consumers and investors suffer so that producers may thrive, remains intact.

Japan was already a rich and modern country, as China still is not, by the time trade friction intensified, in the 1980s. More important, its leading companies were often competing head-to-head with established high-value, high-tech companies in the United States: Fujitsu against IBM, Toshiba against Intel, Fuji against Kodak, Sony and Matsushita against Motorola, and on down the list. Gains for Japanese companies often meant direct losses for companies in America—whether those companies were seen as stodgy and noninnovative, like the Detroit firms, or technologically agile and advanced, like the semiconductor makers.

For the moment, China's situation is different. Its companies are numerous but small. Lenovo and Qingdao are its two globally recognized brand names. But Lenovo is known mainly because it bought the ThinkPad brand from IBM, and a quarter of Qingdao Beer is owned by Anheuser-Busch. Chinese exporters have done best when working for, rather than against, Western companies, as Foxconn (like numerous smaller firms) has in working with Apple. While the Chinese government obviously wants to strengthen the country's brands—for instance, with an aircraft company it hopes will compete with Boeing and Airbus—its "industrial planning" has mainly taken the form not of specific targeting but of general business promotion, as with the incentives that brought companies to Shenzhen.

"Here, you've got nine different suppliers within a mile, and they can bring a sample over that afternoon," Casey told me. "People think China is cheap, but really, it's *fast*."

Other changes included increasing margins in features "to give a lot more white space to readers who spent more time with the magazine, because those walls and walls of type were intimidating," explains Treat, and creating a folio section of more compact pieces "for the shorter attention span reader." Type was also opened up and modernized, making a stronger connection between image and headline, and thereby making it easier for readers to find—and find their way into—articles. Information design and presentation used a lighter touch, so complex data is more comprehensible and accessible.

Navigation was simplified by organizing page number, article title, and magazine name around a short rule at the top, rather than spreading them along the bottom of the page. What was great for readers turned out to be less wonderful for advertisers when it was discovered that the extra white space was being carved out of fractional ads. While advertisers were given time to adjust, delaying the launch of the new design, they eventually came to see that having a slightly smaller ad in a publication with more breathing room held many more benefits than drawbacks.

In keeping with the design intention to improve reader experiences, the circulation department utilized an Internet-based interview system to get subscriber feedback on the new look. "In a secure environment, we were able to post mockups of the redesign, and readers emailed us their thoughts," explains Treat. While they were concerned that regular readers "might be unsettled by too much change, the surveys were confirmatory," he says. "The response was overwhelmingly positive."

While the new, less constrained design is certainly more interesting for the art director to work with, it has also helped the editorial mission of the magazine. "It makes the magazine easier to read, and the design does a better job of delivering the message of each story and the larger editorial mission," says Bennet. "It's served as a much better display case for our stories—it's that simple." He also points out that the design does something not usually associated with serious journalism, but is certainly welcome: "It's just more fun."

Chapter Two:

THE ELEMENTS OF A PAGE

26

ARTHUR **HOCHSTEIN**

INA **SALTZ**

JANDOS **ROTHSTEIN**

NICOLE **DUDKA**

CASEY **CAPLOWE**

EMBRACE THE STRUCTURE

"Each magazine is a continuum of adherence to the template and what hits it every week," says Arthur Hochstein. "It doesn't exist in the perfect world of the designer; it has to exist in the real world." This real world, when it comes to publications, includes the framework of style sheets, font families, front of book, back of book, grids, regular columns, mastheads, specific sections, and more. "Some people hate structure and want chaos all the time," Ina Saltz points out, suggesting these people would perhaps not make the best publication designers. "I like some sense of orderly progression," she continues. "I need to know that there's a cycle that is repetitive and dependable, it's not all up for grabs every single time; you're not reinventing the wheel every month." For Saltz, as for many publication designers, structure enhances rather than limits her creativity. "I think of creativity as flowing water," she explains. "For me, if I have a narrow pipe, it goes faster and further; if it's a wide pipe, it just trickles."

Jandos Rothstein, magazine design director, educator, and book and blog writer, also sees the grid as a way to enhance creativity. He compares publication design to jazz: There are only so many rhythms in music, but you can bring in instruments in whatever way you want, he points out. "What the grid does for you as a designer is give you the structure in which you build pages. It helps with the mechanics of putting it out every month, is a timesaving tool, gives you something to work against and work with. Sure, there are magazines that have been built on no grids, but those magazines had one designer doing everything, so there was a continuity and visual vocabulary because it all came from one person. With a grid, you have regularity and rhythm, but you still have quite a bit of freedom." Nicole Dudka also finds plenty of room to move within the grid. "One of the things that I always say is that it's a canvas, not a page. Try not to focus too much on the grid and the structure and the restrictions, but let the artful part drive your design. Once you have a good concept, photo, or illustration, you can let the restrictions and grid fall into place around it."

Great magazines usually create an architecture at the outset—or in redesign—that provides flexibility. At *GOOD* magazine, "We have very consistent sections, but some of these sections are very freeform," explains Casey Caplowe. For example, different artists create several loosely thematic spreads for the "Graphic Statement" that comes before the table of contents in each issue; different designers are given the opportunity to create interpretations and representations of statistical information in the "Transparency" section; the "Op Ed" portion features a different illustrator each month. "All these sections are opportunities where we've created frameworks and then invite people to participate and interpret them each time," Caplowe says. "We don't have a firm, dogmatic idea of what *Good* is. It's an exploration. There's a foundation that's ours, but a lot of the details are other people's."

The structure Pentagram partner Luke Hayman created for the redesign of *Time* magazine is flexible enough to accommodate a variety of editorial content and images so readers have the comfort of knowing they are in the specific world of *Time*, even as they encounter striking artwork, familiar columnists, and the occasional surprise.

Dashboard WASHINGTON MEMO ... NEWSREEL ... LOVE THE U.S., HATE THE U.S. ... A SAFER RIDE IN IRAQ ... MORTGAGE MELTDOWN ... LEXICON **Verbatim** "I SHOULD HAVE FOCUSED ... LESS ON MY PERSONAL MORAL VIEWS" **People** THE SCORE ... DIDDY AND SNOOP: HAS HIP-HOP HEALED? **Milestones** BYE-BYE, BETTY ... CAPTAIN AMERICA SALUTED ... LAST WORD: BRONX FIRE FUNERAL

Briefing

2007 | #13

THE MOMENT

The Confession Procession. These are days of absolution in the nation's capital

"MISTAKES WERE MADE," Attorney General Alberto Gonzales admitted when pressed about the purge of eight U.S. Attorneys viewed as unfriendly to the Administration. "Mistakes were made," President Bush agreed the next day. It's a bad sign when officials are left quoting Nixon spokesman Ron Ziegler, whose handling of Watergate set the standard for nonconfessions as well as nondenials. Flamboyant apology has never been in the Bush script. This is an Administration known for firing people for independence, not incompetence. But campaign season has arrived, subpoena power has changed hands, and suddenly everyone is in a purgative mood.

This was Gonzales' second round in as many weeks, having joined FBI chief Robert Mueller in admitting how far the FBI had stretched the Patriot Act in order to probe the phone and bank records of 52,000 people suspected of terrorism. Setting the pace in the accountability race was Defense Secretary Bob Gates, who fired the Army Secretary for not firing those responsible for the Walter Reed scandal.

In private life the conscience is our secret police, driving us to repent, but in public life contrition is often more about opportunity than obedience. With epic misconduct on every front page—the Vice President's man a convicted perjurer, the sacred trust of wounded soldiers betrayed—there was a window for anyone accused of more commonplace crimes to wipe the slate clean.

In public life, contrition is more about opportunity than obedience

Newt Gingrich confesses his serial marital sins to Focus on the Family founder James Dobson and wins absolution; Mitt Romney admits the error of his earlier tolerance of abortion rights. John Edwards seldom misses a chance to repent of his vote for the war, to highlight Hillary Clinton's refusal to do likewise. As for paying for past mistakes, Barack Obama took care of $400 worth of parking tickets left over from his law-school days—two weeks before he announced his candidacy.

Talk is cheap when confession plays as entertainment on daytime TV. In politics, as in church, there's no telling when penitence is sincere, for God alone knows the human heart. But it's a useful test in judging character to ask whether admitting failure comes at a cost—or a discount. —BY NANCY GIBBS

TIME March 26, 2007 15

WORLD

The Truth About Talibanistan

Islamic militants have turned the borderlands between Pakistan and Afghanistan into a new base for al-Qaeda. An inside look at the next battleground of the war on terrorism

BY ARYN BAKER

KABUL, AFGHANISTAN

THE RESIDENTS OF DARA ADAM Khel, a gunsmiths' village 30 miles south of Peshawar, Pakistan, awoke one morning last month to find their streets littered with pamphlets demanding that they observe Islamic law. Women were instructed to wear all-enveloping burqas and men to grow their beards. Music and television were banned. Then the jihadists really got serious. These days, dawn is often accompanied by the wailing of women as another beheaded corpse is found by the side of the road, a note pinned to the chest claiming that the victim was a spy for either the Americans or the Pakistani government. Beheadings are recorded and sold on DVD in the area's bazaars. "It's the knife that terrifies me," says Hafizullah, 40, a local arms smith. "Before they kill you, they sharpen the knife in front of you. They are worse than butchers."

Stories like these are being repeated across the tribal region of Pakistan, a rugged no-man's-land that forms the country's border with Afghanistan—and that is rapidly becoming home base for a new generation of potential terrorists. Fueled by zealotry and hardened by war, young religious extremists have overrun scores of towns and villages in the border areas, with the intention of imposing their strict interpretation of Islam on a population unable to fight back. Like the Taliban in the late 1990s in Afghanistan, the jihadists are believed to be providing leaders of al-Qaeda with the protection they need to regroup and train new operatives. U.S. intelligence officials think that Osama bin Laden and his deputy, Ayman al-Zawahiri, may have found refuge in these environs. And though 49,000 U.S. and NATO troops are stationed just across the border in Afghanistan, they aren't authorized to operate on the Pakistani side. Remote, tribal and deeply conservative, the border region is less a part of either country than a world unto itself, a lawless frontier so beyond the control of the West and its allies that it has earned a name of its own: Talibanistan.

28

Photographs for TIME by Balazs Gardi

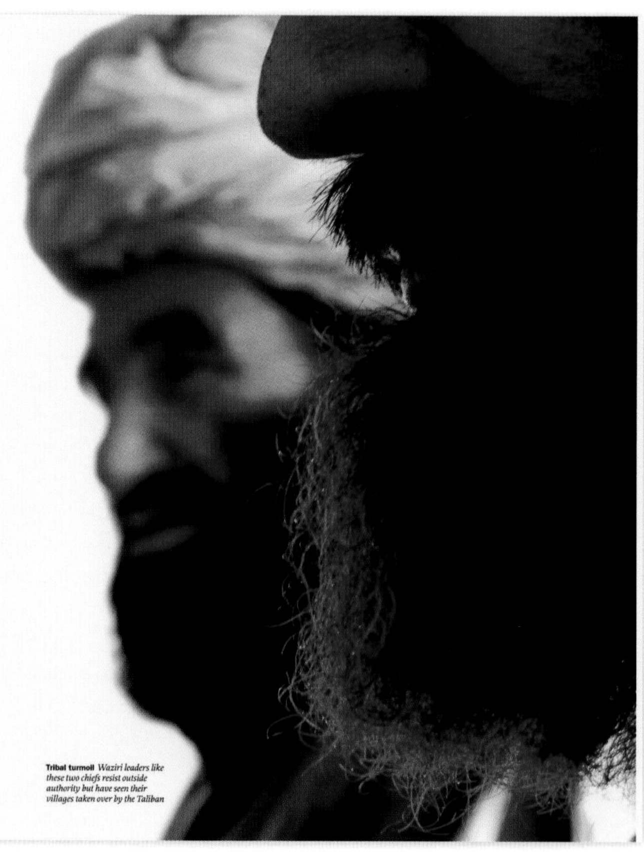

Tribal turmoil *Waziri leaders like these two chiefs resist outside authority but have seen their villages taken over by the Taliban*

27

INA **SALTZ**

TODD **SIMMONS**

KALLE **LASN**

FORGET THE STRUCTURE

There are other publications where consistency of structure is not only less necessary but actually impedes the editorial mission. Magazines less interested in the mass-market—literary, youth market, rabblerousing, niche, and others—have developed audiences that expect and embrace change. Ina Saltz points to, for example, the Transworld family of skateboarding, snowboarding, BMX, motocross, and surf magazines, which maintain their edgy vibe by constantly changing their look—even their logos—to keep themselves up to date and relevant with their hyped-up, adrenaline-fueled, youth-market readers.

The all-volunteer literary magazine, *Matter*, foregoes not only structure but also more fundamental navigational devices, such as a table of contents. Todd Simmons, the magazine's publisher, explains, "We want to start with the work, rather than the table of contents or an editor's note. We try to make it hard to navigate because this makes it more direct and immediate. We want the reader to start on the cover and go straight through as if every part were as important as every other." For the crew at *Matter*, standard procedures are something to be challenged. "We try to question and investigate for ourselves what value common practice has, and how it adds or subtracts from the experience," Simmons says. "Until you do without something, what do you really know about it? Or, until you make it your own, how do you know it completely? We want to make sure we're not doing something for the sake of doing it, because there's so much busy-ness in the world already."

Adbusters is another magazine where repetitive structure is outright rejected as overly constricting to both the magazine and its readers. "The trap that a lot of art directors have fallen into is they think their job is to just somehow follow a formula," Kalle Lasn says. "Every now and again they redesign, but then there is a new formula, and the job of the designer becomes rote and boring and just filling in the grid." *Adbusters* seeks to shake up the world by shaking up each issue. "Every magazine should be as close as possible to a one-off. You should design it from the bottom up, because if you start with a grid, you're lost before you start. The formula that I have is to have a single, powerful narrative, one seamless story line that flows from front cover to back cover in one passionate, existential blast." A formula which, while not for regular readers of supermarket tabloids, is central to Lasn's mission of creating meaningful debate on important social issues of our times.

The literary magazine *Matter* arranges each issue, very loosely—around a theme. The magazine also does away with traditional front material, or makes things like the table of contents "virtually useless or so hard to decipher that most people flip past them immediately," says publisher and editor Todd Simmons.

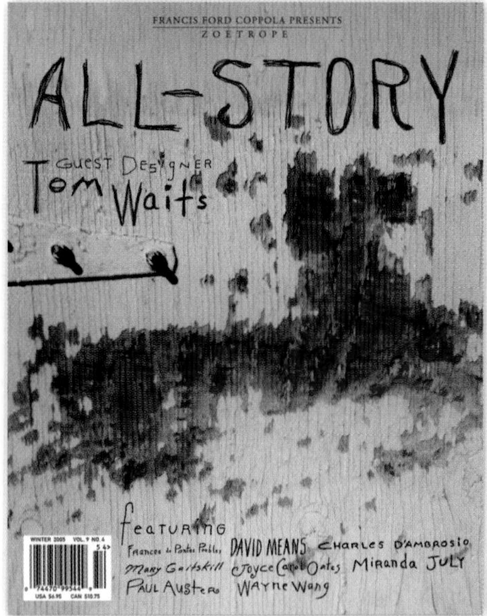

***Zoetrope: All-Story* engages a different artist—usually from various nonpublication media—to design each issue of the publication. This issue was designed by musician, Tom Waits.**

28

MICHAEL **RAY**

ENHANCE THE IMMEDIACY OF THE MEDIA

"What's great about magazines," says Michael Ray, editor at *Zoetrope: All-Story*, "is that because they are disposable, they can be continually reinvented." *Zoetrope* maximizes this opportunity to be a moving target by asking a different person, usually a non-graphic designer who is an artist in some other medium, to design each issue. Musician Tom Waits, photographer Marilyn Minter, and actor Tim Roth are just a few of the magazine's guest designers, who may or may not connect their ideas to the literary content or call on the staff designer for assistance. "The independence versus interdependence between magazine staff and artist varies from issue to issue," says Ray. "There's this really interesting potential when we sit down together. As far as we're concerned, the farther from magazine design that this artist's principal pursuit is, the better. The more unexpected, the better."

However, even this stretching of boundaries does have its limitations. "There's always some sort of negotiation," Ray concedes, clicking off the necessary compromises between art and practicality. "On a basic level, we want to make sure the text is readable; we don't want to challenge our readers unnecessarily. We want to be respectful of the writers as well, so we present their work in a format that can be consumed as easily as possible. We need to have a barcode. It's nice to have the logo at the top so it can be seen on the newsstand." Beyond these concerns, there are the actual stories themselves. "In each issue, we publish six to eight stories or one-act plays," Ray explains. "But otherwise, the magazine is a surprise." And *Zoetrope* recognizes that this element of surprise will inevitably limit its readership. "This is not an impulse buy in the checkout line of a supermarket," says Ray. "We have an entrenched readership who knows what to look for. And they like finding something new in our approach every time."

Left and below: *Zoetrope: All-Story* designed by performer, Will Oldham

Calisthenics, Poison Ivy, Final Cut

Woody Allen

As a one-time hatchling chloroformed and shanghaied each summer to various lakeside facilities bearing Indian names where I struggled to master the dog paddle under the baleful eyes of capos otherwise known as counselors, my attention was pinioned recently by something in the back pages of the *New York Times Magazine*. Amongst the usual dumping grounds where well-heeled parents might stash their sniveling issue and savor a comatose July and August were ads for such trendy modern specialties as basketball camp, magic camp, computer camp, jazz camp, and perhaps the most glamorous of all, film camp.

Apparently somewhere amidst the crickets and ragweed a teenager with a yen for montage can idle away his sunny vacation learning to churn out Oscar-winning dialogue, proper camera angles, acting, editing, sound mixing, and, for all I know, the correct way to buy a home in Bel Air complete with valet parking. While less dream-weaving adolescents are busy foraging for arrowheads, a number of budding von Stroheims actually get to make their own original movies, a far hipper summer project than, say, braiding a lanyard to dangle one's skate key.

This pricey inspiration seemed a long way from Camp Melanoma, run by Moe and Elsie Varnishke in Loch Sheldrake, where I suffered the dog days of my fourteenth year playing dodgeball and keeping the calamine-lotion industry solvent. It was not easy to picture a mom-and-pop couple like the Varnishkes running anything resembling so chic a venue as film camp, and only the fumes of a smoked whitefish I was deconstructing at the Carnegie Deli induced sufficient hallucinatory molecules to conjure the following correspondence.

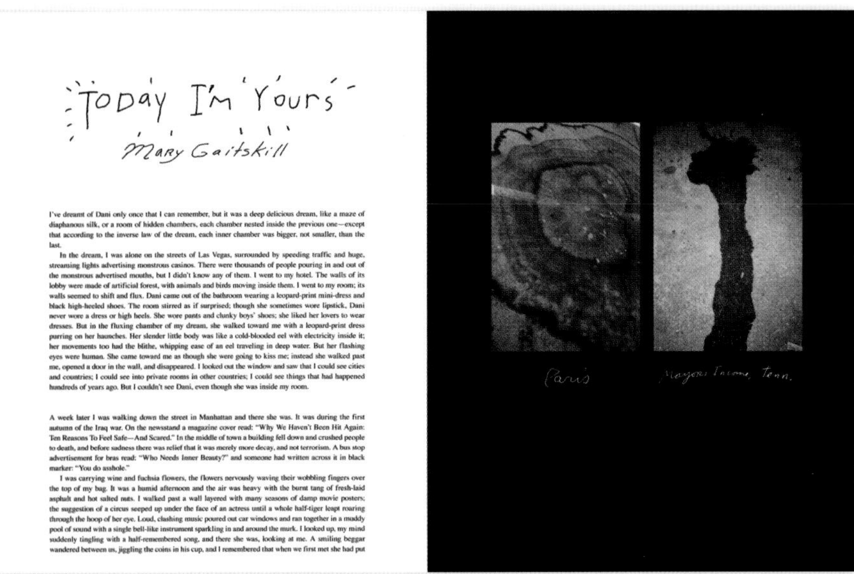

Today I'm Yours

Mary Gaitskill

I've dreamt of Dani only once that I can remember, but it was a deep delicious dream, like a maze of diaphanous silk, or a room of hidden chambers, each chamber nested inside the previous one—except that according to the inverse law of the dream, each inner chamber was bigger, not smaller, than the last.

In the dream, I was alone on the streets of Las Vegas, surrounded by speeding traffic and huge, streaming lights advertising monstrous casinos. There were thousands of people pouring in and out of the monstrous advertised mouths, but I didn't know any of them. I went to my hotel. The walls of its lobby were made of artificial forest, with animals and birds moving inside them. I went to my room; its walls seemed to shift and flux. Dani came out of the bathroom wearing a leopard-print mini-dress and black high-heeled shoes. The room stirred as if surprised; though she sometimes wore lipstick, Dani never wore a dress or high heels. She wore pants and clunky boys' shoes; she liked her lovers to wear dresses. But in the fluxing chamber of my dream, she walked toward me with a leopard-print dress purring on her haunches. Her slender little body was like a cold-blooded eel with electricity inside it; her movements too had the blithe, whipping ease of an eel traveling in deep water. But her flashing eyes were human. She came toward me as though she were going to kiss me; instead she walked past me, opened a door in the wall, and disappeared. I looked out the window and saw that I could see cities and countries; I could see into private rooms in other countries; I could see things that had happened hundreds of years ago. But I couldn't see Dani, even though she was inside my room.

A week later I was walking down the street in Manhattan and there she was. It was during the first autumn of the Iraq war. On the newsstand a magazine cover read: "Why We Haven't Been Hit Again: Ten Reasons To Feel Safe—And Scared." In the middle of town a building fell down and crushed people to death, and before sadness there was relief that it was merely more decay, and not terrorism. A bus stop advertisement for bras read: "Who Needs Inner Beauty?" and someone had written across it in black marker: "You do asshole."

I was carrying wine and fuchsia flowers, the flowers nervously waving their wobbling fingers over the top of my bag. It was a humid afternoon and the air was heavy with the burnt tang of fresh-laid asphalt and hot salted nuts. I walked past a wall layered with many seasons of damp movie posters; the suggestion of a circus seeped up under the face of an actress until a whole half-tiger leapt roaring through the hoop of her eye. Loud, clashing music poured out car windows and ran together in a muddy pool of sound with a single bell-like instrument sparkling in and around the murk. I looked up, my mind suddenly tingling with a half-remembered song, and there she was, looking at me. A smiling beggar wandered between us, jiggling the coins in his cup, and I remembered that when we first met she had put

Zoetrope: All-Story designed by musician, Tom Waits

29

LUKE **HAYMAN**

ADAM **MACHACEK**

LET THE MATERIAL CREATE THE STRUCTURE

More mainstream publications naturally adhere to a more formal and recognizable architecture. "There is a real pattern that most magazines follow, with a clear logic," Luke Hayman points out. "There is a table of contents, with the editor's note and masthead and letters section up front, with lots of small stories that don't develop into longer pieces, then longer stories, then features in the middle or the end." This inherent structure gives a designer not only the raw material to develop the design but also a way through the material. "It's a logical pacing," Hayman notes.

Even when the publication does not have a well-established structure, a designer should let the form of the final piece develop organically from the material provided. Adam Machacek says, "I think the rules come out themselves with each project, during the process. In most cases, the client comes with two piles: texts and images. Sometimes, these are very well organized and edited, and then it's easier to foresee the structure of the book." However, as a young, two-person shop, Machacek and his partner don't generally get clients as buttoned-up or well established as those that tend to appear on the doorstep of Hayman's Pentagram office. "Mostly, it's all just mixed up," says Machacek, "And so together, with the author, we are editing, planning, and building it up like a house."

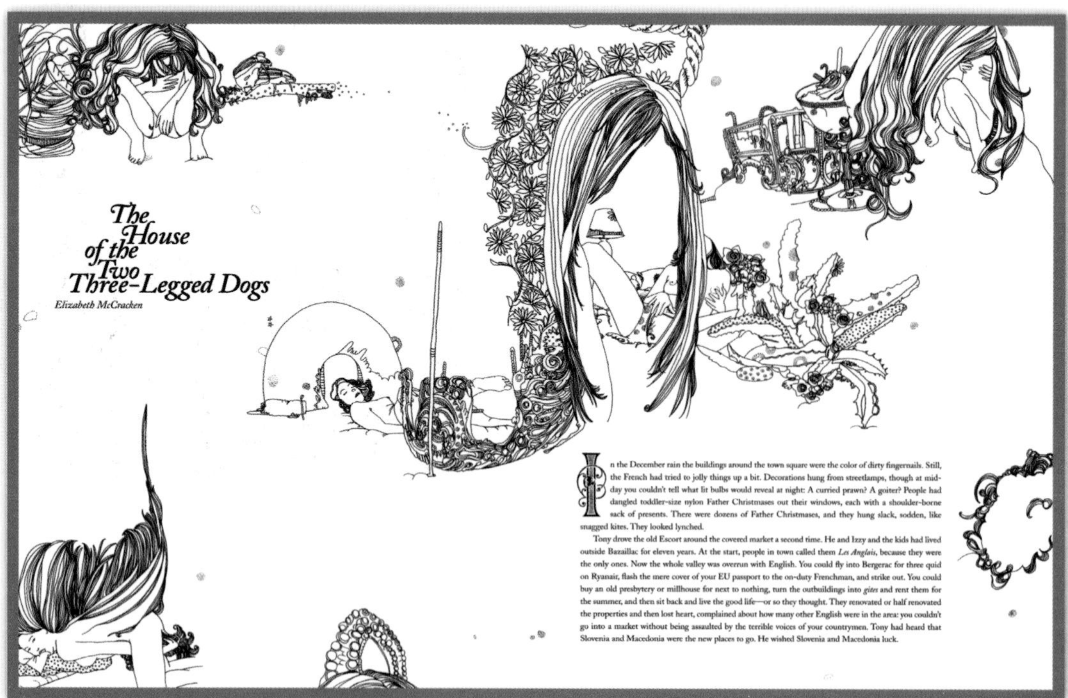

The House of the Two Three-Legged Dogs

Elizabeth McCracken

In the December rain the buildings around the town square were the color of dirty fingernails. Still, the French had tried to jolly things up a bit. Decorations hung from streetlamps, though at midday you couldn't tell what lit bulbs would reveal at night: A curried prawn? A goiter? People had dangled toddler-size nylon Father Christmases out their windows, each with a shoulder-borne sack of presents. There were dozens of Father Christmases, and they hung slack, sodden, like snagged kites. They looked lynched.

Tony drove the old Escort around the covered market a second time. He and Izzy and the kids had lived outside Bazaillac for eleven years. At the start, people in town called them *Les Anglais*, because they were the only ones. Now the whole valley was overrun with English. You could fly into Bergerac for three quid on Ryanair, flash the mere cover of your EU passport to the on-duty Frenchman, and strike out. You could buy an old presbytery or millhouse for next to nothing, turn the outbuildings into *gites* and rent them for the summer, and then sit back and live the good life—or so they thought. They renovated or half renovated the properties and then lost heart, complained about how many other English were in the area: you couldn't go into a market without being assaulted by the terrible voices of your countrymen. Tony had heard that Slovenia and Macedonia were the new places to go. He wished Slovenia and Macedonia luck.

Zoetrope: All-Story **designed by performer, Will Oldham**

30

DEVELOP A STRUCTURE THAT IS SIMULTANEOUSLY LINEAR AND NONLINEAR

ARJEN **NOORDEMAN**

DAVID **ALBERTSON**

"The main thing that's different about book design versus other kinds of design," says Arjen Noordeman, "is that you have to think about the story developing. It's an experience that has a timeline like a movie." While this is especially true of narrative books, where readers generally start with the cover and dutifully turn the pages one by one, people may enter the "story" of an art book or magazine at different points, looking at pictures and reading articles here and there. "You have to build up the experience," says Noordeman, "but also create an overarching structure that can work nonlinearly."

The structure needs to be solid so readers feel firmly in the grip of the editorial viewpoint, and yet flexible enough that they can express their own browsing and reading eccentricities. "Really good graphic design points the reader in the right direction so they're looking at the right thing at the right time," says David Albertson. "It's about structuring the magazine experience so it's functionally enjoyable. Sometimes you see a publication where every page pretty much looks the same, the photography looks the same; it doesn't look like anyone was working hard to bring it to you. A publication like that could be successful, but it makes me sad," he notes.

A special edition for fall 2007 featured a mid-magazine flip, with half of the magazine dedicated to the usual short stories and the other half to a movie by magazine founder and director Francis Ford Coppola.

31

DESIGN A SYSTEM THAT ENGAGES PEOPLE, OVER AND OVER AGAIN

CHRIS **VERMAAS**

JESSICA **FLEISCHMANN**

SCOTT **STOWELL**

To create a magazine that provides functional reader benefits—and keeps readers coming back—designers need to put even more attention on the basics. "Think about choice of typefaces, point sizes, structures within the layout, imagery, paper stocks, use of space, and so on to express the editorial elements; they all have to work together," says Chris Vermaas, partner with Chin-Lien Chen in the Office of CC in the Netherlands. "You can see a successful publication design as well-functioning machinery that directs the already embedded knowledge of your audience about how to read and use a magazine."

Jessica Fleischmann, of the Los Angeles design studio still room, finds herself focusing on two critical implements: "Structure and typography are super weighted in publications," she observes. "I believe in getting out of the way of the work and for design to support the content, so I have to have strong conceptual and functional reasons for choosing typefaces and developing structure. In addition to image selection and pacing, my voice, as a designer, is going to show mainly through type and structure." Part of why structure is so important, and yet needs to remain flexible, is that you don't always know what's going to happen within the confines you've created. "You're working with something over a number of pages, so you have to make sure that it's really going to function and it's going to make the argument or statement that you want to convey over all those pages, knowing that the content is shifting."

These shifts happen not just over the hundred or so pages of a single magazine but over many iterations. "A striking difference between publication design and other fields of graphic design is that in publication design, the stage, the medium, and the platform are set up to be in use for years," says Vermaas. "They must offer enough flexibility to generate every issue as a separate entity. The challenge is in creating this diversity within unity." For Scott Stowell, of the New York design studio Open, this challenge is his favorite part of publication design. "What I love about magazines," says Stowell, "is that it's creating a system within each magazine, but at the same time, the system has to work over time. Each issue has to be new but the same." For Stowell, playfulness is critical to engagement. "The constraints of an assignment are like setting up the rules of a game," he says. "So if you set them up well, you can play a game that's very fun, but different every time."

Morf is a magazine on the history and theory of design, directed and distributed to Dutch design students to "enhance their knowledge on the history and theory in their field. To stress the seriousness of this mission, we kept the design plain, yet gave the publication a face that could be recognized," according to Vermaas and his partner Chin-Lien Chen.

32

LET YOUR DESIGN BE THE NINTH THING

MICHAEL **RAY**

At *Zoetrope*, guest designers are given an exceptional amount of leeway. Because the magazine uses a different (usually) non-designer to create each issue, the usual boundaries, rules, and conventions are not necessarily broken as they simply don't apply. Each issue is a one-off, an opportunity to explore some creative obsession or preoccupation that will, intentionally, never come again. "Fundamentally, when I say that the design supports the text, what I hope is just that it doesn't interfere with the text," says Michael Ray. "But fundamental to our mission is to give the guest designers as much freedom as possible. We're giving them the magazine and saying, do whatever you want to do. If you want to mimic the stories in mood or narrative, go ahead, but if you don't want to, you don't have to."

What this creates in each issue is a tableau of multiple visual and literary voices moving to their own internal rhythms, which may or may not have much to do with one another but are individually coherent, artistic, well crafted, and expressive. According to Ray, "Some artists read the stories and some don't. Some don't want to be influenced. They feel like the most obvious thing to do is create a visual manifestation of the writing. These guys are looking at designing an issue once and maybe never again, so they want to take more risks and do something unexpected. I've heard it repeatedly from artists that the magazine has eight stories and they want their design to be a ninth thing."

33

JEREMY **LESLIE**

KALLE **LASN**

CHALLENGE THE GIVENS

Design is, by nature, the merging of creative impulses with pragmatic considerations. There's always an audience, a budget, schedules, sales goals, and the limits of producing something in the particular time space continuum of planet Earth. It is from these demands and realities that rules are born. Unfortunately, because so many magazines are facing not only these same considerations but also trying to grab a piece of the same consumer pie, they end up with similar solutions. "Magazines have all begun to really look the same in terms of how they present themselves," Jeremy Leslie remarks. "There are a lot of techniques and wise words about how front covers should appear, how to make it sell, how the newsstand is a very particular environment, and how to be successful there. Various people can give you those five, ten, or fifteen rules, but what I enjoy doing is challenging those rules."

However, there's no point in creating difficulties just for the sake of being a contrarian. Every challenge must have a purpose in mind, a goal in sight, a means to an end. Leslie offers this advice: "I always look at a brief for what we can challenge, where we can make a difference, how we can make it stand out from the competition, not by being different for the sake of being different, but by looking for what will work for the magazine and best represent the client," he says.

Kalle Lasn, as would be expected, expands his idea of rule-breaking all the way to the most basic underpinnings of what publications are doing in the larger world. "Throughout the history of magazines," he fulminates, "it's always been the case that there are commercial publications, and I don't care if eight out of ten of them are that way, but I lament that 99.9 percent are that way, and 99.9 percent of the designers are going along with it." He longs for a day when designers are doing more than catering to commercial interests. "I lament that there's not one of ten that go against the grain. I lament the fact that our culture has become so commercialized, so homogenized, that there's no dissenting voices speaking back. This speaks of a culture that's a dinosaur." The answer, he believes, is in challenging the status quo by asking bigger questions and demanding more interesting answers. "Our culture has lost its soul and its passions, and the designers have, too. To hell with the rules," he concludes. "The real movers and shakers are rule breakers."

34

IF YOU'RE GOING TO BREAK THE RULES, KNOW WHAT THEY ARE

MARCUS **PIPER**

INA **SALTZ**

MICHAEL **RAY**

CHRIS **VERMAAS**

As in life, so it is with magazines: Sometimes the best way to bring attention to a limitation is to step beyond it. "Breaking the rules is the way to add pace to a publication," says Marcus Piper. "By breaking the rules, you can stop the reader in their tracks, get their attention, and remind them they are inside your publication, engaging with it." However, randomly ignoring all conventions and expectations leads simply to chaos that benefits neither the reader, nor the publication or publisher. As Ina Saltz says, "Rules can be broken in divinely successful ways, but it takes someone who knows what they are doing to break the rules well."

The smartest effects of rule-breaking come when the intention is somehow contained within the act itself. "Regarding the conventions of magazine design," says Michael Ray, "it's most interesting to break them if you first know what those conventions are and why you're breaking them." It helps if your readers know about them as well. "For every new graphic problem, we believe in defining a new set of rules," Chris Vermaas says. "We present the users with the basic structure, the rhythm, the size, the known, the hierarchy, and so forth. Once the graphic parameters are set, it becomes possible to show your audience when the 'rules' are being broken. Using an italic, a shifted baseline, a double word space, starts to stand out, starts to get its meaning, and will not be seen as a mistake."

integration became an urgent concern. Since it was also clear that most people did not have the necessary mental baggage to found such integration on a rational conception of the functioning of machines, it had to be on an irrational conception. Thus the machine became eroticized—a living organism. ↵
A side effect of this development is that a truly functional streamline, for things that really have to go against the wind, has never materialized. The air resistance of current cars is hardly lower than that of those before 1930. Modern car bodies, then, are not really streamlined—they are *tumescent*. This explains why cars, mixers, and vacuum cleaners rarely have flat or singly curved surfaces: the characteristic shape is the slightly swollen surface. It is a physiological form that reminds one of the puffing up of a taut membrane by pressure from within. Our technical design reflects a disgust of pure geometric shapes. Like machines, after all, geometric shapes are rational forms, constructs of the mind, abstractions, nonexistent in nature. Apparently most people have far more affinity with the incomprehensible than with the abstract. [TB]

184-185 Turn on the Light: postscript

AUTHOR	DUTCH TEXT
Marjan Unger	page 102

Chin-Lien Chen observes that students of graphic design in the Netherlands, as opposed to those in the US, hardly read theory, but that their final work still betrays visual force and professionalism. Chen thus raises the larger issue of how students of design should deal with theory. ↵
It turns out that the correlation between theoretical skills (asking students to read and write a lot) and design skills is largely speculative. Of course it is important to be articulate, also for designers, but there is also the risk that schools will merely produce theory-minded designers who quickly end up in teaching positions or other jobs that keep them from doing what they were trained to do. ↵
As art history instructor I always hated it when my colleagues complained about their students' limited knowledge. How much did they themselves know when finishing their formal education? My own knowledge was fragmented at best, and only later on it developed into something more substantial. Indeed, knowledge of art and design history is the kind of knowledge that has to grow on you. We all have our individual frame of reference, and it is important to demonstrate to students how we built our knowledge by drawing causal relationships between the various historical practices, artists and periods, as well as by simply telling stories about what we know. I must add that I have also had many colleagues who did so. Therefore I feel that instructors at Dutch design schools can perfectly explain future designers how to tackle theoretical concerns. ↵
As for students, at any moment you are free to start exploring and deepening your knowledge of art and design, and how it specifically applies to your own work and interests. [TB]

185-188 On Pottery

AUTHOR	DUTCH TEXT / IMAGES
B. Majorick	page 107

ABOUT THE AUTHOR
B. Majorick is an alias of sculptor/typographer J.J. Beljon [1922-2002].

ORIGINALLY PUBLISHED IN	YEAR
"Ontwerpen en verwerpen. Industriële vormgeving als noodzaak", Em. Querido, Amsterdam	1959

VIEW IMAGES IN COLOR
www.morf.nl

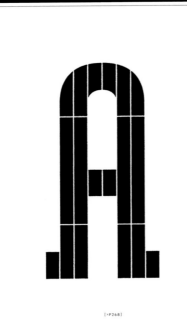

[›P268]

145-163 Taste and Fashion [Chapter XVIII]

AUTHOR
James Laver

ABOUT THE AUTHOR
James Laver [1899-1975], British art critic and fashion historian.

FIRST PUBLISHED IN	YEAR
Taste and Fashion. From the French Revolution to the Present Day, George G. Harrap & Co., London	1937

INTRODUCTION
In the concluding chapter of his book *Taste and Fashion* James Laver captures the fashion cycle in a straightforward timeline, which has become known as 'Laver's Law'. As the driving force behind this cycle he saw the evolution of taste, which in turn is determined by economic and social factors. In the second part of this text he argues that the continuous changes in taste are not only reflected in dress, but also influence our appreciation of interior design and architecture.

We have now pursued for a hundred and fifty years the complex story of the evolution of European dress. We have sketched its main outline and pursued the subject through some tempting bypaths, and we have seen many seeming trifles take on an unexpected significance in the light of historical perspective. Only the superficial will consider such a subject a waste of time, for although the history of feminine elegance and the history of culture are not precisely the same thing, their courses are curiously

Morf, designed by Office of CC

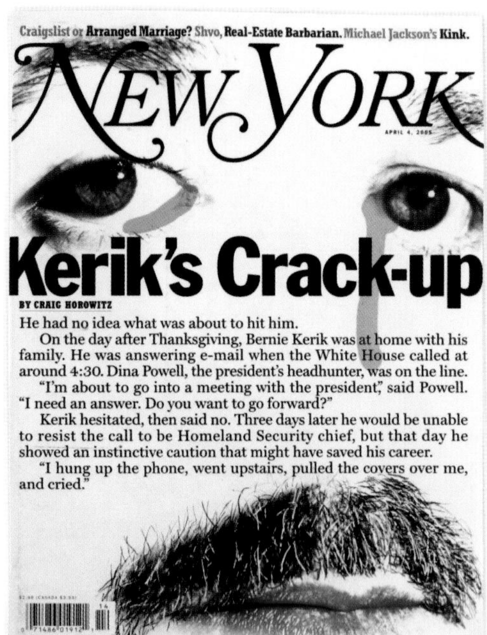

Craigslist or Arranged Marriage? Shvo, Real-Estate Barbarian. Michael Jackson's Kink.

NEW YORK

APRIL 4, 2005

Kerik's Crack-up

BY CRAIG HOROWITZ

He had no idea what was about to hit him.

On the day after Thanksgiving, Bernie Kerik was at home with his family. He was answering e-mail when the White House called at around 4:30. Dina Powell, the president's headhunter, was on the line.

"I'm about to go into a meeting with the president," said Powell. "I need an answer. Do you want to go forward?"

Kerik hesitated, then said no. Three days later he would be unable to resist the call to be Homeland Security chief, but that day he showed an instinctive caution that might have saved his career.

"I hung up the phone, went upstairs, pulled the covers over me, and cried."

35

LUKE **HAYMAN**

INA **SALTZ**

AREM **DUPLESSIS**

SIMPLIFY TYPE

Because the primary role of type in a publication is to convey information and provide guidance throughout the activity of reading, most publication designers recommend using just a few fonts, in a systematic way. "Usually," says Luke Hayman, "the rule of thumb is to simplify. Two families of fonts are typically what I go for." Ina Saltz agrees and amplifies. "In general, you want to work within two to three type families max: one for body copy, a sans serif for contrasting other elements, such as bylines, captions, and so on, and maybe a display type for large headlines that would have a little more refinement." But, she hastens to point out, there is no reason to let this limit also be a constraint. "If you choose well," she explains, "within each family, you will have a broad array of weights, slopes, width. Some type families have up to fifty members, but those families are designed to work well together. The choice of which of those three families will work together is a complex thing, and many factors need to be considered, such as type classification, the designer's taste, and again, the needs of the magazine."

At the *New York Times Magazine*, "We design with only two typefaces," says Arem Duplessis, "Stymie and Cheltenhem, both of which have been redrawn for the magazine." Again, this apparent limitation proves no brake to creativity. "This helps elevate the level of invention," he notes, "while keeping the magazine familiar and cohesive. Even with such a limited arsenal of fonts, it's always a real challenge packaging such diverse subject matter. Let's see, Next Gen Robots and a story about workplace discrimination?" In publication design, there are enough complications for a designer to contend with without adding the unnecessary confusion of competing fonts.

Above and opposite: *New York* magazine, as redesigned by Luke Hayman, kept some iconic elements, such as the magazine title, while bringing in a variety of other type treatments to delineate special sections like the back-of-the-book events listings.

STRATEGIST
SPECIAL: Fall 2005 Runway Report, page 44
PAID WEDDING NOTICES: THE STIGMA 39
THE ACTOR/DESIGNER LOOK 40
VINTAGE TEES IN THE EAST VILLAGE . 42
MAP NO. 8: 125TH STREET 54
MANHATTAN VALLEY DISCOVERED . . . 56
NEW MAKEUP TRENDS. 57
THE BEST BET
FEBRUARY 28, 2005 | NEW YORK 37

WAKING WITH THE FISHES
The last mornings of the Fulton Fish Market.
PHOTOGRAPHS BY BENJAMIN LOWY

36

LUKE **HAYMAN**

CARIN **GOLDBERG**

USE LOTS OF TYPEFACES

While Luke Hayman says "Typically I look to simplify," he concedes that there are exceptions—such as the multi-award-winning *New York* magazine. "It had a lot more tangents and nuance and subject material," he explains. "And there were historical references to the early days of the magazine, as well as a font we used only for the listings. It was unusual."

These special cases can certainly work, as long as they have a reason for being and are handled with insight and intelligence. As Carin Goldberg explains, "Generally speaking, you go with the rules of thumb that call for one setting for text, and then creating a hierarchy of typographic choices for heads, bylines, etc. But, that's just the template you start with, and from there, you can expand and move in any direction. You could use 150 typefaces, of course, if the content calls for that. These rules of thumb simply provide a baseline for developing voice and tone. These rules and choices create the engine that will propel the magazine." As with any complex construction, start with a strong foundation and build upward and outward from there.

Above and opposite: The clarity of the type treatments in *Gallup* magazine, as designed by Carin Goldberg, are not only fresh and easy to grasp but are also a demonstration of the magazine's values.

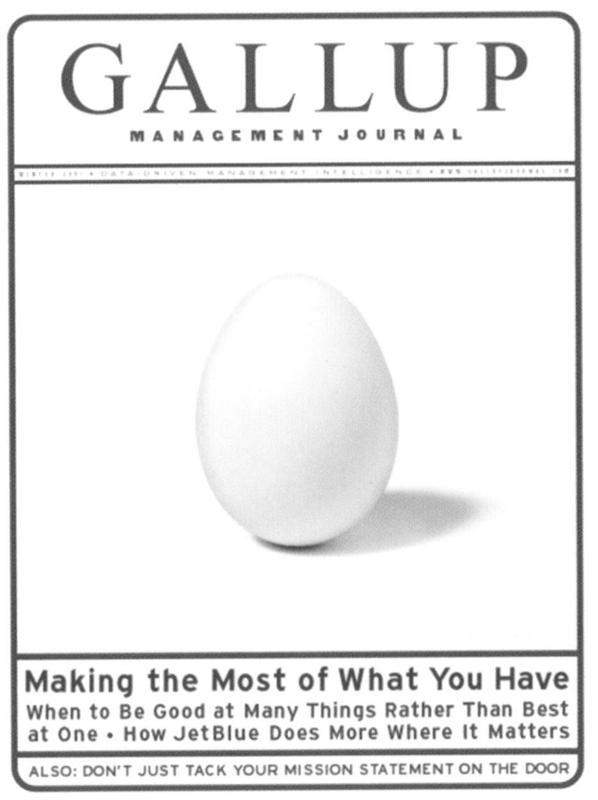

GALLUP
MANAGEMENT JOURNAL
Making the Most of What You Have
When to Be Good at Many Things Rather Than Best at One • How JetBlue Does More Where It Matters
ALSO: DON'T JUST TACK YOUR MISSION STATEMENT ON THE DOOR

37

USE TYPE AS A BRANDING ELEMENT

INA **SALTZ**

CARIN **GOLDBERG**

Publications use type at many levels, but they all work together to create a navigational system that helps readers understand and find their way through the content to determine what they want to read. A headline offers a certain kind of information that is distinctly different from what's in a caption; reading the masthead or calendar listings is a different experience from reading a piece of investigative journalism. While type's primary role is to be read, it can and should do double and triple duty as an identity and branding element, as well. "Type is there to communicate, to establish the personality of the magazine, and to advance the mission of the magazine," Ina Saltz explains. "Type also has a personality, and it communicates style and content. So the choice of typeface is extremely important to the identity of the magazine, and it functions to separate and distinguish the magazine from its competition." Like any graphic design endeavor, getting the tool of type to live up to this important challenge requires extra work from the designer. "When designers, art directors, and editors have a high level of courage and vision," says Carin Goldberg, "the typography can and should be an integral component in conjunction with the photography and illustration, and that's when things get exciting."

***Gallup* magazine, designed by Carin Goldberg**

38

ARJEN **NOORDEMAN**

MAKE TYPE ENTERTAINING

"Beyond legibility, the first thing that comes to mind when I think about type is entertainment," says Arjen Noordeman, describing a quality not normally associated with fonts but clearly present in his numerous hand-drawn type explorations. "I want to evoke an emotion or story," he says, "so before you realize what it is, it transports you to a certain mood or atmosphere." Sometimes experiments do go wrong, and when it comes to type, the results can be illegible or suggest confusing aesthetic directions. "Sometimes, it backfires, I have to admit," says Noordeman. "But it's often better to just take a stand and please 40 percent of the people instead of trying to please everyone and ending up pleasing no one. The alternative is playing it safe, or just boring people. There's a place for that," he says, "but it's not my place."

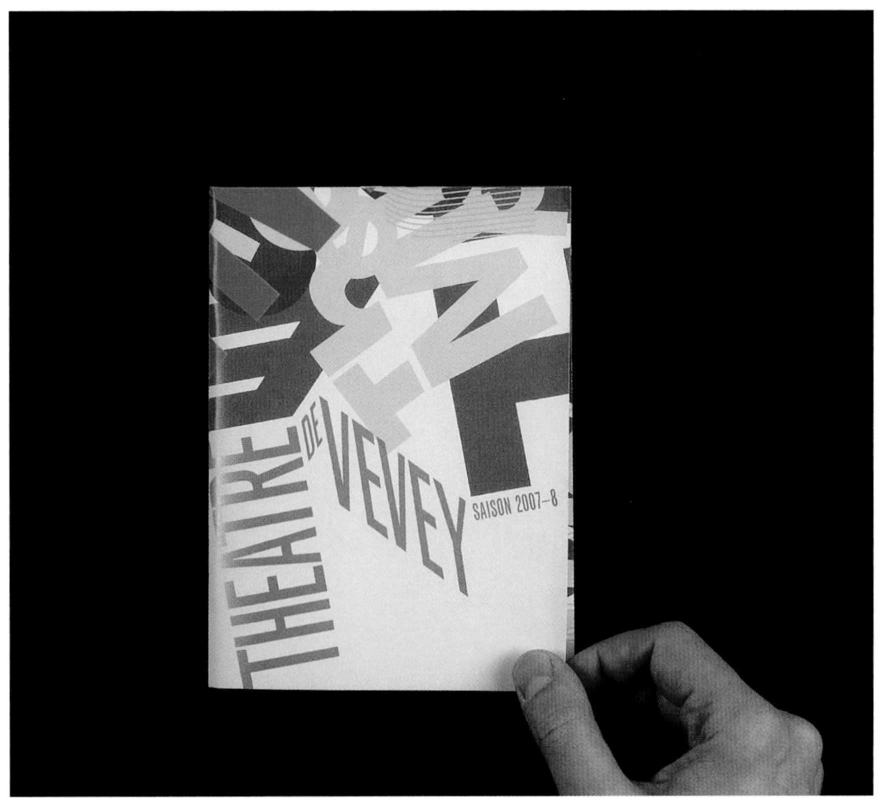

The catalog for this theater company, designed by Welcometo.as, includes a fold-out poster that interacts with the program, creating a changing kaleidoscope of different images and messages, along with information about events. See how it unfolds on the following pages.

39

LET THE IMAGES DO SOME OF THE WORK FOR YOU

ADAM **MACHACEK**

LUKE **HAYMAN**

AGNES **ZEILSTRA**

"Great images make a big part of the job done," says Adam Machacek. "If we are lucky and have great images to work with, our design becomes far less visible." And also allows him to put his attention toward the other aspects of graphic design. "Instead, we focus more on the rhythm and context in which the images are shown. We focus more on papers, typeface, and production details." Images can, and in many cases should, set the tone for these other design exercises. When redesigning *New York* magazine, Luke Hayman notes that the magazine "wanted to become smarter, with more attitude and assuming a greater intelligence of the audience." While the design needed to express this shift, "a lot came through with the photography," says Hayman, "which was quite sophisticated and arty."

Of course, great images are not guaranteed. "Sometimes I work with photos I don't like," says Agnes Zeilstra. "But I have to see it as a challenge to make a beautiful page." In some cases, this requires manipulating the materials provided to make them more interesting or greater than the sum of their parts. "When we receive mixed images, such as bad photocopies and low-resolution screenshots together with serious pictures, then we have no mercy, and we start to cut, draw, Photoshop, destroy, and distort wherever we can—of course, within the concept or rules that we've developed for each publication," says Machacek.

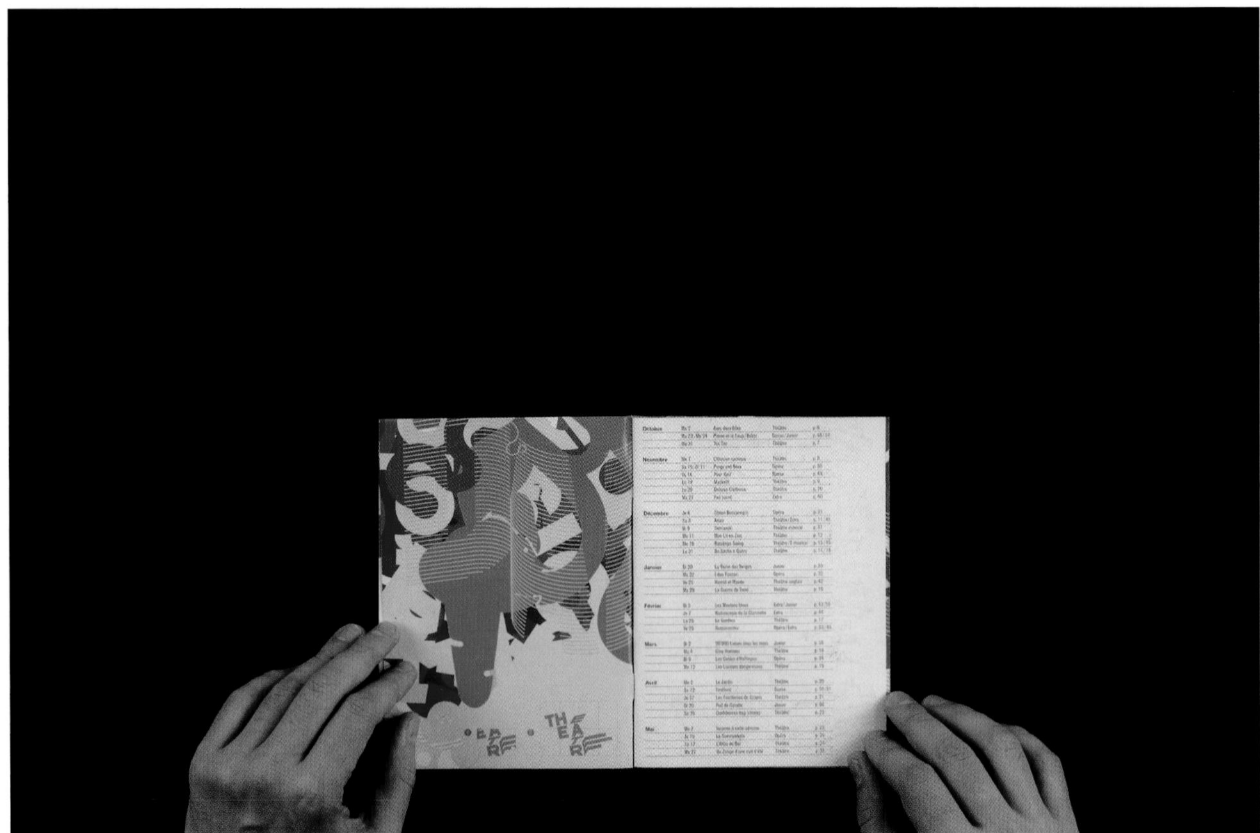

Theater catalog designed by Welcometo.as

40

KEEP IN MIND WHERE THE MAGAZINE WILL LIVE IN THE WORLD

LUKE **HAYMAN**

MICHAEL **RAY**

Magazines get to their audiences in two principal ways: through the mail or off the newsstand. This creates logistical issues that a designer must be aware of. As Luke Hayman suggests, "You have to ask yourself, 'Where will this magazine live in the world?'" In some cases, Hayman says, he's worked up two covers for a publication, one with a large area for the address label and another that addresses the unique demands of the newsstand. "It's very much a part of design to consider how it will work on the newsstand. You look at it from a distance and adjust the scale. You want impact, so you may have to make it less elegant—hopefully you can do both at the same time. I have done something that's larger, more aggressive for newsstands. When I've worked on magazines that are 95 percent subscription, it's a different need, because you know it's not competing next to *Us* magazine."

Zoetrope is mostly subscription-based, so it is less concerned about how it will get attention, or even be recognizable, on the newsstand. "We encourage people to reinvent the title," says Michael Ray, recalling one designer who split the masthead and had a barcode on the front and back. "Some people didn't recognize it. And it created major headaches for our newsstand distributors," he concedes. "But it's our mission to be as open to these artists' ideas as possible and manifest them in as many ways as we can."

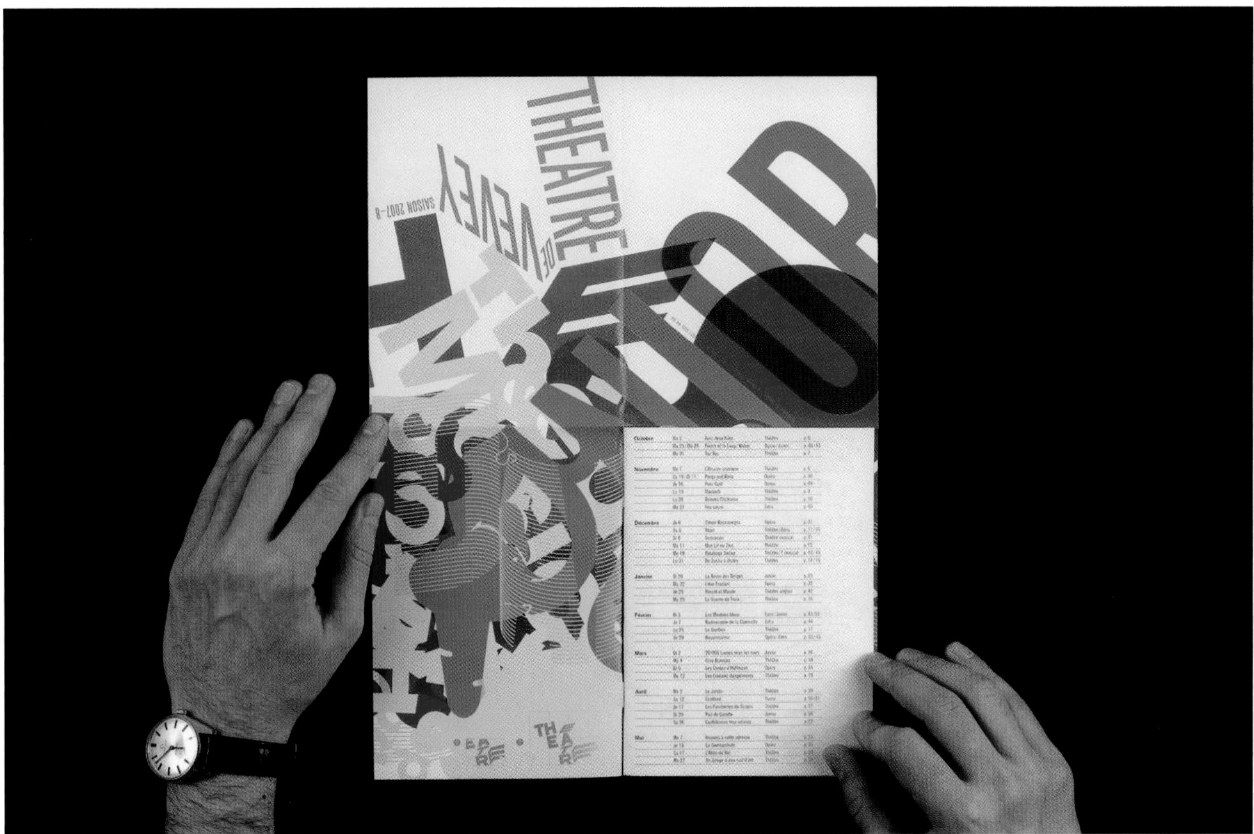

41

MICHAEL **RAY**

RESPECT PRACTICAL LOGISTICS

While *Zoetrope* may not concede much territory to the demanding environment of the newsstand, the magazine does have to take into consideration certain practical logistics, just like any other. "We started as a tabloid," says Michael Ray. "Out of Francis Ford Coppola's nostalgia for the broadsheets from the 1930s." (Director Coppola is the founder of *Zoetrope*.) Unfortunately, reality got in the way of this particular vision. "The problem was that because it's a small magazine, and we're shipping it out, magazines were arriving to subscribers shredded. Newsstands didn't want to carry them; they didn't know how to stock anything that broke conventional dimensions."

Even though the sizing had been integral to the original goals, respect for both the contributors and the readers forced a change in execution. "We liked the idea of a magazine that was the product of so much effort drawing on the talents of so many artists, and yet was ultimately fragile and temporary. While we liked that idea, we also wanted the magazine to succeed and find readers, and we wanted to be fair to those subscribers who, issue after issue, received shredded magazines." So *Zoetrope* was reinvented in a more conventional format, complete with traditional binding and semigloss or newsprint paper, according to each artist's preference. The content remains the same, and readers don't have to tape pages back together to read them.

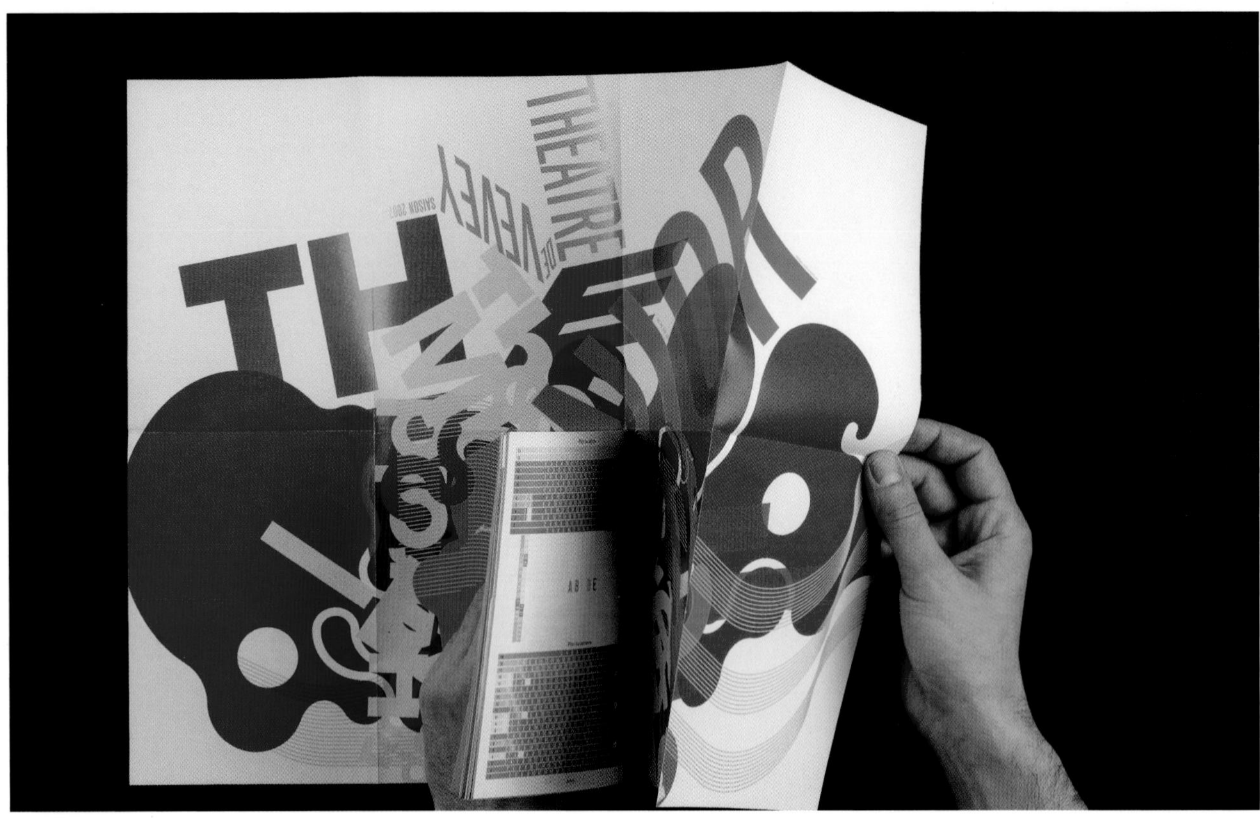

Theater catalog designed by Welcometo.as

42

INA **SALTZ**

MAKE SURE THE IMAGE AND WORDS WORK TOGETHER

The most frequent mistake that Ina Saltz sees is images and words working against, rather than for, each other. "The biggest and most common mistake," she says, "is when the words and image do not send the same message. Sometimes words don't apply to the image, or the other way around. They shoot each other in the foot instead of enhancing and amplifying each other." This mistake is especially egregious on magazine covers, which are supposed to instantly telegraph a strong and cohesive message that grabs attention and entices people to pick up, open, and buy the magazine.

THEATRE
DE VEVEY
JUNIOR

THEATRE
DE VEVEY
JUNIOR
20'000 Lieues sous les mers
Poil de Carotte

43

INA **SALTZ**

LUKE **HAYMAN**

PAY ATTENTION TO WHERE THE ADVERTISING IS

Most publications, unlike other graphic design projects, include advertising. This puts the designer in the unique position of incorporating what someone else, usually with a completely different agenda, has created. To maintain editorial as well as design integrity, the designer therefore has to be on the lookout for perceived conflicts of interest between advertising and editorial. "The readers' perceptions influence everything," Ina Saltz explains, "and there will often be jarring or confusing adjacencies from advertising to editorial. The conflict might involve any number of factors, from too-similar type treatments or images, to confusion because of the way elements are arranged, to conflicting or confusing subjects and backgrounds. Wherever the reader may experience a disconnect or a miscommunication," she says, "a good designer will create clear separation. Someone needs to oversee the advertising and editorial adjacencies."

Luke Hayman offers a couple of pragmatic ways to handle these "concussions" when they occur. "There's a stage of magazine design where you get to see ads next to the editorial," he says. "If it looks as though there's an editorial conflict or the pages visually merge, then you have to have a discussion with the ad manager and publisher to ask if ads can be moved. Other times, I've just created a clear boundary so the pages that face ads have, for example, a rule going down the gutter, so editorial doesn't bleed into the gutter and never actually touches an ad." These and many other fixes are available to the designer; the important thing is to make sure that the fixing gets done wherever it's needed.

44

INA **SALTZ**

LUKE **HAYMAN**

CREATE A FEATURE WELL

"Within the framework of the magazine, there should always be an editorial well," says Ina Saltz, "which is a series of spreads, uninterrupted by advertising, where the editorial voice can be most clearly heard. This gives the readers a chance to bond with the magazine and creates reader loyalty, which is what is deeply desired." Luke Hayman points out that the well also serves "the requirements of advertising, which likes to be up front. But the goal is always to have a section, hopefully of features, that can be uninterrupted by advertising. Not every magazine has this, but it's better if they do." Better, not only for the reader, but for the designer, as this well is the one place where their page designs can stand on their own, without the visual noise and clutter of advertising.

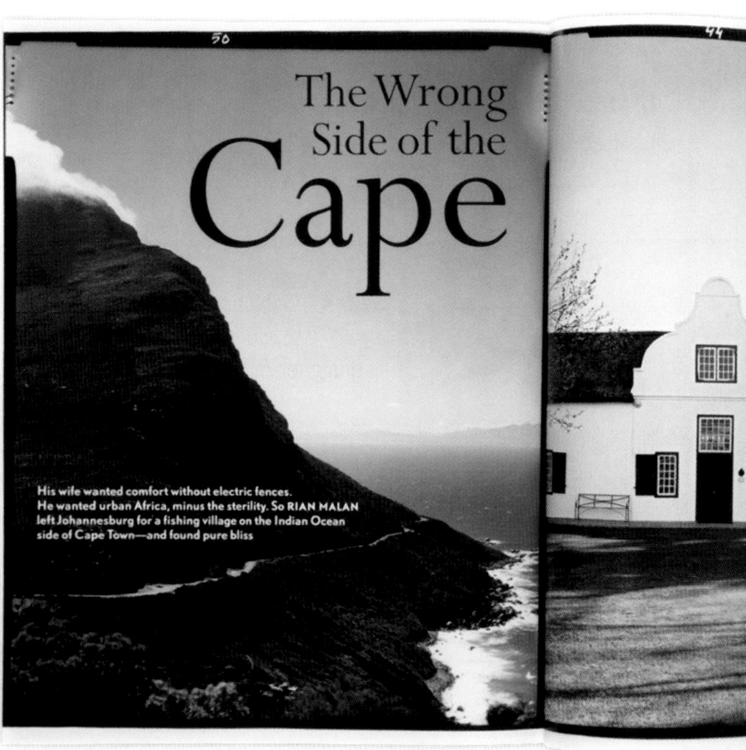

Travel & Leisure, as designed by Luke Hayman, lets powerful images and simple type tell the story of the stunning locations and elegant travel destinations that readers expect to see in its pages.

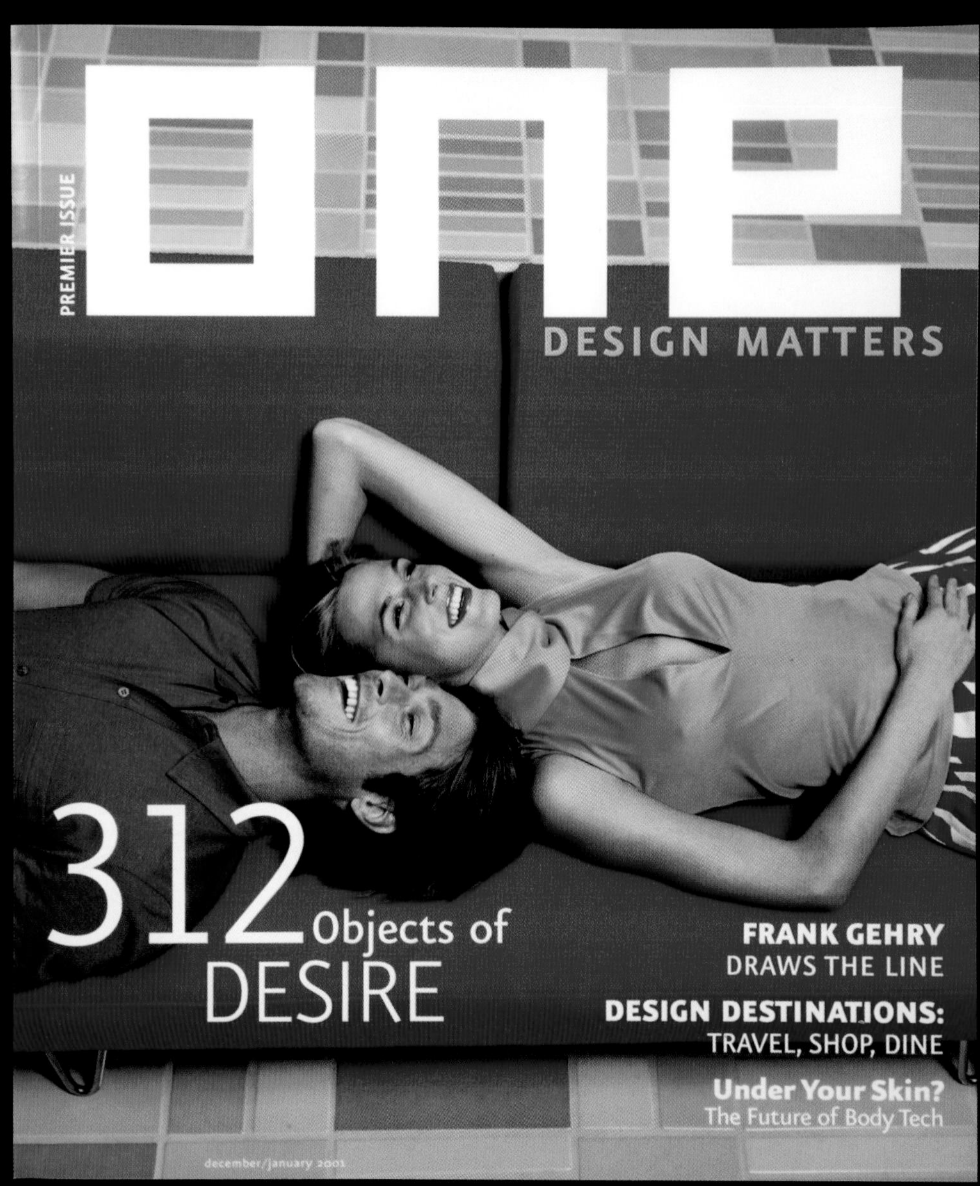

One, designed by Albertson Design, was a national consumer magazine that sought to "bring the growing national obsession with design to a general audience."

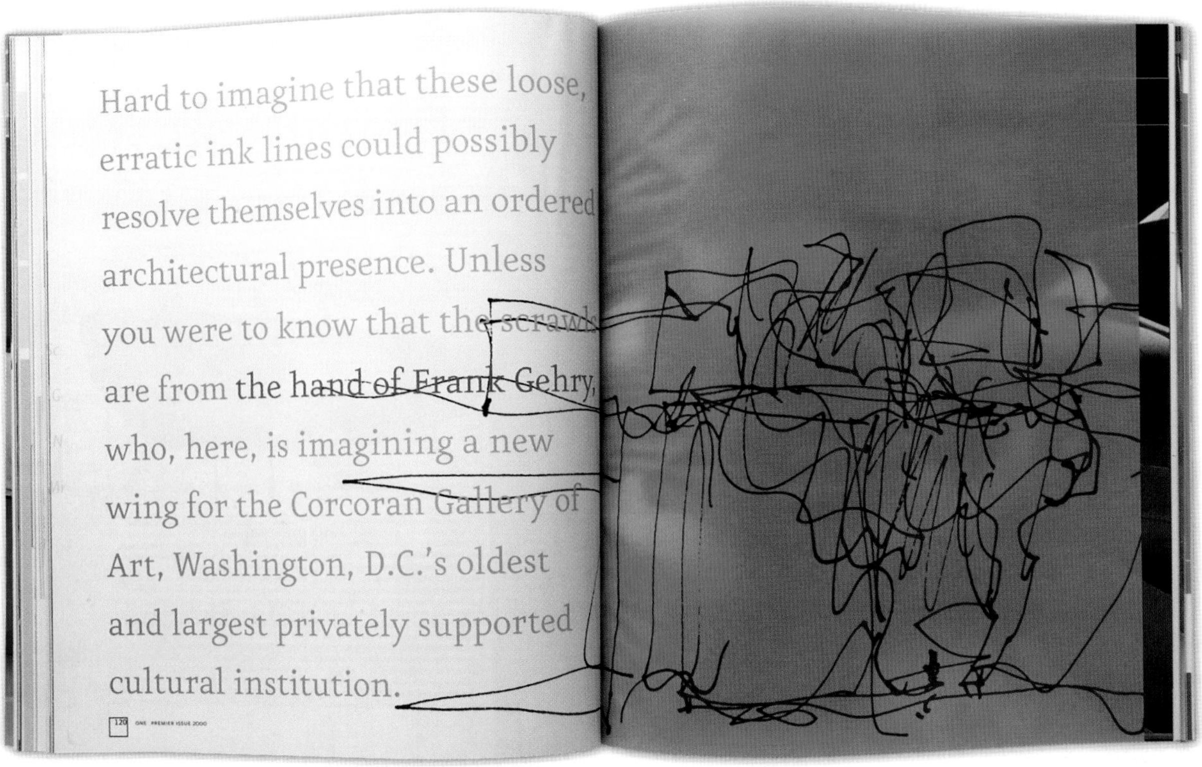

Hard to imagine that these loose, erratic ink lines could possibly resolve themselves into an ordered architectural presence. Unless you were to know that the scrawls are from the hand of Frank Gehry, who, here, is imagining a new wing for the Corcoran Gallery of Art, Washington, D.C.'s oldest and largest privately supported cultural institution.

45

SPEAK SOFTLY

LUKE **HAYMAN**

In addition to sharing the same space between two covers, editorial content must also compete with advertising for the reader's attention. Advertising is rarely subtle, and often covers similar topics as the articles. This can dilute the editorial mission and create confusion for readers who may be unsure of how to comprehend what they're looking at. Luke Hayman provides an example and a solution from one of the magazines he's worked on: "In *Travel & Leisure*, the editorial has stiff competition from the advertising, which is everywhere, is strongly designed, and has the same kind of imagery. So it's important to make editorial look like editorial and stand apart from the advertising. Sometimes, by stripping out color and making the editorial quieter, it stands out more."

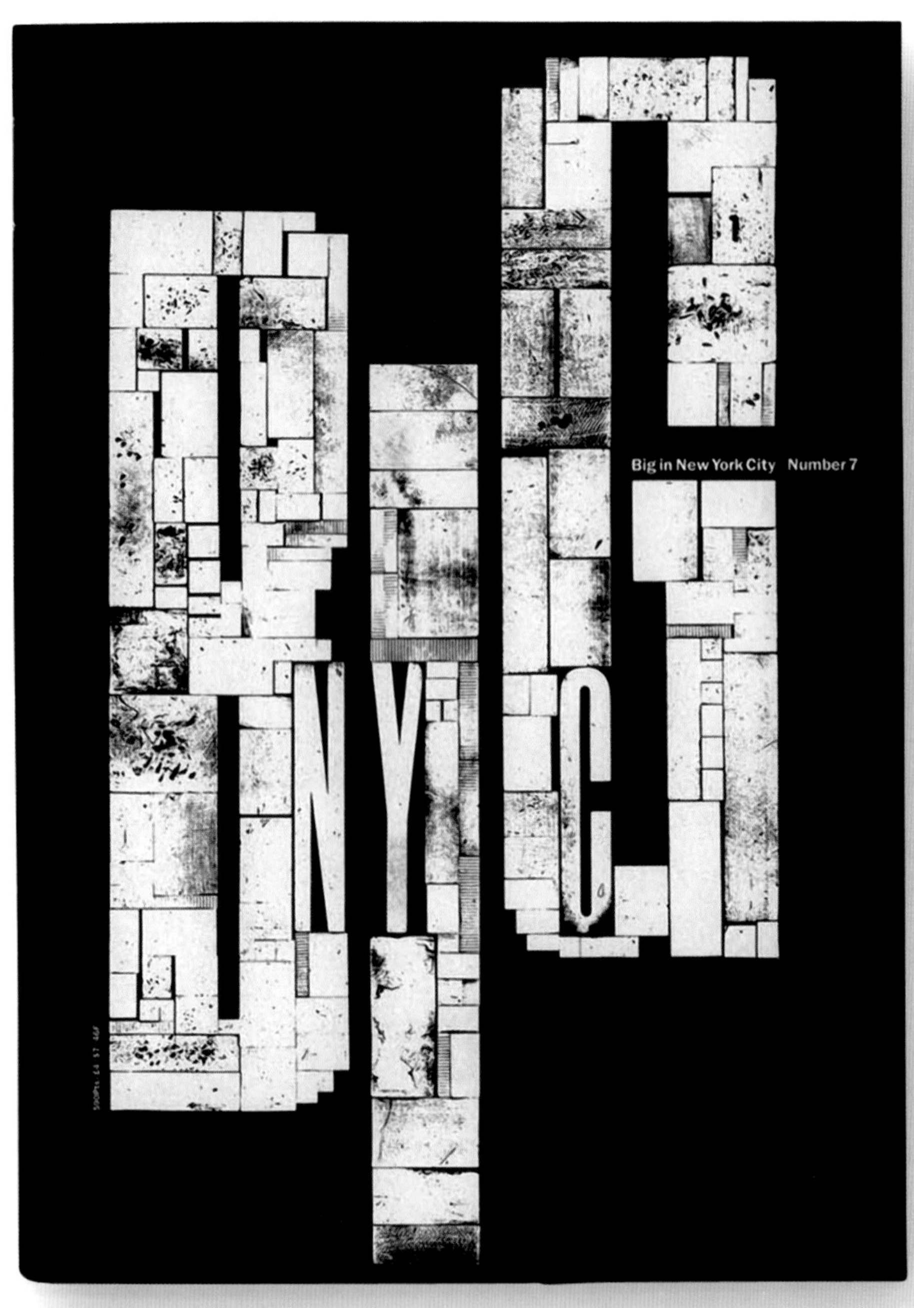

Bold images and confident type in black and white ensure that each spread of *Big* magazine, designed by Frost Design, makes a singular statement without distracting design back flips.

46

INA **SALTZ**

MAKE IT A PHYSICAL OBJECT

In the end, a magazine is something that will be picked up, held in hand, flipped through, brought to the sofa, beach, chair, or bed. Especially in this day of computer-generated everything, the quality of the physical experience of paging through the finished piece is critical to the success of any publication. "I am a firm proponent of setting up a wall where every page of the magazine is put up so everyone on staff can see them, even if they are reduced in size," says Ina Saltz. "This allows the magazine's pacing and flow to be visualized. Designers and editors typically work on one story or layout at a time. When you can see the flow of the pages from one story to the next, it is a good way to spot mistakes that might not otherwise be evident, such as too-similar headlines or type treatments in contiguous stories. It's also a good idea to have a binder with sleeves where pages are slipped in so everyone can see the facing adjacencies. This gives you the added advantage of allowing you to page through the magazine as a reader would." Whether it's a wall, table, floor, or binder, all publications must get out of the computer and into the hand before design is finalized. It's as much a designer's job to consider what readers will do as what they will see.

47

AREM **DUPLESSIS**

STEVEN **HELLER**

JEREMY **LESLIE**

AVOID OVERUSING DESIGN DEVICES

"I tend to lean toward the 'less is more' approach, which especially helps with a title like the *New York Times Magazine*," says Arem Duplessis. The point is that design should not be distracting. "I like the little tweaks that bend the design to force thought. But please, nothing over the top," he continues. "One twist and that's it; no layers. The idea should be concrete and confident." Steven Heller similarly cautions designers against mindlessly doing design gymnastics. "It's things like using asterisks too much, hairlines too much, having multiple typefaces on pull quotes." he says. "It's the things that are seen over and over and just become thoughtless. It becomes this thing that people did, and someone thinks it looks cool, so it gets done ad nauseam. You have to have some restraint." The way to maintain this restraint? Question each thing you put on the page. "My big belief is that everything on the page has to be there for a reason," says Jeremy Leslie. "Everything has to have a purpose and not be there just for decoration." He goes on to recommend ruthless self-editing. "There are a host of little additions and tricks and visual elements that get added to the page because something else doesn't work or because the design wasn't right in the first place," he says. "For example, if you place the caption in the right place, you don't need an arrow, because it will be obvious what picture the caption is talking about. A lot of these additions are just lazy shorthand, and if the page was designed with more consideration and care, you wouldn't have had to add those tricks in."

48

VINCE **FROST**

LUKE **HAYMAN**

WHEN REDESIGNING, START WITH A DISCUSSION

"If it's a redesign," says Vince Frost, "we want to work with the editor and publisher to understand what's wrong, to really try to understand all the problems and what their day-to-day work life is like so we can improve things not just visually, but by putting systems in place. We can help them not just with the design, but with the way they work." In addition to uncovering problems from the past, when redesigning a magazine, it's important to understand the agenda for the future.

"It starts with discussions with the editor and their vision for the magazine and what that is," says Luke Hayman. "It's trying to find the reasons they want to change, what works and what doesn't work, feeling around the project and trying to get a sense of what they're trying to achieve, the tone, the functional issues, and the structure."

In most cases, the process will be evolutionary, rather than revolutionary. After all, if the editors want a radical change, they could, and probably should, simply start a new magazine. "Magazines tend to evolve," says Hayman. "They try to remain contemporary so they don't feel as if they're aging with a generation. Editorially, they're not saying they're becoming a new magazine. I think that when magazines say they want to attract a new or broader audience, essentially what you're trying to do is make it more contemporary to serve that purpose."

49

ARTHUR **HOCHSTEIN**

BRING IN AN OUTSIDE VOICE

When *Time* magazine wanted to embark on a redesign, they called Luke Hayman at Pentagram. "The reality is that an outside designer can come in, and they're empowered to make more change than a staff art director," says Arthur Hochstein. "When you hire someone from outside and are paying good money for them, you're supposed to do what you're told." Not to mention, the outsider generally has a long record of successful publication design. "The editors can count on the designer's history of doing good work, solving problems, and having a vision," Hochstein points out. "And that allows editors to relax a little."

This process does not absolve the in-house designer from responsibility. It's his job to shepherd the new design system through internal processes and ensure that the design integrity is maintained, even as it evolves to accommodate changing needs. "I'm finding myself being a guardian of what's been done," says Hochstein. "In the first few issues, you're planting the seed, and then over the course of time, you try to remold it to make it work better and serve the editorial needs a little better. I see my role as being an advocate of the work that's been done." If the in-house art director does not perform this role, then the magazine design tends to drift, become diluted or confused, and soon enough, you're back to needing a design overhaul to regain clarity.

Big magazine, designed by Frost Design

50 BE RESPECTFUL OF THE IN-HOUSE TEAM

VINCE **FROST**

LUKE **HAYMAN**

Not all in-house art directors see the value of bringing in outside designers for a fresh perspective. "When the editor or publisher decides to go externally, it pisses off the people working on it," notes Vince Frost. "They have egos and pride and the idea of someone else doing the redesign is difficult because they're doing the day-to-day work and they have habits and systems in place to make their lives easier. They get upset because the redesign means that they're going to have to learn new systems." Understanding this situation is the key to working productively within it. "It's always quite a difficult process, and when you come from the outside, it really shakes things up," says Frost.

So, an outsider needs to be a diplomat as well as a designer, and the job becomes managing the people as well as the publication. "For *Time* magazine," says Hayman, "we worked closely and collaborated with the staff so they had ownership, too. We weren't forcing anything on them." And accept that in spite of your best efforts, the design you create may not last more than a few issues. "I don't think you can ever really guarantee that a design will be taken forward," says Hayman. "The more your design serves the needs of the publication and the staff working on that publication, the more likely it is that they will embrace it, protect it, and carry it into the future."

51 MAKE THE MOST OF THE FORMAT YOU HAVE

NICKI **KALISH**

While the functional requirements of printers, the post office, budgets, and reader expectations mean most magazines end up being similar sizes and even utilize similar paper stock, the special sections of newspapers present different challenges and opportunities. "One of the biggest problems with newspapers is paper," notes Nicki Kalish. "Because everything prints terribly on newsprint."

However, the sheer size of a newspaper makes other, more interesting things possible, even on newsprint. "You can do things on a much larger scale in a newspaper that you can't do in a magazine," she says. "So you can do something big and grand, where you're more limited by size in a magazine." For Kalish, special sections have a hybrid quality to them. "I try to design my covers as if they were magazines," Kalish says. "They don't have a real newspaper look, and fall into a slot of their own. The scale is very different, and falls in between a spread and a poster. I think that when the covers are successful, they could be blown up as a poster." Seeing one's work, whatever the original form, pinned up on a wall as a poster is the ultimate compliment.

Big magazine, designed by Frost Design

The Dining Out section of the *New York Times*, designed by Nicki Kalish, uses photography to provide an unexpected spin on a seasonal topic and illustration to convey a complicated—and amusing—concept.

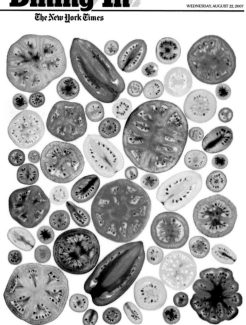

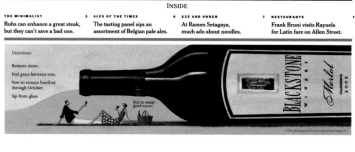

C M Y K Nxxx,2007-08-22,F,001,Bs-4C,E1

Dining In

The New York Times

F1

WEDNESDAY, AUGUST 22, 2007

Of Church And Steak: Farming For the Soul

PHIL MANSFIELD FOR THE NEW YORK TIMES

GOD'S WORK Sister Mary Ann Garisto farms organically at Sisters Hill Farm in Dutchess County, N.Y.

By JOAN NATHAN

HOWARD, S.D.

NEAR a prairie dotted with cattle and green with soy beans, barley, corn and oats, two bearded Hasidic men dressed in black pray outside a slaughterhouse here that is managed by an evangelical Christian.

What brought these men together could easily have kept them apart: religion.

The two Hasidim oversee shehitah, the Jewish ritual slaughtering of meat according to the Book of Leviticus. The meat is then shipped to Wise Organic Pastures, a kosher food company in Brooklyn owned by Issac Wiesenfeld and his family. When Mr. Wiesenfeld sought an organic processor that used humane methods five years ago, he found Scott Lively, who was just beginning Dakota Beef, now one of the largest organic meat processors in the country.

Mr. Lively adheres to a diet he believes Jesus followed. Like Mr. Wiesenfeld, he says the Bible prescribes that he use organic methods to respect the earth, treat his workers decently and treat the cattle that enter his slaughterhouse as humanely as possible.

"We learn everything from the Old Testament," Mr. Lively said, "from keeping kosher to responsible capitalism."

Humane, sustainable practices like Mr. Lively's are articles of faith for many Americans concerned with the way food gets from farm to plate. But they are even more deeply held matters of faith for a growing number of farmers and religious groups. In the past few years protecting the environment has emerged as a religious

Continued on Page 2

OWEN FRANKEN FOR THE NEW YORK TIMES

When in France, cook as the French do, in classes that do not take much time. Page 5.

A GOOD APPETITE

Melissa Clark

So Many Tomatoes to Stuff in a Week

OF all the produce that tastes amazingly better in season —peaches and apricots, strawberries and peas — none inspires the same cultish devotion as summer tomatoes.

Meaty and succulent, their velvety flesh enclosing a fragrant jelly of golden seeds and dripping with sweet pink juice, summer tomatoes are everything their cold-weather counterparts aren't, including cheap and abundant.

Right now farmers' markets are rich with them: a dizzying profusion of scarlet beefsteaks, mini red and orange cherries and luminous lumpy heirlooms ranging from mild yellow Striped Germans to tart, intense, mauve-hued Brandywines. Swooning in their midst, I can't seem to walk away without bags of them.

Once I get them home, though, I'm left wondering, What the heck am I going to do with all these tomatoes? How fast I can consume my purple Krims and Green Zebras before they ooze into a sticky puddle?

As I contemplated my most recent load of beauties, in hues from amethyst to gold and even a few unripe greens, it almost seemed a shame to eat them. But it would be more of a shame not to.

If I really wanted to take full advantage of their delectability, and to eat them every day, a plan was in order. So I summoned all the great tomato dishes I've ever eaten, compiling a list of the easiest, most varied and most tomatoey of the lot.

I spent the next week in decadent tomato revelry. Here's a chronicle of my grand tomato tour.

DAY 1: PAN CON TOMATE I could eat this Catalan dish every single day for as long as good tomatoes hold out. It resembles bruschetta, but instead of cubing the tomatoes as a topping for garlic- and olive oil-rubbed toast, all you have to do is squeeze their guts directly onto the bread.

Of all the dishes, this one benefits the most from using an ultraripe tomato, still warm from the farmers' market. When you halve it, its insides practically flow out of their own accord. But be careful: one step beyond ultraripe and you are in trouble. Yes, alas, it is possible to buy a terrible August tomato. Supermarkets are full of the same

Continued on Page 4

And on the seventh day, she made marmalade: recipes, Page 4.

PHOTOGRAPHS BY FRANCESCO TONELLI FOR THE NEW YORK TIMES

INSIDE

CMYK Nxxx,2007-08-01,F,001,Bs-4C,E1

N F1

Dining Out

WEDNESDAY, AUGUST 1, 2007

The New York Times

In Dense Stews From Senegal, Intriguing Secrets

By MATT LEE and TED LEE

WITH its spotless new white-tile floors and gleaming stainless-steel ovens, the basement kitchen of Patisserie des Ambassades, a French cafe in Harlem on Frederick Douglass Boulevard, has the fit and finish of a laboratory. On a recent weekday morning, its two resident scientists — bakers in starched white coats — glazed mixed-berry tartlets and spread crème Chantilly over thin sheets of millefeuille pastry on a long steel table.

But at the table's opposite end was the kitchen's resident artist, Ken Alice N'doye, preparing thiebu djen (cheb-oo JEN), Senegal's national dish of rice cooked in a tomato-based fish stew. Although Ms. N'doye, 31, an owner of the cafe, also wore a crisp chef's coat, her every move sprung from sensual, rather than technical, cues.

"In Senegal, we never measure," Ms. N'doye said, as she reached deep into a large can of tomato paste and pulled from it a fistful of thick red purée, which she massaged into a small bowl of warm water. In a stew pot on her stovetop, chopped onions, red bell peppers and tomatoes sizzled toward their combustible limit in hot oil.

Our journey to this unusual pastry kitchen began a year before and a few blocks south at Africa Kine, a Senegalese restaurant on 116th Street. We loved the stews on the menu there — dense, richly flavored concoctions that seemed kin to the gumbos we grew up eating on the coast of South Carolina. And yet in these dishes (and in others we sampled at Le Baobab, another Senegalese restaurant in the neighborhood) we also discovered new flavors that were as thrilling as our first tastes of fish sauce or kaffir lime. We set out to forage for ingredients.

Fred R. Conrad/The New York Times

FLAVORFUL STEW Ken Alice N'doye making a Senegalese lamb stew.

The blocks around 116th Street and Frederick Douglass Boulevard make up the most densely settled Senegalese quarter in the city. As in Senegal, which until 1960 was a colony of France, Islam is the predominant religion and French the default language, heard wafting out of hair salons and among groups of men in bright robes gathered outside the mosque on Frederick Douglass. Directly across 116th Street from Africa Kine, we shopped at Darou Salam Market and Nawel Keur Mame Asta Walo, neatly organized emporia where we bought a few Senegalese staples: bags of crumbly, broken rice, a tub of unsweetened peanut butter and a bottle of palm oil. But nothing we cooked over the weeks that followed had half the depth of flavor we'd encountered on 116th Street.

So we set out to talk our way into the kitchen of a Senegalese home cook who could show us some of the techniques and ingredients we'd been missing. Gorgui N'doye, an owner of Patisserie des Ambassades, said he knew just such a person: his wife.

The N'doyes opened their bakery with a loan from the Small Business Administration in 2002, and brought to Harlem's Senegalese quarter a cafe like those of their native Dakar, Senegal's capital, where excellent baguettes may be as common as they are on the

Continued on Page 4

Arnold Roth

INSIDE

Fine Diner To Riffraff: Tipsy Tales Of 4-Star Benders

By FRANK BRUNI

THE Bordeaux was flowing, the foie gras abundant and the well-heeled epicures at Daniel were having a refined old time when suddenly all eyes turned toward a table against one wall and all conversation ceased.

Jean-Luc Le Dû, a sommelier in the restaurant, looked in that direction, too. And he saw her: the woman making like a dancer on a pole at Scores.

She stood facing the rest of the dining room. First she took off a vest or a jacket, as best Mr. Le Dû remembers. Then she went to work on her blouse.

Just as she was getting to her bra, the maître d'hôtel got to her. Thus her drunken, wobbly stint as a stripper ended, and so did her dinner. She and her date, a smiling, sloshed man who had seemingly egged her on, were escorted to the door.

"She was not necessarily attractive or young, so it was disruptive," complained Mr. Le Dû, who left Daniel several years ago and now owns a wine shop in Greenwich Village. "If she were beautiful, it might have been different. People might have been cheering her on."

At Daniel? Hard to believe. But then Mr. Le Dû's story provides a reminder that a 1985 Burgundy casts the same dark spell as a 2007 peppermint schnapps. That in a four-star temple as surely as a starless dive, some diners drink too much: way, way too much.

And that when they do, they act in all the expansive, untamed and humiliating ways you might expect, transplanted to settings in which you don't expect them. The inebriation comes at a higher price, but it looks much the same. It looks randy. Sloppy. And — how best to put this? — sickly.

That's one of the most striking lessons in a book about the restaurant Per Se to be published by William Morrow in the fall.

In "Service Included: Four-Star Secrets of an Eavesdropping Waiter," Phoebe Damrosch re-

Continued on Page 5

THE POUR

Eric Asimov

A Simple Thirst, a Great Cab

SNOHOMISH, Wash.

THE issue, a scant four decades ago, was simple.

"I couldn't find any decent wine in Washington," Alex Golitzin recalled.

It was back in 1967, after Mr. Golitzin and his wife, Jeannette, had moved to the Seattle area. They had come from San Francisco, where you could find decent wine, after Mr. Golitzin, an engineer, got a job with the Scott Paper Company.

Puget Sound was beautiful. To the west you could watch the sun set over the Pacific Ocean. To the east you could see the rugged snow-capped peaks of the Cascades. But Mr. Golitzin was thirsty, and when he complained about it, his uncle had a simple solution.

"He said, 'Why don't you make it yourself?' " Mr. Golitzin remembered during an interview here in early July.

Fine advice, since his uncle was André Tchelistcheff, legendary enologist for Beaulieu Vineyard, who was instrumental in the 20th-century development of the California wine industry.

In the 1960's Mr. Tchelistcheff began consulting in one of the early efforts to grow vitis vinifera, the European vine that is the source of all the great wine grapes, in eastern Washington. There were fewer than half a dozen commercial wineries operating there, but Mr. Tchelistcheff, who died in 1994, sensed potential for fine wine.

Inspired by his uncle's possibly flip suggestion, in 1974 Mr. Golitzin began to make his own wine in his garage in a glade here about 45 minutes northeast of Seattle. That little experiment grew into Quilceda Creek Vintners, and that garage is now a trim, handsome winery housing one

Continued on Page 6

SANDY SOIL The Galitzine Vineyard of Quilceda Creek Vintners in central Washington.

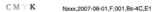

52

SCOTT **STOWELL**

CREATE MULTIPLE ENTRY POINTS

As much as reading a publication is generally defined as a linear experience, rarely does someone pick up a magazine, open to page one, and methodically follow the prescribed route to the back of the book. Blame it on the effect of the Internet, information overload, or our growing impatience and shortening attention spans, but the fact is that people skim, jump around, and flip through pages. Designers must work with this reality, without overwhelming the page with directive starbursts and bold type. "You get the sense from a lot of magazines that there's a kind of desperation," says Scott Stowell. "There are these screaming headlines, and you get this feeling that it's amped up so far that it's saying, 'please read us before we go out of business.' It's off-putting because I don't want to be sold once I've already bought the magazine." The way to avoid this used-car salesman approach is to make every spread interesting and engaging on its own terms and within the larger context of the publication. "The idea," according to Stowell, "is to offer a lot of entry points for people, so you can pick it up anywhere and start reading. It's like creating a smorgasbord."

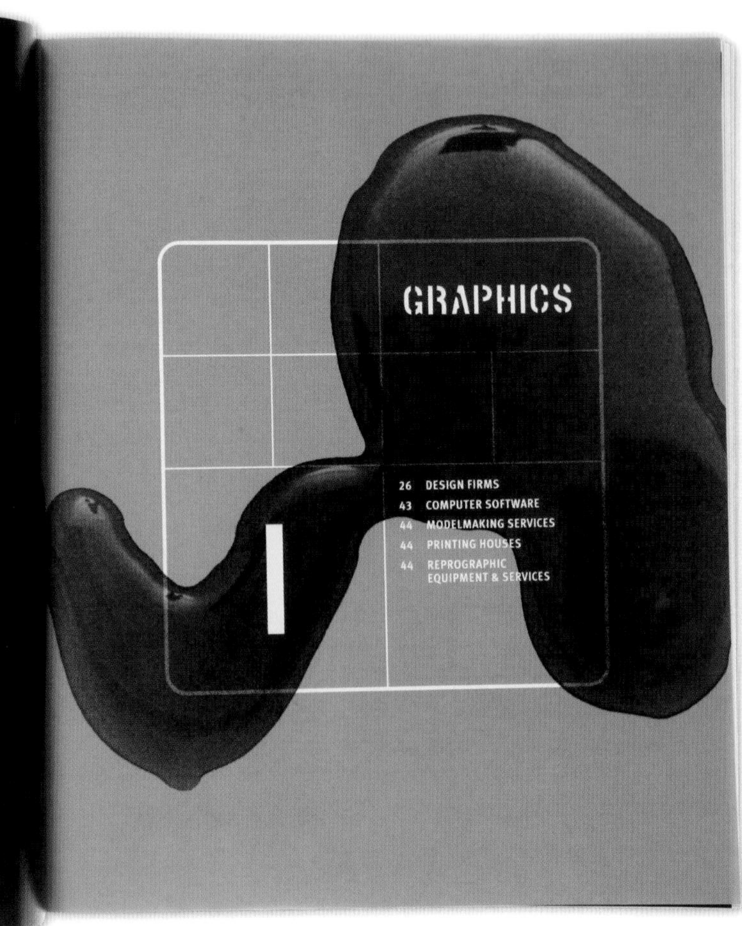

The most unassuming of shapes and objects can become fertile fodder for magazine layouts as shown in these *ID Design Sourcebook* spreads, art directed by Luke Hayman; a spill of liquid and a cluster of capacitors become beautiful images when paired with a graphic and type that enhances without competing.

53 LOOK BEYOND PUBLICATIONS FOR INSPIRATION

AREM **DUPLESSIS**

CHRIS **VERMAAS**

NICOLE **DUDKA**

One of the ways to avoid copying other designs, and therefore design mistakes, is to look for ideas and thought-starters beyond the printed page. "I think the most common mistake in editorial design," Arem Duplessis says, "is looking only to other magazines for inspiration. There are so many magnificent things in the world. Magazines, as beautiful as they can be, are not the be-all-and-end-all."

"Our inspirations come from many areas of interest: the books we've read, the places we've visited, the ordinary objects and events of our daily life, our own cultural backgrounds, and the education we've received," says Chris Vermaas. Nicole Dudka finds ideas simply by walking in the world. "Always keep your eyes open," she says. "I find inspiration in a lot of stuff around me—music, a poster design, a sign, a CD cover, a greeting card. They all can spark an idea or teach you something aesthetically." A digital camera along with a willingness to see things with a fresh eye can also provide just the refresher a designer needs when faced with yet another blank page. "It's easy to get in a rut with the daily grind of deadlines and such," Dudka notes. "But if you can find inspiration in the things around you, it will keep the creativity flowing. I got a digital camera and it changed my life," she says. "I took pictures of different things I could use for reference or that could be used as a basis for an illustration. It might be random stuff, like textures, outdoor venues, little flyers for a simple event." Inspiration is all around—you just have to open your eyes to it.

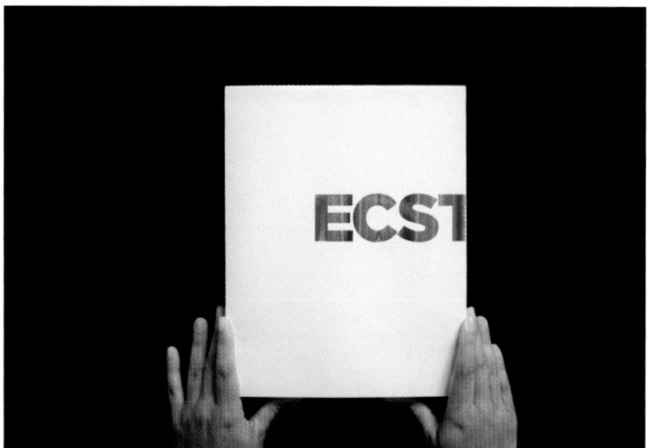

***Ecstasy*, designed by Counterspace, uses a few special techniques that exactly capture the mood of the content in this book about a museum show of artwork that explored altered states.**

54

USE SPECIAL EFFECTS

ARJEN **NOORDEMAN**

MICHAEL **WORTHINGTON**

ADAM **MACHACEK**

When designing a book or publication, there are many techniques—beyond manipulating type and images—to make it unique. "You can design a book in a number of ways," says Arjen Noordeman. "You can pick paper and focus on visual design, or you can make it a more tactile experience. Could it be a box, or incorporate metal, wood, or plastic? Could it be injection molded? There are so many things you can do, and often, if you can express a concept with a material, it enhances the narrative of the material without being overly direct."

Remember and work with the tactility and dimensionality of a publication. "It's important to consider the materiality of the book," says Michael Worthington, a partner at the Los Angeles design studio, Counterspace. "How do you experience it as an object? How does it open, what kind of paper is it printed on? What size is it? Sometimes," he continues, "these are things that are much harder to learn, because before you experience them, you have to imagine them. Even if you print out the pages, you don't experience the materiality."

Adam Machacek has utilized a variety of special techniques that not only enhance the story a particular piece is telling, but ask the reader to become more physically involved with the publication in hand. For example, he and his partner made a book jacket that can be unfolded into a poster, included a set of promotional stickers inside the front cover of a catalog, made a map that folds out of the cover of a booklet. "From the feedback we've had, these little details made people remember the publication and have fun with it," says Machacek. "And we had fun creating them as well."

However, these techniques are used "only when we think it's appropriate to the project." And this is perhaps the most important point—when overused, design effects become overwhelming or irrelevant. "Special techniques are about setting a mood and a tone," says Worthington. "In the worst case, they can become gimmicks with no relationship to the content; in the best case, they make the book an object where the content and technique gel together so you don't notice the special effect, it's just the right effect for that book. When you have a design idea, it should communicate to the audience even when you're not there to explain it."

ASY
E

CSTASY
IN AND ABOUT ALTERED STATES

Part of a large body of experiential sculptural works called Synchro System meant to induce trance-like states in the viewer, Carsten Höller's *Upside-Down Mushroom Room* (2000) is "a materialized hallucination": "It is not you and the object: the object and you are you."[1] Before entering *Upside-Down Mushroom Room*, visitors make their way through the ninety-eight-and-a-half-foot-long pitch-black hallway *Gantenbein Corridor*, a reference to the protagonist in Swiss writer Max Frisch's novel *Mein Name sei Gantenbein* (1964), who pretends to be blind in order to observe the true nature of his friends, ultimately discovering that he cannot rely on his assumptions about how the world operates. The same effect holds true as one leaves the darkness of the corridor and emerges into an entirely different realm where the ceiling and the floor have switched places. Seeming to sprout directly from the ceiling, nine ten-foot-high fly-agaric mushrooms—the potent red and orange variety common in German folklore and stories by the Brothers Grimm—rotate upside down at various speeds, while spotlights embedded in the floor flood the room with a disorienting white glow.

This particular mushroom species appears throughout Höller's works of the late 1990s as a symbol of the artist's desire to question perception, as well as a direct reference to the mushroom's role as the main ingredient in the intoxicating ritual drink, or soma, of the ancient Vedic peoples, as chronicled in R. Gordon Wasson's book *Soma: Divine Mushroom of Immortality* (1968), a key reference for Höller. Rather than functioning as a means for hallucinatory escapism, his interest in fly-agaric mushrooms signals a decidedly critical aim. The notion of change and transformation of perception harkens back to one of the central themes of Höller's work: the investigation of doubt as a radical critique of Enlightenment rationalism. Like Theodor Adorno and Max Horkheimer, he distrusts the understanding of subjectivity in modernity as a fixed and fully formed ego capable of mastering nature. As completely unnatural as the *Upside-Down Mushroom Room* seems, Höller's installation actually replicates the upside-down projection of images onto the retina before the brain inverts what one sees. Höller's installation asks what would happen if one could perceive images prior to this "corrected" vision.

Gloria Sutton

notes

1 Carsten Höller, in "Carsten Höller: The Synchro System and Yours," *Flash Art*, no. [illegible] (May–June 2000): [illegible]

Carsten Höller

Ecstacy, **designed by Counterspace**

55 DON'T STOP AT DESIGN

VINCE **FROST**

Your responsibility as a designer does not end when you turn over the digital files. Once you've created the virtual product, you want to make sure the real one will measure up. "Be totally on top of the process or things fall apart quickly," says Vince Frost. "You can design a great book, and then the publisher decides to use some crappy paper or reduce production values." Of course, a designer may not have a say or be able to influence every aspect of how the final piece is made, but you should try to exert quality control wherever possible. Speak up, ask questions, and get involved to ensure the complete integrity of the final piece you worked so hard to design so beautifully.

56 WORK WITH A GOOD PRINTER

BRETT **MACFADDEN**

ADAM **MACHACEK**

You've used up hours, consumed caffeine, and spilled sweat selecting images, making the most of the grid, selecting typefaces, getting the captions just right—don't put all that hard work in the hands of a low-cost printer. (Unless you're looking for some kind of grunge effect.) Brett MacFadden, senior designer at Chronicle Books, puts it succinctly: "Sub-par printing is bothersome." Even more, working with a good printer can create opportunities you didn't consider. "It's important to work with a good printer, even if it costs a little more," says Adam Machacek. "A good printer gives you advice, and a bad printer or binder may spoil all the time you invested."

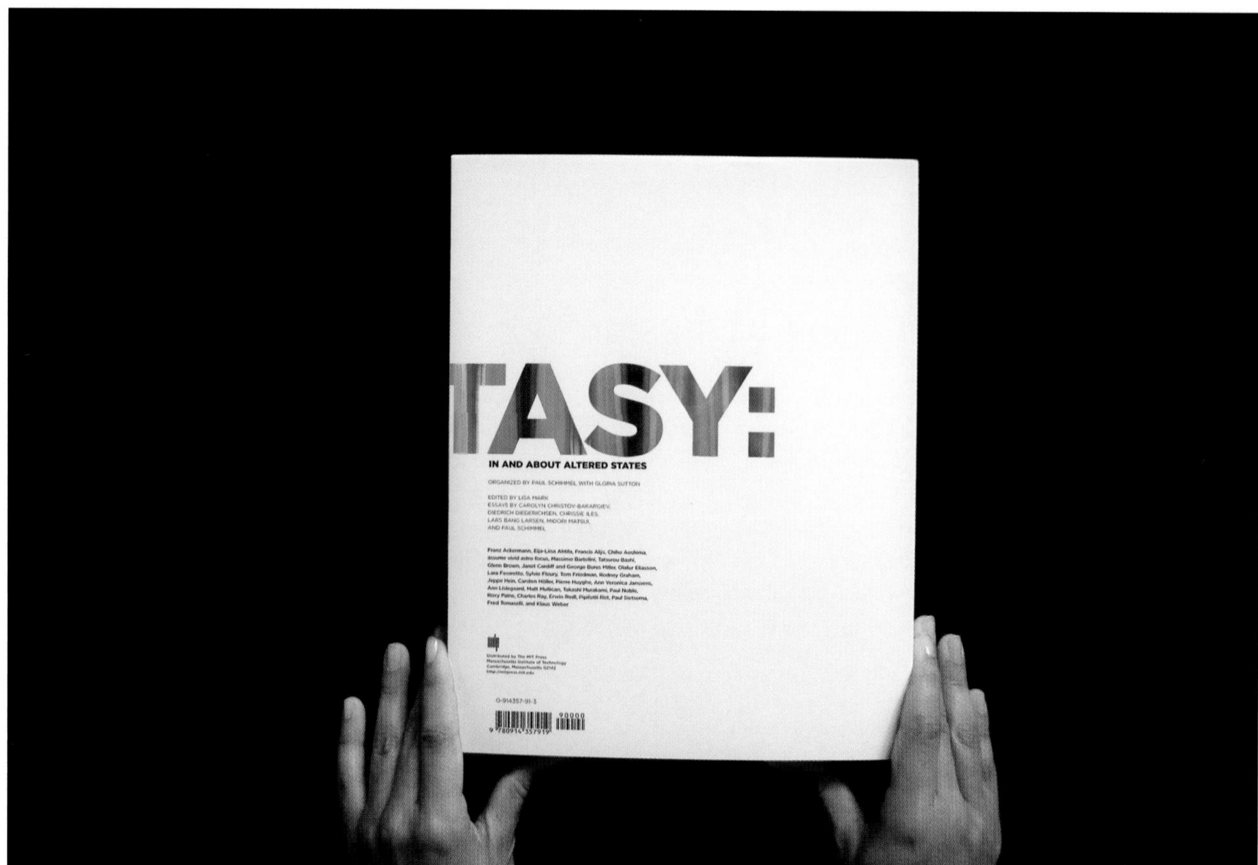

***Ecstacy*, designed by Counterspace**

57

GO AHEAD, TAKE CREDIT

INA **SALTZ**

Publications offer designers something few other graphic design projects can—the opportunity to sign your own work. "When you're an editorial designer, your name is on the magazine," points out Ina Saltz. "That's so satisfying to me. You're credited for your work in a very visible way. Your parents may still not understand what you do, but they can see your name there."

DECONSTRUCTING A SPREAD

Grids, fonts, faces, feature wells.... In any publication, there are numerous design elements that have to work together in ways that are often invisible to the reader. Here, and on pages 102 and 103, Scott Stowell of Open pulls back the curtain on several spreads of *GOOD* magazine to reveal what's really going on behind the scenes and beneath the surface of the page.

This essay by Alice Twemlow asks questions about what good design is (or is not).
The "Design Solutions" section revealed the structure of the magazine.
These icons indicate the content of each story.
We contrast the type grid with images that bleed off the page.
All type and images align with a consistent baseline grid.
Each part of the "Design Solutions" issue used a different "guest typeface."
These photos were shot digitally by Jorge Colombo.
This area at the bottom of each page is the "Infobar."
This black dot is the "Design Solutions" logo, inspired by the logo for the Museum of Modern Art's classic "Good Design" shows.
The *GOOD* grid is made up of 7 equal columns. We combine them to make larger columns for text and images.
Design Solutions
Better-than-it-has-to-be Design
introduction by ALICE TWEMLOW
photographs by JORGE COLOMBO
For many, the AK-47 is a classic in the annals of good design. But good for what and for whom?
How do we know what's up? pages 66-67
How do we make our mark? pages 68-69
How do we understand each other? pages 74-75
How do we work with the machines? pages 76-77
How do we stay safe? pages 84-85
How do we not trash the place? pages 86-87
EXIT 3E
EAST
6
17M
Goshen
SUPPORT IN
FOR IRAQ

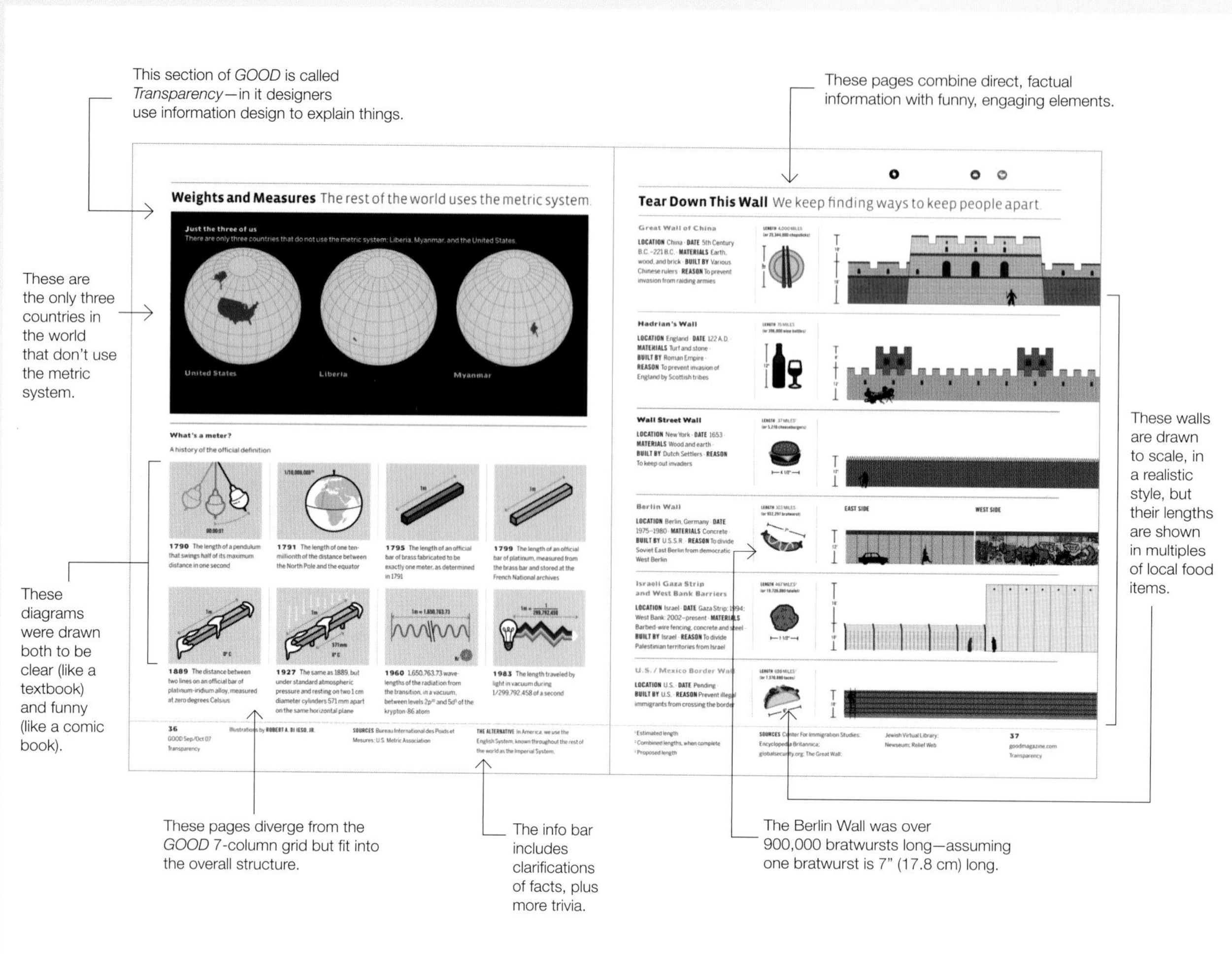

This section of *GOOD* is called *Transparency*—in it designers use information design to explain things.
These pages combine direct, factual information with funny, engaging elements.
Weights and Measures The rest of the world uses the metric system.
Just the three of us
There are only three countries that do not use the metric system: Liberia, Myanmar, and the United States.
United States
Liberia
Myanmar
These are the only three countries in the world that don't use the metric system.
What's a meter?
A history of the official definition
These diagrams were drawn both to be clear (like a textbook) and funny (like a comic book).
Tear Down This Wall We keep finding ways to keep people apart.
Great Wall of China
Hadrian's Wall
Wall Street Wall
Berlin Wall
EAST SIDE
WEST SIDE
Israeli Gaza Strip and West Bank Barriers
U.S. / Mexico Border Wall
These walls are drawn to scale, in a realistic style, but their lengths are shown in multiples of local food items.
These pages diverge from the *GOOD* 7-column grid but fit into the overall structure.
The info bar includes clarifications of facts, plus more trivia.
The Berlin Wall was over 900,000 bratwursts long—assuming one bratwurst is 7" (17.8 cm) long.

***GOOD* magazine, designed and deconstructed by Scott Stowell of Open**

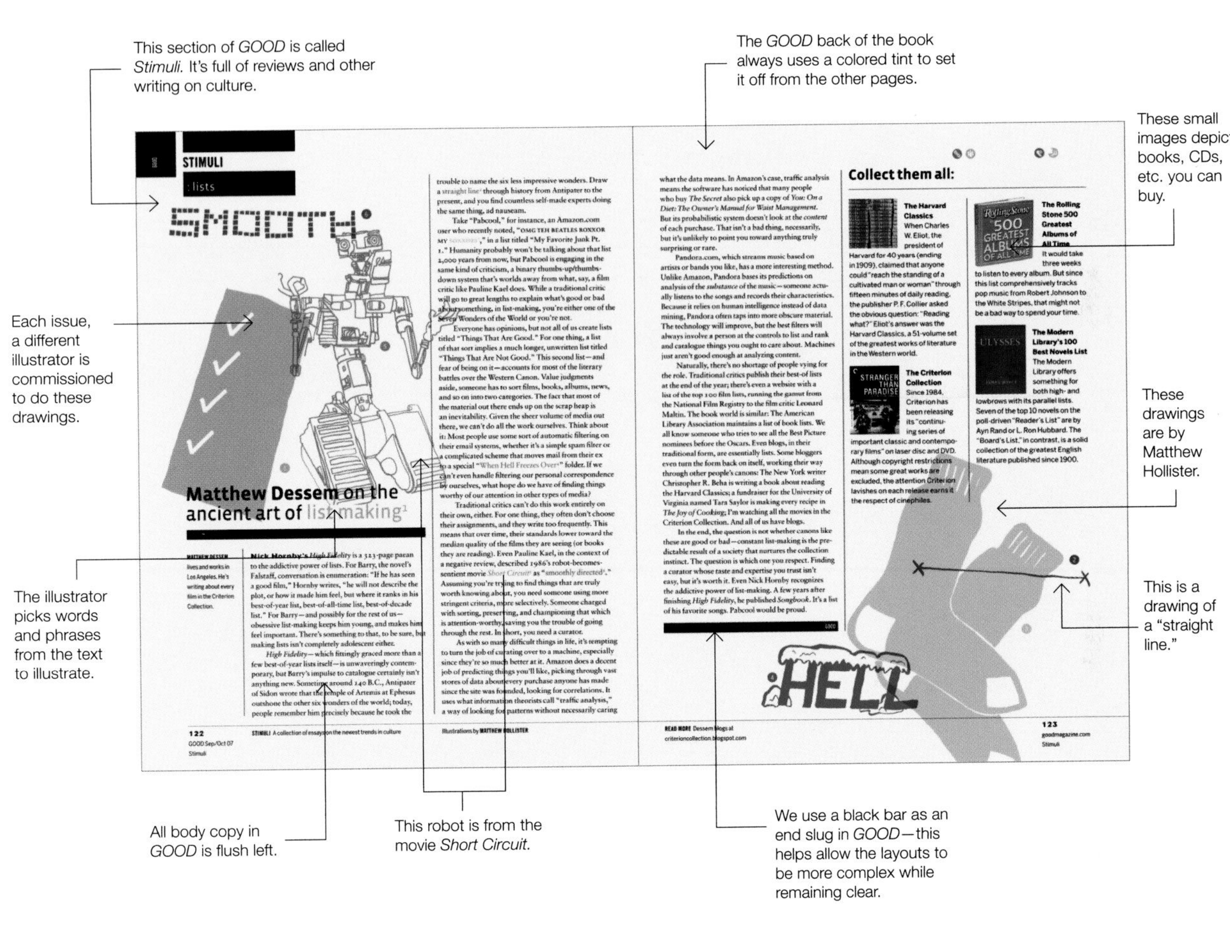

This section of *GOOD* is called *Stimuli.* It's full of reviews and other writing on culture.
The *GOOD* back of the book always uses a colored tint to set it off from the other pages.
These small images depict books, CDs, etc. you can buy.
Each issue, a different illustrator is commissioned to do these drawings.
These drawings are by Matthew Hollister.
The illustrator picks words and phrases from the text to illustrate.
This is a drawing of a "straight line."
All body copy in *GOOD* is flush left.
This robot is from the movie *Short Circuit.*
We use a black bar as an end slug in *GOOD*—this helps allow the layouts to be more complex while remaining clear.
STIMULI
:lists
SMOOTH
Matthew Dessem on the ancient art of list-making
Collect them all:
HELL

Chapter Three:

WORKING WITH EDITORS, ILLUSTRATORS, AND INFORMATION

***Red* magazine, designed by Agnes Zeilstra, captures the lifestyle of the busy European woman juggling family, fashion, career, and friends.**

58

JEREMY **LESLIE**

INA **SALTZ**

THE EDITOR IS YOUR FRIEND AND YOUR PARTNER

In publication design, notes Jeremy Leslie, "Essentially you have an editor and an art director on equal footing. A good editor has to have an understanding of design even if they don't design, and a senior designer has to have a good understanding of words. The best magazines come from the best teams." Like most great partnerships, the one between editor and designer should be based on building personal and intellectual rapport—you may be fortunate and stumble upon an ideal situation, but it's more likely that you'll need to create it. "You're never going to have a great budget, great editor, great staff, and great subject matter all in one," Ina Saltz points out. "But if you have a great relationship with your editor, then it's a good job no matter what any of the other factors are. Because it's all about the power of the merging of visuals and content, there has to be a partnership and a trust and mutual reliance and respect. And to that end, the art director has to appreciate the power of the written word and the editor has to have good visual instincts." When all those elements come together, you get not only a magazine of excellence, but a gratifying personal experience as well. "Working with great editors is like a drug," laughs Saltz. "It's very addictive and very satisfying."

***Red* magazine, designed by Agnes Zeilstra**

59

ARTHUR **HOCHSTEIN**

THINK LIKE AN EDITOR

The best way to understand an editor and get more out of them is to try and think like one. As Arthur Hochstein notes, "Editors tend to see designers as a rare, sensitive species, like tropical plants or African violets. But if you can talk the language of editors, they'll bring you into the process more." Exactly how does a designer learn to enter the editorial mind? "You have to think about how something translates to a reader, rather than just how it looks," Hochstein advises. "You have to see design as a visual narrative, not just a decorative process. This is a huge distinction, because some designers just think about the arrangement of things, but we have a story to tell."

Tel je zegeningen

Peggy Saman

'Ik ben steeds meer van *de makkelijke*'

Meer en meer vrouwen komen erop terug. Zes ballen in de lucht houden hoeft niet meer voor hen. Maar hoe pak je dat aan, want je wilt toch werken, veel aandacht aan je gezin besteden, uitgaan en sporten? Simpel, omarm de attitude of gratitude.

Vrienden van mij die geen kinderen kunnen krijgen, gaan twee broertjes uit Oekraïne adopteren. Mijn vriendin vroeg laatst: 'Heb je nog een advies voor me, voor als ik straks ineens twee kinderen heb?' Nu is mijn vriendin een van de meest praktische en georganiseerde vrouwen die ik ken. Ze heeft haar leven perfect op orde. Ze vergeet geen enkele verjaardag, zegt tegen iedereen op het juiste moment precies de juiste dingen, ziet er altijd geweldig uit, sport vijf keer per week, kookt zeven dagen per week gezond, weet alles in huis te vinden, en verspilt ook nog eens geen geld.

'Dat het allemaal niet perfect hoeft te gaan straks,' zei ik. 'Het geeft niet als je huis een chaos is, als je 's avonds een pizza in de oven doet. Het geeft niet als je kinderen raar gekleed gaan. Een kind is veel gelukkiger met een ontspannen moeder, dan met eentje die de hele tijd bezig is haar ambitieuze programma uit te voeren.'

Later dacht ik: dat is precies het tegenovergestelde van wat ik zelf doe. Ik ben altijd bezig mijn programma uit te voeren. Als ik op zaterdagochtend wakker word, heb ik al een hele lijst in mijn hoofd met dingen die er moeten gebeuren. Boodschappen doen, cadeautjes kopen voor verjaardagen, kinderen naar de kapper, kinderen nieuwe schoenen, boeken terugbrengen naar de bibliotheek, zwemles, borrel bij de buren. En dan is zondag voor familiebezoek, klussen in huis, afspraken met vrienden, werk. Laatst zei mijn vriend: 'Er is nooit ruimte voor iets spontaans.' Ik was het hartgrondig met hem eens. Alleen: wat te schrappen?

Live life to the max

Wat cultuursociologen opmerken is dat er een generatie van 'maximaliseerders' is ontstaan: mensen die zo veel mogelijk uit hun leven en tijd willen halen. Kinderen, een uitdagende baan, interessante reizen, een boeiend cultureel leven, een omvangrijk sociaal netwerk; ze willen alles. Misschien komt het doordat er voor vrouwen tegenwoordig nog maar zo weinig beperkingen zijn om het leven in te richten zoals ze zelf willen; bijna alles kunnen we zelf bepalen. Dat geldt ze- >

De genoegennemers

'Perfectionisme is niet mijn struikelblok, ik probeer bewust geen *superwoman* te zijn. Maar het kost me wel moeite om alle dingen die ik wil doen een plek te geven naast elkaar. Ik heb er bewust voor gekozen om me op drie gebieden te concentreren: werk, gezin en spiritualiteit. Mijn werk is altijd belangrijk voor me geweest en er moet ook brood op de plank komen. Daarnaast wil ik graag een goede moeder zijn. En mijn man en ik maken onderdeel uit van een meditatiegroep die wekelijks met de kinderen bijeenkomt. Dat vind ik even genoeg.

Ik dacht: ik kan alles wel halfhalf gaan doen, maar dat vind ik niet leuk. Ik ga niet meer tot diep in de nacht uit, sport past even niet meer in mijn leven, ik heb mijn naaicursus niet vervolgd, en mijn danscursussen uitgesteld. Omdat ik mijn aandacht niet over al die vlakken hoef te verspreiden, heb ik meer diepgang dan ik vroeger had.'

Peggy Saman (34), loopbaancoach voor vrouwen

tekst: **Annemiek Leclaire** | fotografie: **Manon van der Zwaal**

STYLING: MARRIT MULDER | VISAGIE: SIDDHARTHA @ VIEW AGENCY, RITA SERANO

74 Red

Red 75

60

GREAT PUBLICATIONS ARE NOT DEMOCRACIES

INA **SALTZ**

CARIN **GOLDBERG**

VINCE **FROST**

The very best publications start with the very strongest of ideas. This perspective usually emanates from the office of the founder or editor. "A magazine has to have a strong editorial voice," says Ina Saltz. "It's not a democratic process. The mission needs to be strongly defined, and everyone on staff needs to contribute to that mission and that voice." Because there are so many, sometimes competing, elements that need to go into a magazine—advertising, templates, editorial, features, illustration, photography, and more—it's important for designers to eschew anything that might dilute this core vision. "The best scenario for any project is to cut out the middlemen and decision making by committee," notes Carin Goldberg. "Get to the person whose vision is on par with yours. A magazine is like making a baby, and it's always best for the family to be like-minded and collaborative."

As a designer, working with editors in this way should be exhilarating and edifying. "The experience of working with editors has taught me so much about design and about communicating," says Vince Frost, who feels that he learns the most when he's pushed the most. "I love it when an editor comes to you and says, 'I want three stories on this page,' and you just want to put one big picture there. Yes, he's making my life difficult, but actually that's fun. He knows something I don't. He knows there's a reason for connecting these three stories, so I say, 'Let's make it work.' It's exciting."

"Stoner caught the best moments in a surfer's life."
—Art Brewer
Matt Warshaw is the former editor of Surfer magazine and has been writing about surfing since 1984. He is the author of Surf Movie Tonite! (Chronicle Books) and The Encyclopedia of Surfing. He lives in San Francisco.
Jeff Divine is the photo editor of Surfer's Journal and held the same position at Surfer magazine for more than twenty years. He lives in San Clemente, California.
Published in association with surfer magazine
Jacket design by Brett MacFadden
Manufactured in China
www.chroniclebooks.com

***Photo/Stoner* collects the work of one of surfing's most legendary photographers. In the book, images are grouped in a way that brings attention to the elegance of the design as well as the artfulness of the photographs.**

61

BRETT **MACFADDEN**

CONSULT WITH THE SALES AND MARKETING STAFF

Sales and marketing staff are important resources who can bring critical perspective to the design process. "Sometimes sales and marketing people bring really concrete information that's great to have," Brett MacFadden notes, such as facts and statistics on sales, demographics, buying patterns, and more. He offers an example: "I had a New Age book on tips for living longer. We had designed it with a steel blue palette that we thought was cool and relaxing. Sales and marketing looked at it and said the cover needed to be red. The author was a Chinese doctor, so the cover needed to be Chinese red. Designers would avoid this solution because it seems obvious or trite, but when people are out there buying, they don't analyze things the way we do; they go for what seems right, and sales people are great at seeing the clear direction. There are times that we fight back, we feel it's not the right direction, or we think there's an untapped market, because sales often sees the existing, not potential, market. In this case, the Chinese red was the right direction, as the book did extremely well." While the obvious solution may not always seem the right approach to an aesthetically astute designer, designers need to recognize that their taste does not always reflect that of the buying public, and that the buying public keeps them in business.

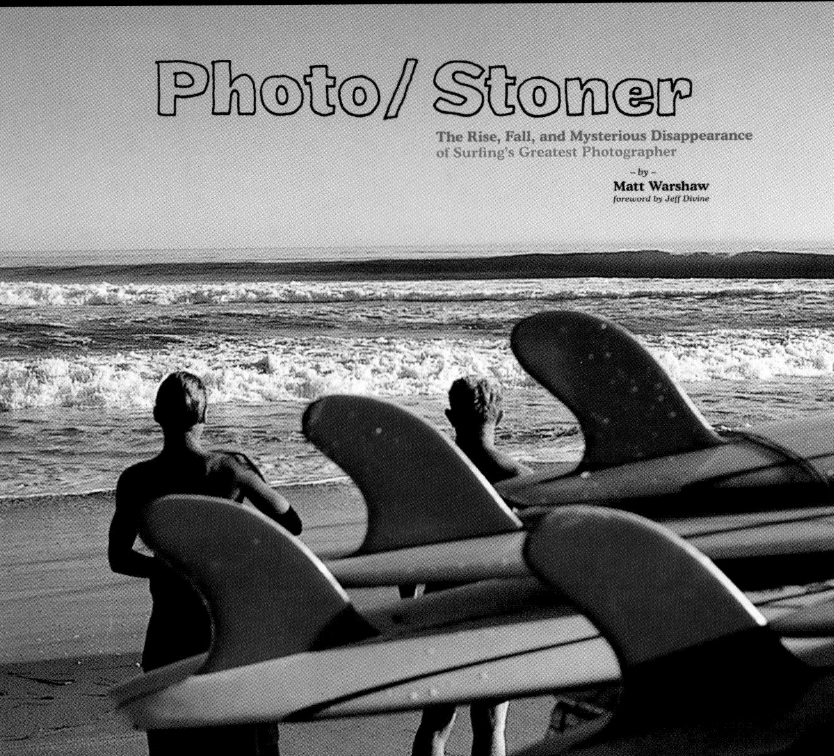

$40.00 U.S.

In 1965, Ron Stoner was the best surf photographer in the business. He captured the balmy beaches, bikini-clad girls, and achingly beautiful waves of Southern California in the full Technicolor they deserved.

When Stoner set up his Century 1000mm lens beachside to shoot, all the hot locals would paddle out to show off their moves. Stoner turned these local guys into heroes in the pages of *Surfer* magazine: Bill Andrews and Dickie Moon shot from the cliff at Black's Beach; style master Bill Hamilton cutting back at Swami's; Mike Hynson trimming out at Hollister Ranch.

Then, at the zenith of his career, Stoner stumbled off this sunny stage into drug use and mental illness. He was barely working by 1970. By 1977 he was declared missing. In 1991 he was declared dead. His photos disappeared into the *Surfer* archives, where they gathered dust for decades until surf historian Matt Warshaw and photo editor Jeff Divine tracked down all the negatives they could find and handpicked the best of the lot—many of which haven't been seen since the '60s.

In *Photo/ Stoner*, Stoner's strange, dark story is recounted alongside his best and rarest images—photographs that capture an innocent Southern California where there were always plenty of waves, offshore winds, and time to surf. In word and in image, *Photo/ Stoner* is a poignant ode to a lost era, and a lost man.

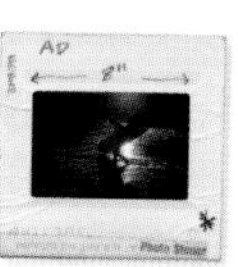

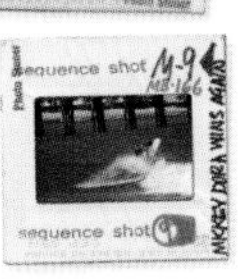

CHRONICLE BOOKS
SAN FRANCISCO

62

MICHAEL **RAY**

MARTHA **RICH**

CREATE OPPORTUNITIES FOR COLLABORATION AND "CHANCE CREATION"

Publications are group efforts, and the more a designer can contribute to creating an environment that enhances teamwork, the better the publication will be. When famed movie director Francis Ford Coppola started *Zoetrope*, according to Michael Ray, "He wanted to mimic the collaborative aspects of filmmaking. The cinematographer, director, actors, producers—all of these people are contributing to one thing. He likes the idea of chance creation." In *Zoetrope*, using artists who are not necessarily graphic designers to develop each issue independent of every other certainly ups the opportunity for unexpected bursts of creativity. "We select the stories and send them off to an artist, preferably someone who has never designed a publication before," says Ray. "Sometimes the artist reacts to the text, sometimes not. When he or she returns the design, it's necessarily out of our control."

For more conventional magazines, designers have the opportunity to create chance collaboration by working with illustrators. As Los Angeles illustrator Martha Rich says, "The more freedom I have, the better. If you have an art director who is nitpicking, it squashes your creativity." She encourages art directors and designers to remember that they're working with an illustrator's ideas, not just their product. "When you hire an illustrator, you're hiring them for their mind," she says. "The best thing for me is to work as a team where they know my strengths and they're using my mind in tandem with their minds to get a great result."

60

61

Unidentified surfers. (Opposite) Lance Carson, Rincon—a *Surfer* cover shot from mid-1967. Stoner's photo was actually shot in the late morning and is green-blue; *Surfer* publisher John Severson "sandwiched" the photo of Carson with his own image of a setting sun.

100

101

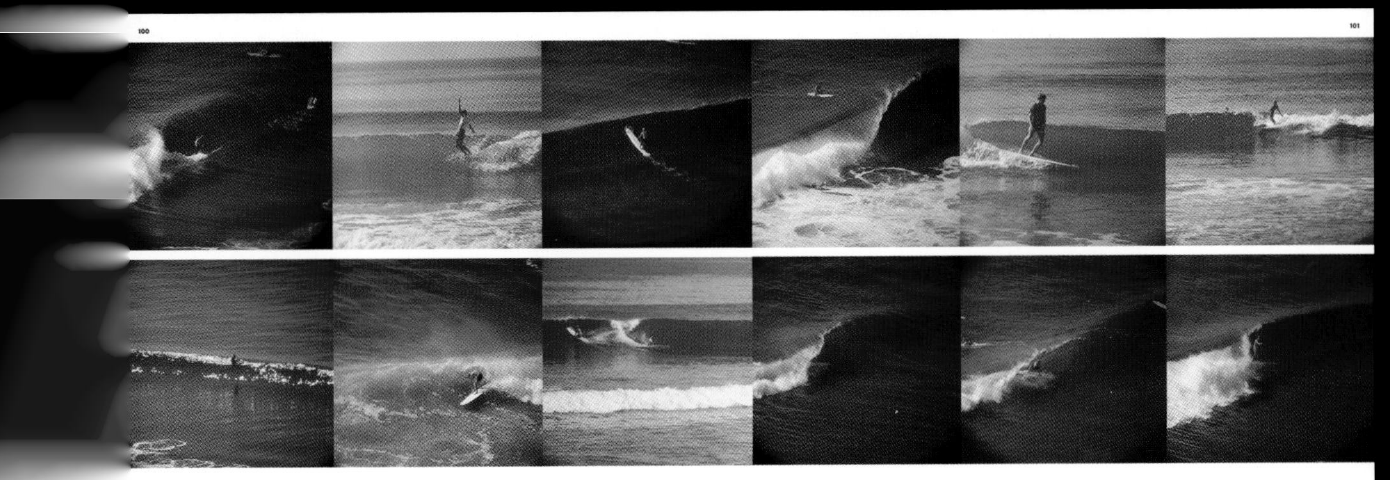

(Pages 98–99) Black's Beach. (Pages 100–103) Most of Stoner's color slides are about forty years old, and those that were stored improperly are now faded or discolored—but eye-catching in their own right.

Photo/Stoner, designed by Brett MacFadden

118

Stoner's ad work: a 1967 photo for Jacobs Surfboards.
(opposite) outtakes from Sherry Haley's
Leopard Spots boutique ads.

119

***Photo/Stoner*, designed by Brett MacFadden**

63 WHEN WORKING ON A LAUNCH, DON'T FORGET ABOUT THE AUDIENCE OF INVESTORS

DAVID **ALBERTSON**

"Prototype work typically focuses on the proof of concept," explains David Albertson. "And that often means you need to convince people with money that it's worth investing in this idea, getting the machine going, getting this brand off the ground. You need to convince people to make a long-term commitment to this venture." Design is central to helping investors see not just what a new publication is, but what it could be. "The prototypical work is very gestural," according to Albertson, "and you work hard on making sure the tone and overall sense has jelled, and that it's hitting a sweet spot people can recognize. You're trying to pretend that it exists, that it's all ready and is a foregone conclusion, so they can see it's real and has legs to it." As challenging as this phase is, the even more difficult work is next to come. "Once you get into a launch, then it becomes, 'How do you fit everything in here and fulfill that gestural promise?' You're trying to match the reality to the dream, and your job becomes a lot harder."

64 ENGAGE WITH THE "THIRD DIMENSION"

DAVID **ALBERTSON**

Publications, even more so than other graphic design projects, involve bringing together different people, agendas, deadlines, and objectives, some of which may be working at cross-purposes. While graphic designers may know plenty about how to make things look good on a page, a publication designer has to juggle a lot more than fonts and pretty pictures. "A lot of graphic designers learn all about combining type and imagery, about using positive and negative space," notes David Albertson, "but I think that they learn less about—and it's harder to learn about—engaging in this third dimension, which is bringing together all of the components and layers and deadlines."

The "third dimension" involves artfully and gracefully keeping the publication world's equivalent of chainsaws, tennis balls, and flaming torches in the design air at one time. Albertson explains: "It's when you have a large photo and a headline and a sidebar and small photos and captions and a slug and a writer and an illustration or diagram, and they're all coming from different places. You may have a creative idea about how to package the thing that you're trying to achieve, but you then have to do the job of making the page well organized and inviting, on deadline. You get squished between a writer who blew their deadline, the photographer who's late, the prepress people who need files, the pressmen waiting to go." Ultimately, it is precisely the multidimensionality of this challenge that makes the final accomplishment of the printed piece such a sweet satisfaction once it's complete.

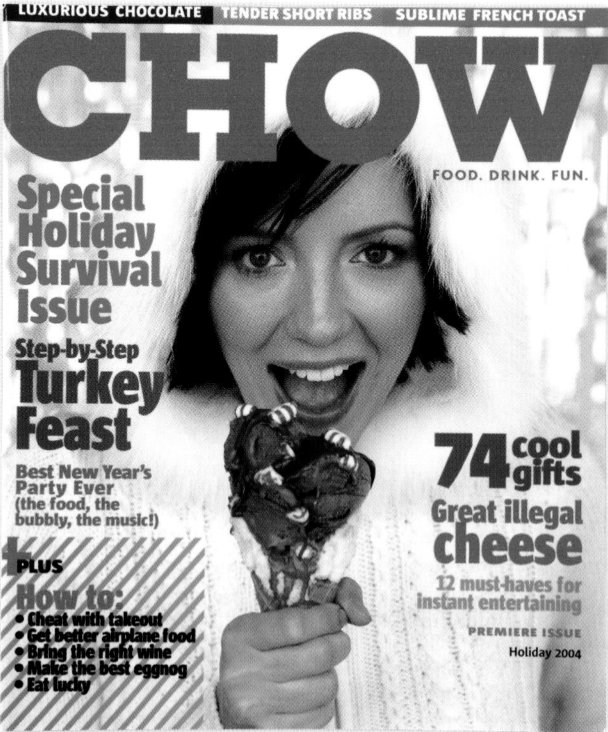

Left and opposite: *Chow*, designed by Albertson Design, is "an alternative food magazine for an info-hungry audience, serving up recipes, restaurants, fast food, and travel in a bold and colorful way with a dash of attitude," according to Albertson.

65

LOOK FOR THE VALUES OF THE CONTENT PROVIDERS

JESSICA **FLEISCHMANN**

ARJEN **NOORDEMAN**

When casting about for a design approach, many publication designers express their respect and admiration for the creative work they're showcasing by amplifying the original artist's vision. "I try to look at the values of the content providers," Jessica Fleischmann explains. "I try to determine if they are interested in creating a private or a public space, and then ask myself how this page and structure can serve as an intimate space or be more outward looking. So there is a reflection of, or a conversation with, the work being represented in the design. I aim to support and dialog with rather than comment on the vision."

This respect for the raw material at hand is especially important when dealing with the work of other artists. Arjen Noordeman designed many art books and catalogs while design director at a modern art museum. "When I was at Mass MoCA," he notes, "the work was about the craft of design and referencing the art itself in the design. Sometimes it worked, but sometimes artists didn't appreciate the graphic design, and they just wanted their work to show; they don't want design to interfere with their work. It's like photographers hate graphic designers who put text over their images." The solution in these, and many other cases, is not to defer to content, but to enhance it. "We started to realize that we should not reference the artwork in our design, but just create a structure that puts the art on a pedestal."

Summer Drinks
sip summer sweetly
Iced tea and lemonade, those brilliant summer staples, get a kick from a mix master

PRIMER EVERYTHING CHOCOLATE
Dark, Rich, and Beautiful What is top quality and relatively inexpensive—and induces euphoria, energy, lust, and joy? Here's our guide to great chocolate, the gift no one ever returns
BY MATT PALMQUIST PHOTO BY ASTERISM
What's New
Why varietals?
"Single origin"
Racy New Bonbons
How It's Made
The Bliss Molecule

A magazine about serious topics, the *Journal of Aesthetics and Protest*, designed by Jessica Fleischmann, works both aesthetics and protest into type treatments by taking a simple font and using it in a totally unexpected way.

66

GET THE RIGHT PERSON FOR THE JOB

NICKI **KALISH**

ANITA **KUNZ**

When working with photographers and illustrators, it's important to embrace their personal skills and style without trying to force a different aesthetic on them. "I think the most important thing is to use the right person for the job," says Nicki Kalish. "I try to match the assignment to the person. Who lives on Cape Cod, or has a certain kind of sensibility, or understands that something has to be cooked a certain way, or that something else has to be funny? I want to start off with the right person." Toronto illustrator Anita Kunz points out that a little bit of legwork will lead an art director to the right illustrator. "If they look through my work, they'll know what they're going to get," she says. But she also feels that responsibility for making the right match lies as much with the illustrator as the art director. "It's all about respect," she says. "I know I'm good at some things and not so good at other things." She's also knows there are times when the best option is to turn an assignment down or pass it on to someone else. "Sometimes I don't think I'm right for the job, but I can think of one or two artists who would be better for the assignment," she says.

Then there are those stories that call for an illustrator with a very specific set of artistic skills and life experiences. "There was a cover about people who drink too much in restaurants," recalls Kalish. "It was kind of funny, because it was about when people go out to very expensive restaurants; they're out to celebrate and they often behave in ways restaurateurs find very trying. We were trying to figure out how to do that cover, and we had an idea of photographing a maître d' at a restaurant with a fountain in the center. But if you saw that image, you wouldn't know it was about people drinking too much; you might think it was about the restaurant or the maître d'. I really thought it needed to be an illustration, and I wanted to call an artist who likes to drink so they would get it," Kalish says, laughing.

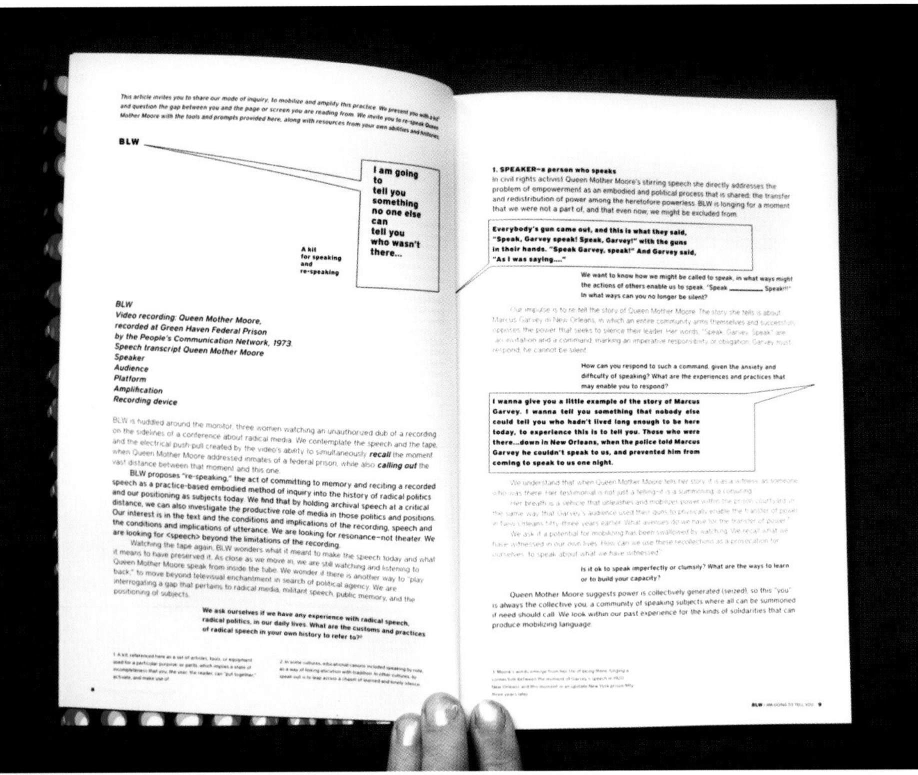
This article invites you to share our mode of inquiry, to mobilize and amplify this practice and question the gap between you and the page or screen you are reading from. We present you with a kit[1] Mother Moore with the tools and prompts provided here, along with resources from your own abilities and histories. We invite you to re-speak Queen

BLW

A kit for speaking and re-speaking

BLW
Video recording: Queen Mother Moore, recorded at Green Haven Federal Prison by the People's Communication Network, 1973.
Speech transcript Queen Mother Moore
Speaker
Audience
Platform
Amplification
Recording device

BLW is huddled around the monitor, three women watching an unauthorized dub of a recording on the sidelines of a conference about radical media. We contemplate the speech and the tape, and the electrical push-pull created by the video's ability to simultaneously ***recall*** the moment when Queen Mother Moore addressed inmates of a federal prison, while also ***calling out*** the vast distance between that moment and this one.

BLW proposes "re-speaking," the act of committing to memory and reciting a recorded speech as a practice-based embodied method of inquiry into the history of radical politics and our positioning as subjects today. We find that by holding archival speech at a critical distance, we can also investigate the productive role of media in those politics and positions. Our interest is in the text and the conditions and implications of the recording, speech and the conditions and implications of utterance. We are looking for resonance—not theater. We are looking for <speech> beyond the limitations of the recording.

Watching the tape again, BLW wonders what it meant to make the speech today and what it means to have preserved it. As close as we move in, we are still watching and listening to Queen Mother Moore speak from inside the tube. We wonder if there is another way to "play back," to move beyond televisual enchantment in search of political agency. We are interrogating a gap that pertains to radical media, militant speech, public memory, and the positioning of subjects.

We ask ourselves if we have any experience with radical speech, radical politics, in our daily lives. What are the customs and practices of radical speech in your own history to refer to?[2]

1. SPEAKER—a person who speaks

In civil rights activist Queen Mother Moore's stirring speech she directly addresses the problem of empowerment as an embodied and political process that is shared: the transfer and redistribution of power among the heretofore powerless. BLW is longing for a moment that we were not a part of, and that even now, we might be excluded from.

We want to know how we might be called to speak, in what ways might the actions of others enable us to speak. "Speak ________ Speak!!" In what ways can you no longer be silent?

Our impulse is to re-tell the story of Queen Mother Moore. The story she tells is about Marcus Garvey in New Orleans, in which an entire community arms themselves and successfully opposes the power that seeks to silence their leader. Her words, "Speak, Garvey, Speak" are an invitation and a command, marking an imperative responsibility or obligation: Garvey must respond; he cannot be silent.

How can you respond to such a command, given the anxiety and difficulty of speaking? What are the experiences and practices that may enable you to respond?

We understand that when Queen Mother Moore tells her story it is as a witness, as someone who was there. Her testimonial is not just a telling—it is a summoning, a conjuring.

Her breath is a vehicle that unleashes and mobilizes power within the prison courtyard in the same way that Garvey's audience used their guns to physically enable the transfer of power in New Orleans fifty-three years earlier. What avenues do we have for the transfer of power?

We ask if a potential for mobilizing has been swallowed by watching. We recall what we have witnessed in our own lives. How can we use these recollections as a provocation for ourselves, to speak about what we have witnessed?

Is it ok to speak imperfectly or clumsily? What are the ways to learn or to build your capacity?

Queen Mother Moore suggests power is collectively generated (seized), so this "you" is always the collective you, a community of speaking subjects where all can be summoned if need should call. We look within our past experience for the kinds of solidarities that can produce mobilizing language.

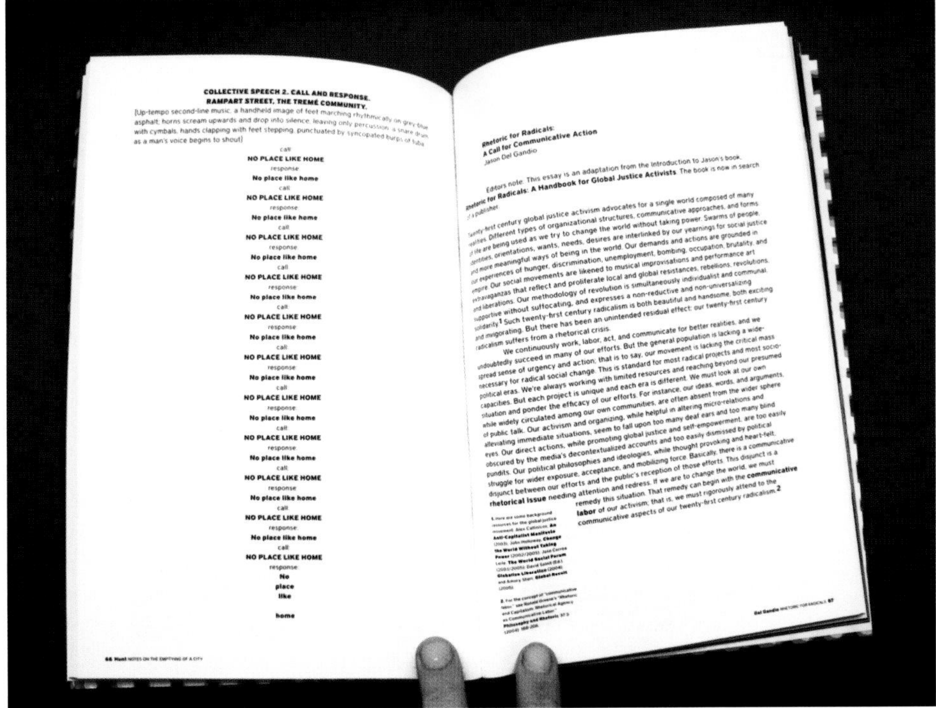
COLLECTIVE SPEECH 2. CALL AND RESPONSE.
RAMPART STREET, THE TREMÉ COMMUNITY.

[Up-tempo second-line music, a handheld image of feet marching rhythmically on grey-blue asphalt; horns scream upwards and drop into silence, leaving only percussion: a snare drum with cymbals, hands clapping with feet stepping, punctuated by syncopated burps of tuba as a man's voice begins to shout]

call:
NO PLACE LIKE HOME
response:
No place like home
call:
NO PLACE LIKE HOME
response:
No place like home
call:
NO PLACE LIKE HOME
response:
No place like home
call:
NO PLACE LIKE HOME
response:
No place like home
call:
NO PLACE LIKE HOME
response:
No place like home
call:
NO PLACE LIKE HOME
response:
No place like home
call:
NO PLACE LIKE HOME
response:
No place like home
call:
NO PLACE LIKE HOME
response:
No place like home
call:
NO PLACE LIKE HOME
response:
No place like home
call:
NO PLACE LIKE HOME
response:
No place like home
call:
NO PLACE LIKE HOME
response:
No
place
like

home

Rhetoric for Radicals:
A Call for Communicative Action
Jason Del Gandio

Editors note: This essay is an adaptation from the introduction to Jason's book, **Rhetoric for Radicals: A Handbook for Global Justice Activists**. The book is now in search of a publisher.

Twenty-first century global justice activism advocates for a single world composed of many realities. Different types of organizational structures, communicative approaches, and forms of life are being used as we try to change the world without taking power. Swarms of people, identities, orientations, wants, needs, desires are interlinked by our yearnings for social justice and more meaningful ways of being in the world. Our demands and actions are grounded in our experiences of hunger, discrimination, unemployment, bombing, occupation, brutality, and empire. Our social movements are likened to musical improvisations and performance art extravaganzas that reflect and proliferate local and global resistances, rebellions, revolutions, and liberations. Our methodology of revolution is simultaneously individualist and communal, supportive without suffocating, and expresses a non-reductive and non-universalizing solidarity.[1] Such twenty-first century radicalism is both beautiful and handsome, both exciting and invigorating. But there has been an unintended residual effect: our twenty-first century radicalism suffers from a rhetorical crisis.

We continuously work, labor, act, and communicate for better realities, and we undoubtedly succeed in many of our efforts. But the general population is lacking a wide-spread sense of urgency and action; that is to say, our movement is lacking the critical mass necessary for radical social change. This is standard for most radical projects and most socio-political eras. We're always working with limited resources and reaching beyond our presumed capacities. But each project is unique and each era is different. We must look at our own situation and ponder the efficacy of our efforts. For instance, our ideas, words, and arguments, while widely circulated among our own communities, are often absent from the wider sphere of public talk. Our activism and organizing, while helpful in altering micro-relations and alleviating immediate situations, seem to fall upon too many deaf ears and too many blind eyes. Our direct actions, while promoting global justice and self-empowerment, are too easily obscured by the media's decontextualized accounts and too easily dismissed by political pundits. Our political philosophies and ideologies, while thought provoking and heart-felt, struggle for wider exposure, acceptance, and mobilizing force. Basically, there is a communicative disjunct between our efforts and the public's reception of those efforts. This disjunct is a **rhetorical issue** needing attention and redress. If we are to change the world, we must remedy this situation. That remedy can begin with the **communicative labor** of our activism; that is, we must rigorously attend to the communicative aspects of our twenty-first century radicalism.[2]

The *Journal of Aesthetics and Protest*, designed by Jessica Fleischmann

67

BE CAUTIOUS WITH ADJECTIVES

NICKI **KALISH**

JESSICA **FLEISCHMANN**

One of the challenges when working with illustrators, photographers, artists, curators, and editors is trying to describe an image or approach that exists only as a fuzzy concept. Even the most specific word or phrase can be easily misunderstood or evoke contradictory images. "I think communicating is really important," says Nicki Kalish. "But I've learned that two people can use the same words and have very different pictures in their minds. So it helps to be very explicit if you want something done in a particular way."

Jessica Fleischmann suggests asking for visual references to back up a verbal description. "I ask them for other works or pieces that they think are relevant. And then I ask them what they like or don't like about it," she advises. "It's good to know their aesthetic preferences, not because I'm going to mimic them, but because it helps me know exactly what they mean. When we use subjective terms, they can sometimes be misinterpreted, so seeing a reference helps me qualify and quantify those subjective words. For example, they may say that they like something interpretive, but then they show me something clean and modern. Or, if they say they like bold typography, well, there's such a range in that description." Plus, getting a very clear idea of where your collaborators stand helps the designer know how far they can move the project. "It helps me know what level of graphic sophistication they have," Fleischmann notes, "so I know how far I can push it."

68

KEEP IT INTERESTING FOR YOURSELF

NICKI **KALISH**

Many publications deal with the same topics over and over. There's the fall issue on foliage or fashion. There's the election roundup or the annual college rankings. As a designer, to keep it interesting for the readers, you have to keep it interesting for yourself. "This is why I try to have variety," says Nicki Kalish, thinking about her latest effort to design a cover about what to do with this year's end-of-season crop of tomatoes, among other repeat subjects. "I talk a lot with editors and photographers so I don't keep getting the same images over and over. It's especially helpful to have an editor who is visual so when you say something like you want to look at a bag of chips from inside, they understand—or simply have faith because what you've done in the past has worked."

augustus, september, oktober 1988 11.50 20e jaargang nr 3
Bijvoorbeeld
vormgeving en kunst
Criteria

Left and opposite: *Bijvoorbeeld*, a magazine on art and design, "shows all types of solutions and surprises based on the same grid," notes Vermaas. While the redesign "revived the magazine," he concedes that "many people were excited by the design, and some were upset by it."

69

ARJEN **NOORDEMAN**

CREATE YOUR OWN BUILDING BLOCKS

While all this emphasis on deferring to provided content and simplifying type and letting illustrators go can lead designers to despair that their job is simply to provide an artful soapbox for other people's creative output, there are many ways they can make their presence on the page known. "I try to create all my own building blocks," says Arjen Noordeman. "So instead of making wild compositions or intense color juxtapositions that get in the way, I would create my own patterns, fonts, and other graphical devices. Through these things, I would create a design that would not overpower the message, but my voice is being heard because I'm creating the building blocks."

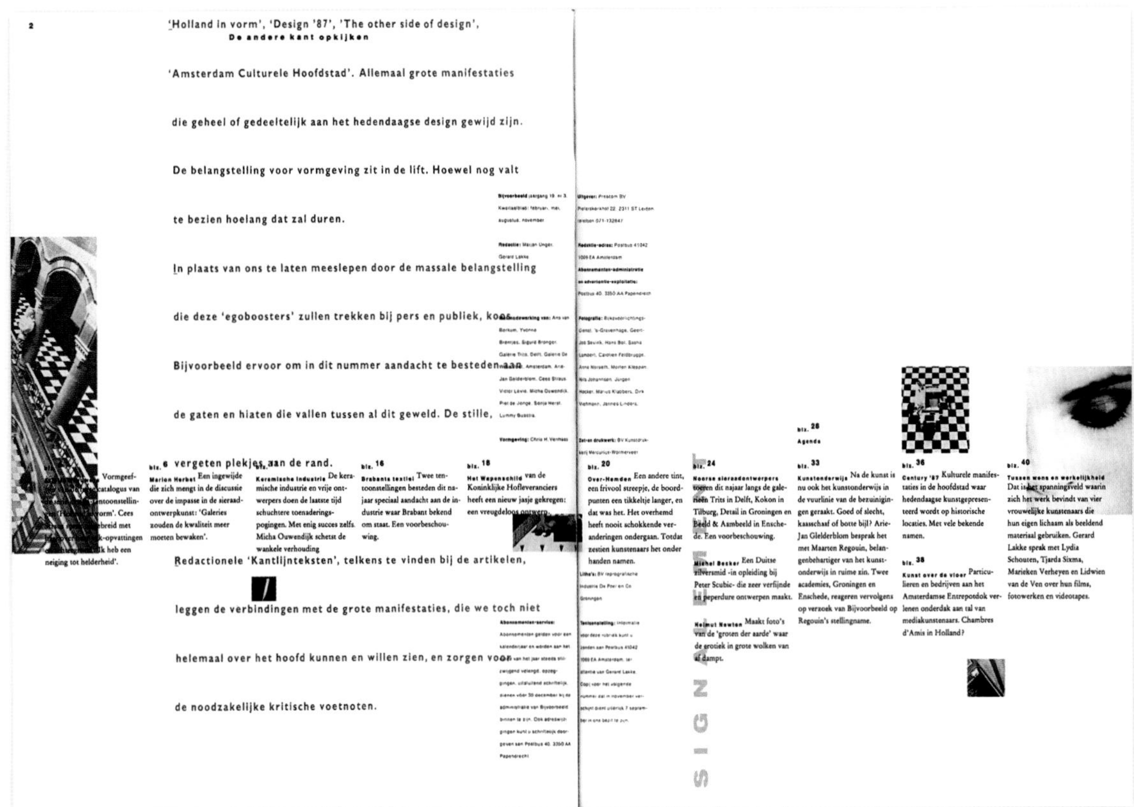
'Holland in vorm', 'Design '87', 'The other side of design',

De andere kant opkijken

'Amsterdam Culturele Hoofdstad'. Allemaal grote manifestaties die geheel of gedeeltelijk aan het hedendaagse design gewijd zijn.

De belangstelling voor vormgeving zit in de lift. Hoewel nog valt te bezien hoelang dat zal duren.

In plaats van ons te laten meeslepen door de massale belangstelling die deze 'egoboosters' zullen trekken bij pers en publiek, kozen we Bijvoorbeeld ervoor om in dit nummer aandacht te besteden aan de gaten en hiaten die vallen tussen al dit geweld. De stille, vergeten plekjes aan de rand.

Redactionele 'Kantlijnteksten', telkens te vinden bij de artikelen, leggen de verbindingen met de grote manifestaties, die we toch niet helemaal over het hoofd kunnen en willen zien, en zorgen voor de noodzakelijke kritische voetnoten.

70

ROBERTO **DE VICQ**

BE SEDUCTIVE

While there are standard, intellectual, objective ways to evaluate the success of a design—is it balanced, does it communicate clearly, does it provide clues to the reader for navigating the piece?—design is an artistic as well as commercial enterprise and, as such, has the power to reach for so much more than mere competency. Design can and should use the tools of its trade to entice and entrance everyone along the continuum of concept to final printed piece. "You still have to seduce the art director; seduce the editor; seduce the publisher, the author and the sales force; and sometimes the agent," says New York city designer Roberto de Vicq, about the craft of book design. If you have all these people clamoring for your work, the reading public will not be far behind.

40

41

Zoet gepeins, zware fantasieën.

Feestelijke dagen in december. Niet zelden zal er op een avond fluweel, satijn en zijde nonchalant over een stoel of aan een openstaande kastdeur hangen. De slaapkamer van een dame, die haar avondtoilet uitkiest. Zacht-glanzend wacht de stof tot ze een lichaam omhult.

Max Bruinsma

In het werk van Lili Dujourie krijgen deze kostbare weefsels een eigen leven. Schijnbaar moeiteloos zweven donkergloeiende of felgekleurde stoffen langs de wanden van de tentoonstellingsruimtes waar Dujourie exposeert. Op het eerste gezicht is het een en al barokke weelde, een soms gemaniëreerd aandoende overdaad van plooiingen. Een spel van draperieën waarin de lichamen van de dragers zijn verdwenen. Maar is dit abstracte vormenspel werkelijk waar het om gaat in Dujourie's kunst?

Er is iets in die verwaaide plooien dat aan geweld doet denken. Een niet zichtbaar woeden, dat langsgetrokken is en alles in een werveling bracht. Zoals een roeispaan, die het water heeft opengescheurd, een draaikolk achterlaat, lang nadat de boot voorbij is. Ook in de draperieën van Lili Dujourie lijkt de herinnering aan een heftige beweging bewaard. Verstild, bevroren: 'Dédié à la nuit, loin des tumultes et du bruit' [1], maar er wel de nagalm van. De achterkant van een tumultueuse handeling. Achterkant mag hier een vergezocht begrip lijken maar die associatie wordt gevoed door eerder werk van Dujourie.

Tegenbeeld Ze is begonnen met conceptuele sculpturen, zware ijzeren platen van ruim een meter in het vierkant, die tegen de muren van de tentoonstellingsruimte geleund stonden. Bij een aantal van die werken was de voorkant onbewerkt gebleven, roestkleurig ijzer, terwijl de achterkant in een kleur geschilderd was, onzichtbaar voor de beschouwer. Slechts een vage gloed op de witte galeriewand verried soms de kleur achterop de panelen. Dat werk ging over gewicht, evenwicht, maar ook over bedekken, verhullen, over het niet-zichtbare, voelbare.

In een serie video-tapes, die Dujourie rond 1972 maakte, treedt de draperie voor het eerst op in haar werk, als bedekker en onthuller van het naakte lichaam van de kunstenares. In een langzame opeenvolging van klassieke vrouwelijke, mijmerende, verleidelijke poses ontrolt zich voor het statische oog van de camera een spel tussen vrouw en kleed. Zich voegend naar de bewegingen van de figuur, is het laken haar tegenbeeld, haar negatief.

Stille getuige Vanaf 1982 is die spiegel zelf het beeld geworden. De dragende figuur is uit het beeld verdwenen. Bij veel van Dujourie's draperieën heb je het gevoel dat, wanneer je seconden eerder de museum- of galeriezaal was binnen gekomen, je de oorzaak van die hevige werveling betrapt zou hebben. Als in een foto die net te laat genomen is zweeft stil maar onmiskenbaar een 'gevolg'.

Of is het misschien beter van slow-motion te spreken? Het werk van Dujourie is driedimensionaal. Bij elke beweging van de beschouwer verschuift er iets in de complexe structuur van vouwen, lijnen, plooien. Dat versterkt het gevoel van 'gevolg', alsof het textiel nog nagolft, nog heel vertraagd antwoordt aan de hand die het tegen de muur geslingerd heeft of het er van heeft losgescheurd.

Lili Dujouri,

Lili Dujouri, 1986
'De Kus'

Bijvoorbeeld designed by Office of CC

71

EDEL **RODRIGUEZ**

LEAVE SOMETHING OUT

There is power in empty spaces, in what is left unsaid, unknown, unsigned. "Sometimes editors don't trust the viewer or reader enough and they want to hand it to them really literally," says New York City illustrator Edel Rodriguez. "But I think readers want to be surprised and want to see some interesting visuals." Rodriguez entices his audience and creates the element of the unexpected by intentionally leaving a little to the imagination. "I want the illustration to be a bit of a tease and get them to read the story. What's the purpose of telling the whole story with one image? You make the illustration lead into the story, but not be the whole story. I try to leave something to be filled in by the reader."

WORKING WITH ILLUSTRATORS

ROB **DUNLAVEY**, NICKI **KALASH**, ANITA **KUNZ**, MARTHA **RICH**, EDEL **RODRIGUEZ**

ANITA KUNZ

ROB DUNLAVEY

One of the distinct pleasures of working on publications is the opportunity to work with other creative people, particularly illustrators. A productive collaboration between art director and artist can result in a stunning image that not only visually interprets a story but also raises the profile and appeal of the entire publication. As Nicki Kalish says, "It's helpful to work with smart illustrators, not just talented illustrators." So, here, in their own words, is advice, counsel, and ideas from four smart, talented illustrators.

ROB DUNLAVEY

ROB DUNLAVEY

ROB DUNLAVEY

NATICK, MASSACHUSETTS

When an art director calls, I usually try to get a quick sense of the editorial quality and how much latitude I have to interpret the text. Since I'm currently working in a variety of styles, I also want to get a sense of where they're at artistically, which often boils down to asking the designer where they saw my work. Sometimes they just have a rough description of the article, and I have to ascertain technical details as well as what mood they're after for my illustration. Sometimes I get a full manuscript, and if I'm struggling with a concept, it's nice to have more content with which to work. I can also sketch directly on the manuscript and work closely with the text. I'm trying to get a sense of the voice of the author, the tone, who the reader is, what I can do to serve or amplify the main points. I get some first impressions, go with them and sketch, then go back and read the manuscript and try to go deeper to see if there's something I've missed.

Throughout the creative process, I'm really interested in the decisions I make and the accidents I discover. You could look at the cracks in the wall or the clouds in the sky or the spill of coffee, and that might be the thing that gets your motor going. When I sketch, I block in the major elements that have to communicate strongly, and then I paint and play with color. My sketchbook is the compost pile from whence many of my ideas come, but I still create final digital art because it's part of everyone's production pathway. The maturation of an illustrator depends on learning to read with the author and art director on your shoulders. It's not about grandstanding with your style or conceptual approach. It's about trying to come up with something that looks good, communicates what's on the page, and hopefully, as a visual communicator, I've made the art be generous enough in concept that it will enlarge the reader's experience of life at that moment in time.

ROB DUNLAVEY

ANITA KUNZ

TORONTO, CANADA

I've been predominantly a magazine illustrator for thirty years. I went into the field because I wanted to be in an industry where my art would be useful as part of a dialog about social, political, and cultural issues. I'm interested in the media and how things are described in magazines. I think that the point of illustration is to entice the reader to read the article, but it also should contain the germ of the idea of the article. I'm looking for what the manuscript is about, but as I'm reading, I'm also looking for things that would suggest interesting images. I try to interpret manuscripts in ways that are not necessarily literal, because the reader can do that on their own, so I look for symbols and metaphors. I'm very conscious of the magazine and the readership of the magazine. If I'm doing something for *Rolling Stone*, I can be more emotional or outrageous, but if I'm working for a literary magazine it has to be more stoic. And of course I have to be mindful that the symbols might be misinterpreted, so I have to be sure that I'm not saying things that I didn't mean to say.

At the very beginning of my career, I was called upon to visually articulate manuscripts. I was given a manuscript and asked to come up with one or more ideas, then I did a final painting and sent it in. In the past few years there's more editorial control, which has to do with the nature of magazines and how they're changing. There's more input from the editor, so it's not quite as creative as it used to be. For a cover, I have to be mindful that it has to be a bold, attractive picture because the cover has to sell the magazine; other than that, I'm blissfully ignorant of what focus groups have to say. Really strong ideas impress me, but I'm also impressed by really strong craftsmanship. This is what makes a good illustration, especially a strong idea. It's all about ideas.

ANITA KUNZ

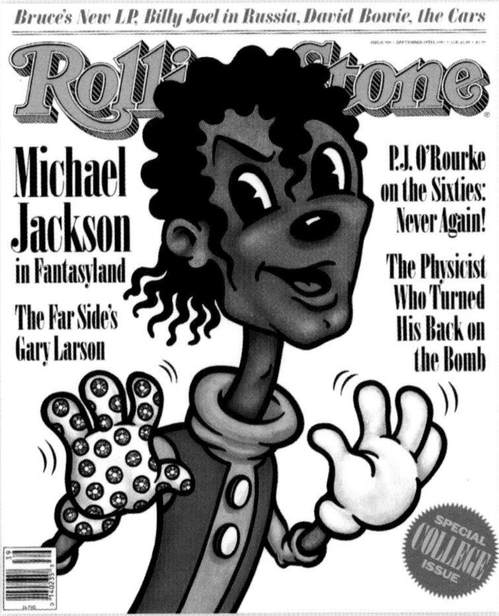

ANITA KUNZ

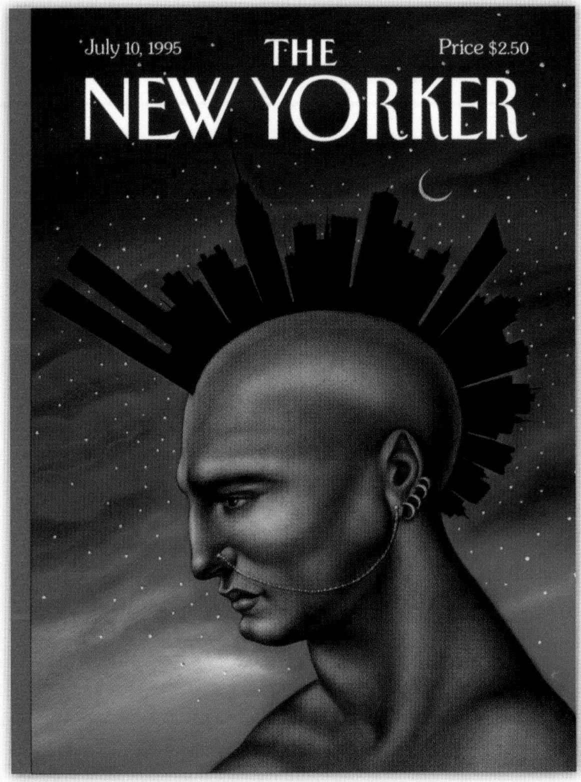

MARTHA RICH

LOS ANGELES, CALIFORNIA

The really good art directors know who they're working with, and they match the project accurately. People have their own signature, so you know what you're going to get. I work better when I'm working as a team, and the art director trusts my judgment, because this usually results in something much better. It's about individual style and trusting the artist—know who you're hiring, give them a little leeway. Don't be nervous; be willing to be open to ideas from the illustrator. There's so many really smart people doing illustration and they have great ideas; you're wasting their talent if you don't let them be part of a team. When I get an article, I read it without taking notes and try to remember what pops out. I try to find the most interesting visual things in there. I always look for something that I'm going to enjoy drawing. Even if it's the most boring article ever, I try to look for something that's going to be interesting for me to draw. You can find weird, good stuff in any article. In fact, illustrators often get hired for boring business articles because they can do something more creative and interesting. The whole job for the illustrator is to draw you in. In illustration, you can manipulate things in any way you want, you can make your own world, and there's freedom to go crazy and wild and be funny. I love where you see someone's hand and humanity in the work. If you're going to be an illustrator, you should develop your own individual point of view and your own work ethic because you have to work hard and you have to really love it. Put yourself into it. Be passionate and don't do soulless work because it shows. Inject your own personality into it. You have to be really confident about your own art and if you don't love it, you shouldn't do it.

MARTHA RICH

MARTHA RICH

MARTHA RICH

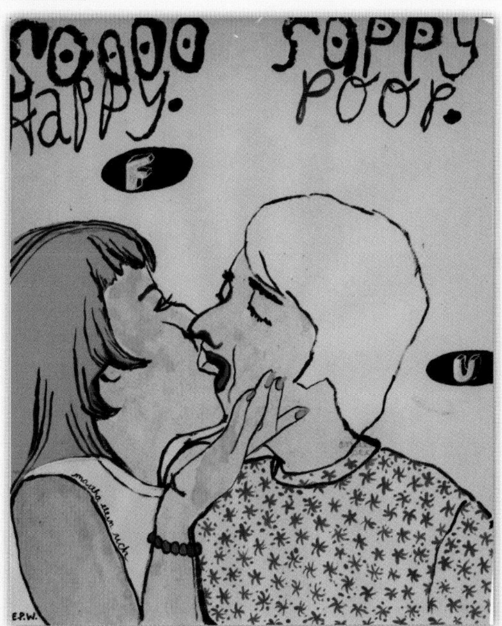

MARTHA RICH

EDEL RODRIGUEZ

NEW YORK, NEW YORK

EDEL RODRIGUEZ

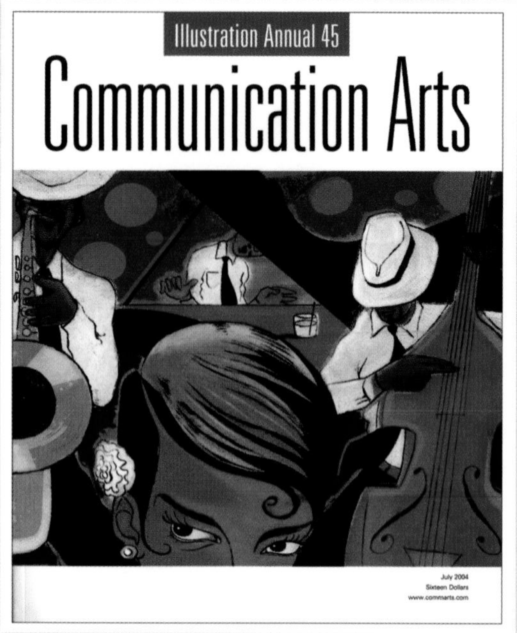

As I read, I start circling things that pop out at me, visual clues or images that are embedded in text. I start highlighting and making connections between things. The magic is trying to take all these things and make something more poetic and personal out of them. For example, I'm working on an article about campaign strategists. When I think of strategy, I think of a guy behind the scenes, or a politician as a sock puppet, and the strategist is a hand going into the sock. A lot of it is unexplainable about how you come up with ideas—it's just something you practice. At the beginning it's hard, but after a while you start to see poetic connections between things. As soon as I read things, there's this rush of imagery that goes on in my head. I do a lot of doodling and then on a separate piece of paper I start to make connections between these disparate doodles.

EDEL RODRIGUEZ

There are times where the editor gets involved and sometimes it can go bad because some editors are very literal and they'll write out what the image should be. If they insist, I'll do it for them so they can see how awful it is. But I'm pretty flexible because I'm an art director too; I'm very open to ideas. I like the whole process, getting out of my comfort zone and working with other people's suggestions. I also really like getting the assignment and then being told to go for it. If right away I get told, 'We want a beach ball,' then all I'm thinking about is the beach ball. The best art directors just give you the subject and then encourage you to come up with something of your own. Illustrations have a certain style of boldness and graphic quality that grabs you. There's more vibrancy and more of a personal touch to illustration. Especially now, with all the digital cameras, it seems that everyone is a photographer. I think creating original pieces of art for a magazine can really brand your magazine and make it stand out. Stock photography is everywhere.

EDEL RODRIGUEZ

EDEL RODRIGUEZ

EDEL RODRIGUEZ

Chapter Four:

THOUGHTS ON BOOKS

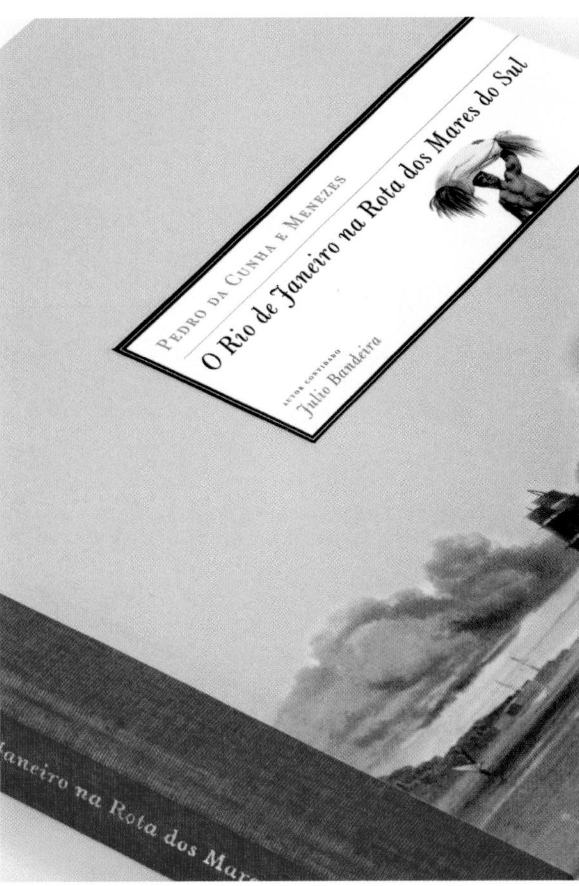

The sophisticated balance of illustration, pattern, and type, in this book, designed by Victor Burton, makes for an elegant object that is a delight to hold, flip through, and make one's own.

72

BE A LOVER OF BOOKS

JASON **GODFREY**

VICTOR **BURTON**

Book design places a unique set of demands on a graphic designer, asking simultaneously for a deep level of engagement as well as a surprising degree of restraint, along with substantive technical skills. On top of this, book design tends to be less lucrative than some other forms of graphic design work. So why do designers choose this media? For love of the objects themselves. "I've always loved books and collected books and thought they were fantastic things," says Jason Godfrey of Godfrey Design in England. "I think that it's the same with anything; you have to have that interest and passion before jumping into these areas."

After all, interest and passion, especially when directed to making something as beautiful and satisfying as a book, are certainly excellent raw ingredients for a satisfying career. Victor Burton of Victor Burton Design Gráfico in Brazil, describes how his lifelong love affair with what lies between two covers led him to design: "Technically I am not a designer. In truth, I consider design an instrument to create what I most love—books," he says. "My grandfather, a Frenchman from Lyon, was a bibliophile, and his library was the object of my fascination and desire since my childhood." This visceral attraction led him to a trainee position at Franco Maria Ricci Publishing House in Milan, Italy, where he was able to turn his obsession into a profession. His design career since then has focused almost entirely on making books that are beautiful enough to inspire the next generation of would-be book designers.

***O Rio de Janeiro*, designed by Victor Burton**

73

ONLY DO A BOOK IF YOU REALLY LIKE THE SUBJECT MATTER

BRETT **MACFADDEN**

VINCE **FROST**

It is no accident that designers use the language of human relationships to describe the process of making a book. While some design projects come and go so quickly they leave no memories behind, books require a different kind of commitment. “Most of my projects are based on things that I have an affinity for,” says Brett MacFadden. “Any book is many months of work, and so you want them to be things that are dear to you.” Books are designed over many months of image and text manipulations—affection for the content will ensure the book continues to hold interest from the beginning to the faraway end of the project.

Like any relationship, that with a book demands some sacrifice as the price for creative satisfaction. “Why go out with someone if you don’t like them?” Vince Frost asks. “Books take a long time to produce and are a phenomenal amount of work. And books don’t pay a lot of money. But I still love doing them.” At the end of the day, simple affection for the things themselves continues to feed the creative spirit of book designers.

***Living the Creative Life*, designed by Maya Drozdz, demonstrates in design the content provided by the contributors, who are working artists in a variety of mostly mixed-media, including collage, assemblage, textiles, beads, and more.**

74

BRETT **MACFADDEN**

MAYA **DROZDZ**

UNDERSTAND THE WHOLE PACKAGE

A book is a product. Like any other, it goes through the full cycle of development, from concepting, to design, through marketing, and then onto life in the crowded and competitive world of a bookstore shelf. To be effective, a designer needs to understand this entire continuum. "We start with a series of meetings," explains Brett MacFadden. "The first is the creative, and that's often before we've even had an accepted bid for the book. We've brought a book to the board, and now we go to the author or agent and make an offer." Nitty-gritty concerns are some of the first things that need to be nailed down. "We have to begin by talking about what the book is going to cost to produce," he says. "We discuss page count, trim size, whether this subject matter inspires certain effects or treatments. Then, once we have a sense of our hard costs, we can calculate the offer."

In all of these considerations, working with the group, gathering information from other departments, and juggling different agendas is critical. "Getting a book off the ground involves talking to a lot of people internally," says Maya Drozdz, partner at VisuaLingual. "The acquisitions editor, the assignment editor, the editorial director, the creative director of the imprint, reps from sales and marketing. It's not only getting to the essence of that book, but also the context of how the book will be marketed and sold, what's going on in this category, the challenges of the context of the book once it's out in the world." While a designer may be itching to get out of the conference room and back to his desk to begin designing, all of these meetings provide important information that will influence the form and look of the book itself. And ensure its eventual success on the shelf.

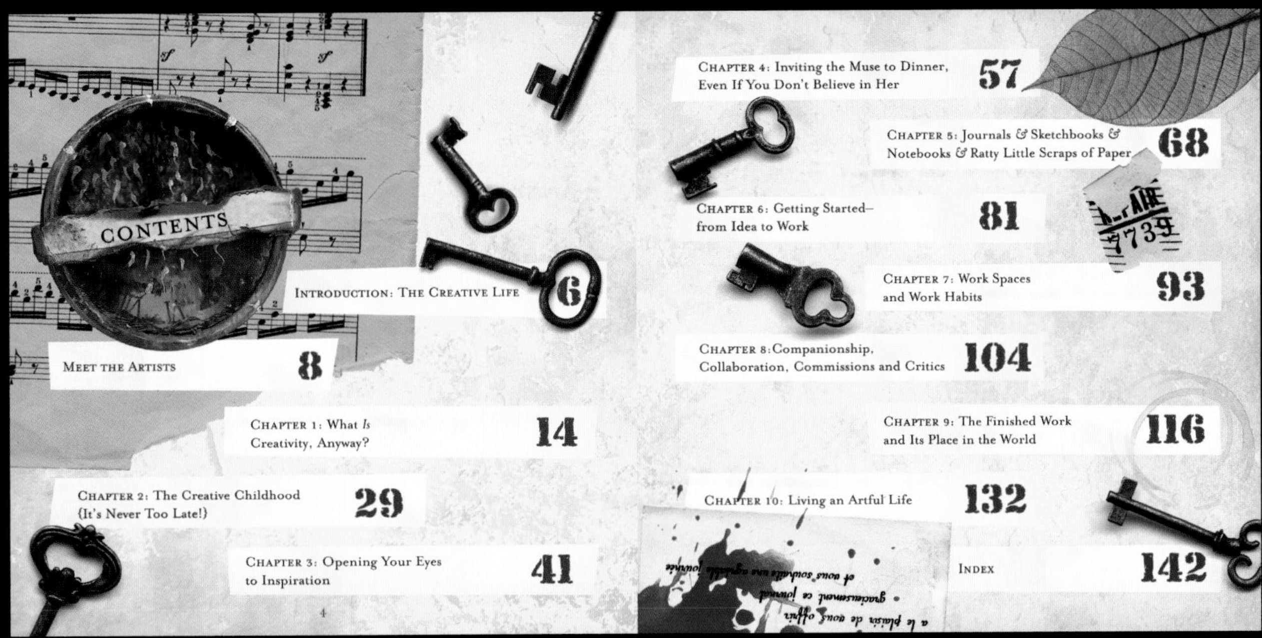

CONTENTS

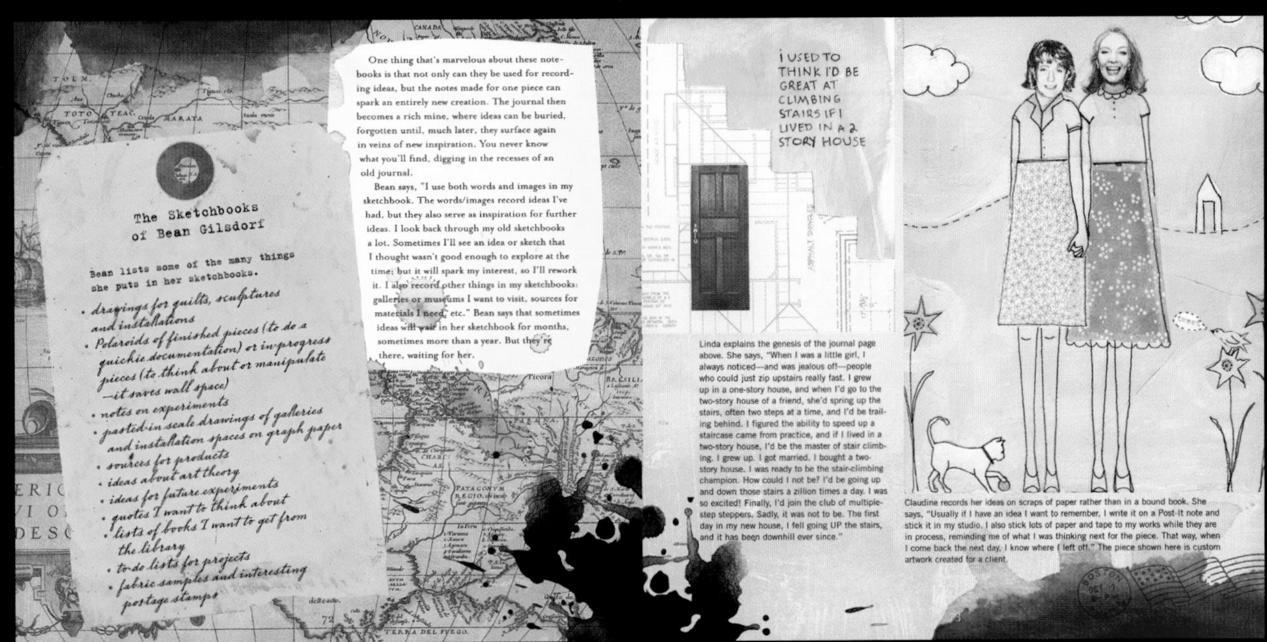

The Sketchbooks of Bean Gilsdorf

Bean lists some of the many things she puts in her sketchbooks.

- drawings for quilts, sculptures and installations
- Polaroids of finished pieces (to do a quickie documentation) or in-progress pieces (to think about or manipulate —it saves wall space)
- notes on experiments
- pasted-in scale drawings of galleries and installation spaces on graph paper
- sources for products
- ideas about art theory
- ideas for future experiments
- quotes I want to think about
- lists of books I want to get from the library
- to-do lists for projects
- fabric samples and interesting postage stamps

One thing that's marvelous about these notebooks is that not only can they be used for recording ideas, but the notes made for one piece can spark an entirely new creation. The journal then becomes a rich mine, where ideas can be buried, forgotten until, much later, they surface again in veins of new inspiration. You never know what you'll find, digging in the recesses of an old journal.

Bean says, "I use both words and images in my sketchbook. The words/images record ideas I've had, but they also serve as inspiration for further ideas. I look back through my old sketchbooks a lot. Sometimes I'll see an idea or sketch that I thought wasn't good enough to explore at the time; but it will spark my interest, so I'll rework it. I also record other things in my sketchbooks: galleries or museums I want to visit, sources for materials I need, etc." Bean says that sometimes ideas will wait in her sketchbook for months, sometimes more than a year. But they're there, waiting for her.

I USED TO THINK I'D BE GREAT AT CLIMBING STAIRS IF I LIVED IN A 2 STORY HOUSE

Linda explains the genesis of the journal page above. She says, "When I was a little girl, I always noticed—and was jealous of!—people who could just zip upstairs really fast. I grew up in a one-story house, and when I'd go to the two-story house of a friend, she'd spring up the stairs, often two steps at a time, and I'd be trailing behind. I figured the ability to speed up a staircase came from practice, and if I lived in a two-story house, I'd be the master of stair climbing. I grew up. I got married. I bought a two-story house. I was ready to be the stair-climbing champion. How could I not be? I'd be going up and down those stairs a zillion times a day. I was so excited! Finally, I'd join the club of multiple-step steppers. Sadly, it was not to be. The first day in my new house, I fell going UP the stairs, and it has been downhill ever since."

Claudine records her ideas on scraps of paper rather than in a bound book. She says, "Usually if I have an idea I want to remember, I write it on a Post-It note and stick it in my studio. I also stick lots of paper and tape to my works while they are in process, reminding me of what I was thinking next for the piece. That way, when I come back the next day, I know where I left off." The piece shown here is custom artwork created for a client.

Living the Creative Life, designed by Maya Drozdz

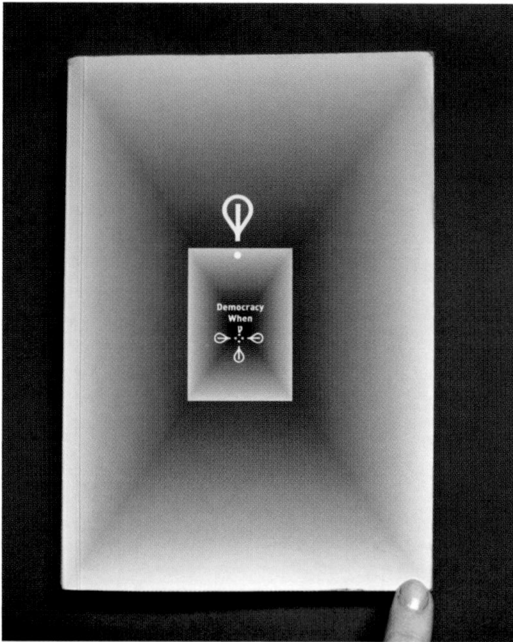

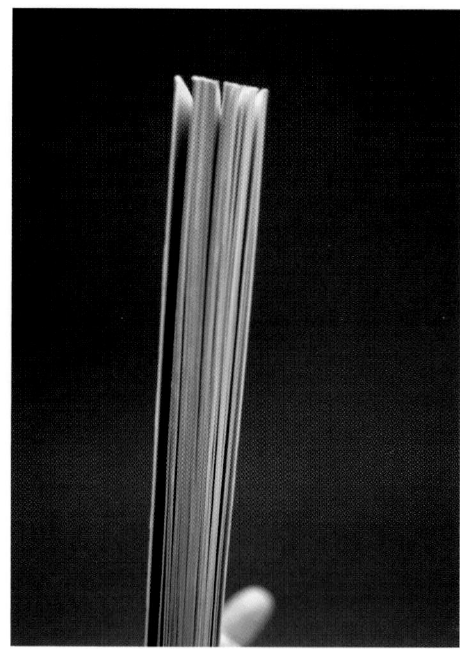

75

START WITH A CONVERSATION

JESSICA
FLEISCHMANN

MICHAEL
WORTHINGTON

While it is not always possible, many book designers, especially those who work on art or museum books, begin their concepting process by discussing the project with the person whose work they are representing. "I start, as much as possible, by having a conversation with the artist, curator, or editor," says Jessica Fleischmann. Michael Worthington begins in similar fashion. "We have a certain process when we work with artists," he explains. "We have a dialog about the way they work."

In both cases, the designers are looking for the artistic sensibility of the work at hand so they can find the best way to graphically represent it. "We tend to sit down and talk with the artist to find out what the show is about and what might be a sympathetic graphic environment to showcase those ideas rather than having some preconceived idea of 'This is cool,'" says Worthington, whose approach should not be seen as a means of limiting designer freedom. It is, in fact, an opportunity for creative minds to work together to come up with something greater than the sum of its parts. "We don't go in with a house style," says Worthington. "We try to make the discussion open and interesting. The artists' work becomes the central point of the discussion, and the project becomes a collaboration."

***Democracy When* utilizes the deceptively simple technique of different-colored papers to visually communicate the diversity of the voices expressed within its covers.**

"THE HOUSE PAINTING PROJECT #1," 2006
Edgar Arceneaux & Kendra Stanifer
in collaboration with the WLCAC & John Locke High School

How does an artist maintain a practice that has a variety of different concerns that pertain to both inside and outside of the intellectualized art world? This question has become the nexus in the organizational structure of the Watts House Project (WHP). Extending from the lineage of Conceptualism and activist practices, WHP attempts to invoke both a postmodern and interdisciplinary approach in its engagement with community. Attempting to avoid the bureaucracy of site-based institutions/organizations, the WHP works as a free-floating agent based within the context of "specific sites" in which we are invited to participate. "Site-specific," initially referring to the relationship between sculpture and site is expanded; Nina Felshin in her book **But Is It Art? The Spirit of Art as Activism** describes "site" not as geographic, but in regards to the issues, needs, and concerns of the public/community, which one is engaging. Yet bringing a practice from an institutionalized art education is not without contention when interfacing with a tangible community concerned with education, economic sustainability, housing, etc. Through each project, WHP aims to address what Joseph Beuys understood as a way of contextualizing and democratizing an art practice in the social realm: "Creation – whether it be painting, sculpture, symphony or novel – involves not merely talent, intuition, powers of imagination and application, but also to shape materials that can be expanded to other socially relevant spheres."

Lida Abdullah

A few days after the Taliban were driven out of Kabul, something quite amazing happened. All the singers, the poets, the artists emerged from their hiding places to see if it was really true. One singer was quoted by a **New York Times** reporter a few days after this happened as asking this: "Is it really safe to sing now?" I could never have imagined that this statement would resonate so much in me. Could never have thought that it would make so much sense now and has probably always been a necessary question for some artists, both here and abroad.

In some sense, the anxiety of the Afghan singer was strangely replicated amongst us also; artists in the US too were asking, and continue to do so, if it was safe to talk about certain issues or to make certain works of art. My answer to this question would always be: No, it really is never safe to sing, to write or to make art, and societies where art has to seek permission about its existence do not make art, but produce propaganda of which all of us have seen much of lately.

So Democracy When?

1) When the emperor or sovereign looks at art and not finding "itself" there lets it live another day, much like Scherezade was allowed a thousand nights to tell her seductive stories. In its infinite desire to control, maybe "it" can be brought out of its domesticity and be made to forget how it got there.

2) When works of art do not contain in them consumable condensations of the same stories that make us parrot the lies as so may facts whose credibility cannot be doubted because it comes stamped with made in USA or the EU.

3) When the experience of art does not mimic the logic of sexual excitement. A+B+C=Orgasm. When it is not just immediate gratification, but a delay or a promise of pleasure later. Of course that is considered decadence and it is unnatural. Democracy Never when art has to serve a purpose, or when it is little more than a prosthetic among others that supplement the quality of one's life.

4) We are always on the way to democracy when the experience of art is more foreplay, which demands some knowledge of the other, some desire to listen to the other, which of course does not have to be a person only. Other ideas, other sensations, other sorrows, other arts.

5) Other Democracies?

problematic 6:67

Democracy When, designed by Jessica Fleischmann

76

VISUALLY EXPRESS THE AUTHOR

CARIN **GOLDBERG**

MAYA **DROZDZ**

VICTOR **BURTON**

Book designers feel a powerful obligation not simply to the nature of the content provided, but to the writer who created it. It's all about one artist understanding another. "We are on the same page, literally and figuratively," says Carin Goldberg. "You and the author become a team, and the goal is to get the voice and spirit of your teammate. There must be a respect for the writer's intent and vision. My responsibility is to have a visual response or reaction to their vision, their art."

To create this "visual response," Maya Drozdz calls upon the tools of marketing as well as the conventions of design. "I try to understand, in my head, what I call the author's brand," she says. "When it works, it's because the author has an aesthetic that's evident, and I can find ways to complement that aesthetic through art directing the photography, and all the design decisions I make throughout the book. Ideally, the aesthetic of the author and designer should come together."

It's important to note that this coming together tends to run mostly in one direction. Because the writer isn't going to change his work to meet the creative desires of a designer, it is incumbent on the designer to bend his own aesthetic will to that of the author. "I don't collaborate with an author," says Goldberg. "The collaboration is by reading the work responsibly." Especially in cases where the author is not only no longer living but also a legend. As Victor Burton says, by way of example, "Above all, I believe that in order to successfully create a cover for an Ezra Pound book, I need to speak graphically about Ezra Pound."

The book that accompanied the 2006 California Biennial at the Orange County Museum of Art features photosensitive ink on the cover, a nod to one of the many effects that southern California sunshine can have on art.

***CaBi 06*, designed by Counterspace**

BECOMING ANIMAL
Contemporary Art in the Animal Kingdom
MASS MoCA

***Becoming Animal*, a book accompanying a show at the Massachusetts Museum of Contemporary Art, Mass MoCA, featured a hand-drawn typeface manipulated to reflect animal parts. Early versions had to be dialed back a bit to increase legibility.**

77

FIND THE GRAPHIC STANCE

ROBERTO **DE VICQ**

BRETT **MACFADDEN**

How, it would be fair to ask, can a designer cram so many different agendas and opportunities from so many different departments onto the small canvas of a book jacket? "It's a little like packaging an animal," says Roberto de Vicq. "The publisher says it is a leopard and the marketing person says we are selling rabbits nowadays, so you have to package the leopard looking like a rabbit." He likens the process to the story of a bunch of mice feeling different parts of an elephant and trying together to determine what kind of animal they have in front of them. "Even when you do the jacket, you can only show the ears of the rabbit. You see only part of it. Even the concept of the rabbit is very general. It's a very difficult combination."

Brett MacFadden tries to solve this conundrum by looking for the "graphic stance of that particular book. Some are fun or jokey, and those have to feel appropriate to the subject, have to feel light, but also have to reach a certain price point. Some may require something more sparkly or jazzy about them." For MacFadden, distribution strategy provides a welcome angle to consider his design approach. "Because a lot of Chronicle books go into gift stores or museums that allows us to represent these projects as packages rather than just reading material." Which is yet another example of how careful consideration of the many issues that need design resolution can sometimes suggest solutions and help focus the design effort.

MOTOHIKO ODANI
Motohiko Odani, who grew up in the historic Japanese city of Kyoto, conflates Japan's past and present in his work. Odani studied at the Tokyo National University of Art and Music from 1995–97, where his traditional craft skills, such as woodcarving, began to show the influences of popular culture. The prolific Odani takes on a wide variety of subjects, ranging from waterfalls, to satellites, to bloodbaths. Odani (along with Yukate Sone) represented Japan at the 2003 Venice Biennial.
Odani's 1997 work Fair Completion anchored his debut solo show, Phantom-Limb, at P-House in Tokyo. Described as a "blood bubble machine," the white plastic and steel sculpture stands three meters high and spews soap bubbles out of a grate on its top. Contained within each bubble is a single drop of the artist's blood, which, when the bubble bursts, splattered onto the white plastic walls. The heat generated from the lights in the gallery then baked the blood into a thin, brown film that coated the walls.
In Phantom-Limb (1997), the viewer is confronted with a familiar Odani aesthetic: the sexualization of innocence. A series of six C-prints depicts a young girl in a white dress, lying on the ground, her hair fanned out under her, with her palms facing upward. The girl's palms are covered in what appears to be blood – the result of her crushing a fistful of raspberries.
Odani's haunting work Erectro (2003), featured in Becoming Animal, presents a taxidermy baby deer with its spindly legs in traction. The deer stands helplessly as its legs are "healed." The assistance of these elaborate medical devices appears more torturous than therapeutic on what may be the cutest and most endearing of all non-human animals.
Odani's cute aesthetic becomes a transformed Garden of Eden in the short video loop Rompers (2003), also featured in Becoming Animal. A young girl with ponytails sits on a tree branch as she sings and swings her legs. Her forehead is mutated, her dress is dangerously short, her toes are elongated, and honey oozes from a gaping hole in the tree. Below her swinging feet, transgenic frogs leap rhythmically to the tinkling pop music in a trance-like circle, and occasionally the girl looks up and snatches a fly with her miraculously lizard-like tongue. This transgenic Garden of Eden feels like a lush, hypnotic MTV video with a nod to Takashi Murakami. Odani's work uninhibitedly embraces the mutant side of nature by overlaying it with the sweetness of honey and the candy-colored palette of Teletubbies.
92
Becoming Animal
Motohiko Odani, Erectro, 2003. Courtesy of Yamamoto Gendai.
93

Becoming Animal, designed by Arjen Noordeman

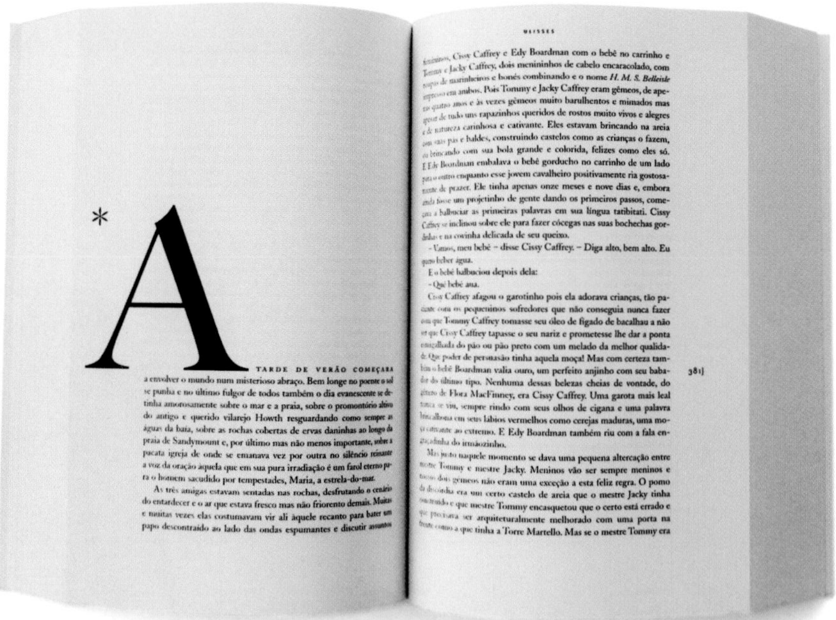

*

A TARDE DE VERÃO COMEÇARA a envolver o mundo num misterioso abraço. Bem longe no poente o sol se punha e no último fulgor de todos também o dia evanescente se detinha amorosamente sobre o mar e a praia, sobre o promontório altivo do antigo e querido vilarejo Howth resguardando como sempre as águas da baía, sobre as rochas cobertas de ervas daninhas ao longo da praia de Sandymount e, por último mas não menos importante, sobre a pacata igreja de onde se emanava vez por outra no silêncio reinante a voz da oração àquela que em sua pura irradiação é um farol eterno para o homem sacudido por tempestades, Maria, a estrela-do-mar.

As três amigas estavam sentadas nas rochas, desfrutando o cenário do entardecer e o ar que estava fresco mas não friorento demais. Muitas e muitas vezes elas costumavam vir ali àquele recanto para bater um papo descontraído ao lado das ondas espumantes e discutir assuntos

ULISSES

femininos, Cissy Caffrey e Edy Boardman com o bebê no carrinho e Tommy e Jacky Caffrey, dois menininhos de cabelo encaracolado, com roupas de marinheiros e bonés combinando e o nome *H. M. S. Belleisle* impresso em ambos. Pois Tommy e Jacky Caffrey eram gêmeos, de apenas quatro anos e às vezes gêmeos muito barulhentos e mimados mas apesar de tudo uns rapazinhos queridos de rostos muito vivos e alegres e de natureza carinhosa e cativante. Eles estavam brincando na areia com suas pás e baldes, construindo castelos como as crianças o fazem, ou brincando com sua bola grande e colorida, felizes como eles só. E Edy Boardman embalava o bebê gorducho no carrinho de um lado para o outro enquanto esse jovem cavalheiro positivamente ria gostosamente de prazer. Ele tinha apenas onze meses e nove dias e, embora ainda fosse um projetinho de gente dando os primeiros passos, começava a balbuciar as primeiras palavras em sua língua tatibitati. Cissy Caffrey se inclinou sobre ele para fazer cócegas nas suas bochechas gordinhas e na covinha delicada de seu queixo.

– Vamos, meu bebê – disse Cissy Caffrey. – Diga alto, bem alto. Eu quero beber água.

E o bebê balbuciou depois dela:

– Qué bebé aua.

Cissy Caffrey afagou o garotinho pois ela adorava crianças, tão paciente com os pequeninos sofredores que não conseguia nunca fazer com que Tommy Caffrey tomasse seu óleo de fígado de bacalhau a não ser que Cissy Caffrey tapasse o seu nariz e prometesse lhe dar a ponta encascada do pão ou pão preto com um melado da melhor qualidade. Que poder de persuasão tinha aquela moça! Mas com certeza também o bebê Boardman valia ouro, um perfeito anjinho com seu babador do último tipo. Nenhuma dessas belezas cheias de vontade, do gênero de Flora MacFlimsey, era Cissy Caffrey. Uma garota mais leal nunca se viu, sempre rindo com seus olhos de cigana e uma palavra brincalhona em seus lábios vermelhos como cerejas maduras, uma moça cativante ao extremo. E Edy Boardman também riu com a fala engraçadinha do irmãozinho.

Mas justo naquele momento se dava uma pequena altercação entre mestre Tommy e mestre Jacky. Meninos vão ser sempre meninos e nossos dois gêmeos não eram uma exceção a esta feliz regra. O pomo da discórdia era um certo castelo de areia que o mestre Jacky tinha construído e que mestre Tommy encasquetou que o certo está errado e que precisava ser arquiteturalmente melhorado com uma porta na frente como a que tinha a Torre Martello. Mas se o mestre Tommy era

381]

78

BEGIN DESIGN WITH THE COVER

MAYA **DROZDZ**

MICHAEL **WORTHINGTON**

Books are different than other publications because so much is riding on the cover. Sure, magazines need compelling covers to get someone to open the magazine, but once inside, there are many opportunities to use the tricks of the design trade to engage the reader. With books, the interiors are frequently much more muted and may be text alone. This means the cover has to do everything, without overdoing anything. "The cover is the face for the book, and it's also the single image that has to encapsulate the whole book," says Maya Drozdz. Because the making and buying cycle of books takes place over many months, the cover also frequently has to sell the book often before there even is a book. "Conceptualizing a cover direction is the first thing that's needed to start marketing the book and preselling it," says Drozdz. "It determines the direction and all the decisions made inside the book."

Designers are often asked to design a cover without much information about what's going to be in between the covers. Sometimes content changes enough from conception to completion that the cover has to change as well. "If you're making a book for a commercial publisher," Michael Worthington explains, "in most cases, the cover gets designed before the book is completed because they want to put it in a catalog or take it to a book fair. However, we always find that if we do a cover first, we do so with the caveat that we'll probably change it. We often find that if we design a cover first, and then we work on the inside of the book for six months and we know what that looks like, then we need to redesign the cover." In these instances, the long lead time gives the book designer an opportunity for a welcome do-over so he can ensure the promise of the cover is delivered when someone opens the book.

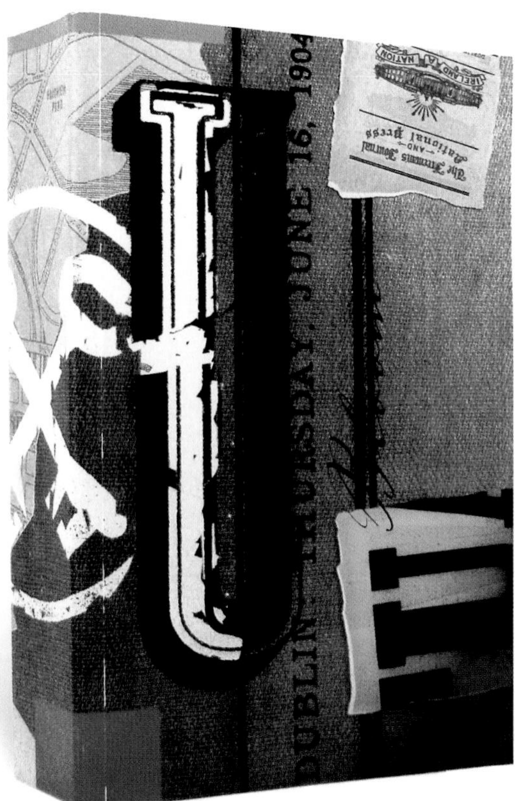

Opposite and above: As designed by Victor Burton, one of literature's most famous classics, *Ulisses*, gets an update, including a jacket printed on vellum and a cover that "once purchased, would have a life of its own, without any commercial information, a purely aesthetic object."

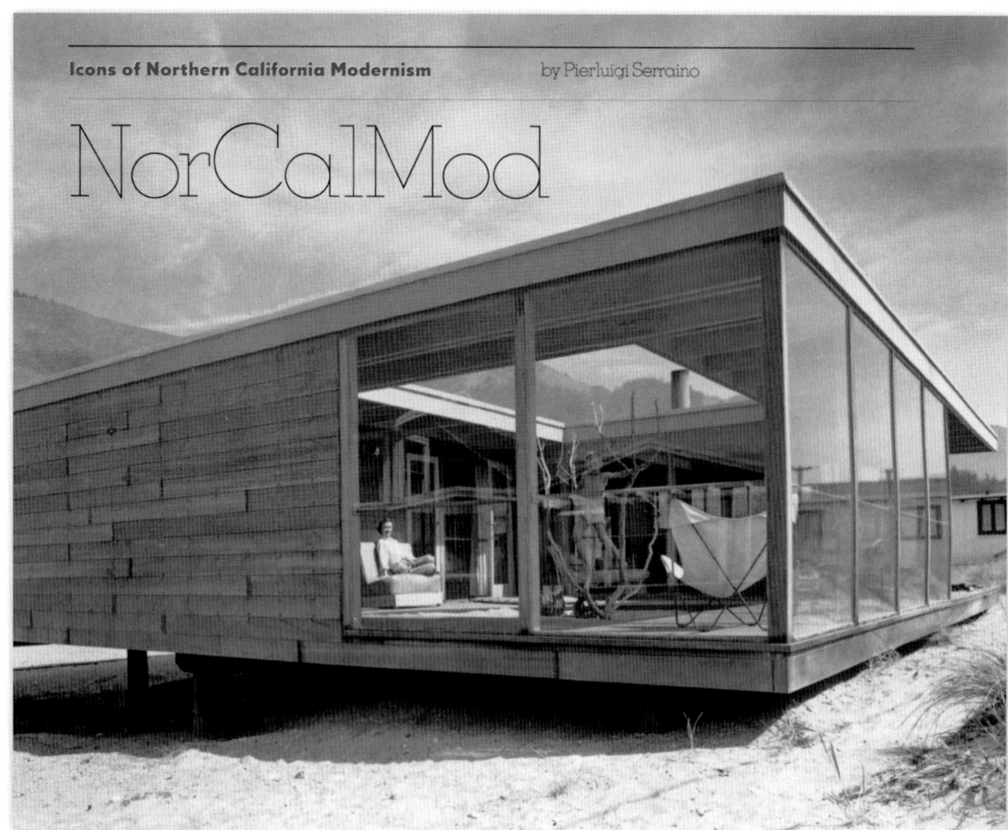

Icons of Northern California Modernism
by Pierluigi Serraino
NorCalMod

79

CARIN **GOLDBERG**

ROBERTO **DE VICQ**

READ IT TO GET IT

While some books require design when they are merely twinkling concepts in an editorial eye, plenty are fully written before they get into the hands of designers. Understandably, time pressures make it impossible for busy book designers to read every word in every book they work on, but it's still important to get an adequate sense of the story. When Carin Goldberg was in the thick of the book design phase of her career, she was creating "100 book jackets a year, minimum," a load that changed the way she worked. "The experience of doing that in such a concentrated way affects the way I responded to the problem solving," she says. For her, this meant reading enough, but not too much. "The times I have read an entire book, cover to cover, have not been the most fruitful. I've either liked it too much, or not enough, or became too invested, and that leads to subjectivity," she notes. "As soon as I intuitively know it, I put the book down." Roberto De Vicq follows a similar procedure. "I read until I have a jacket," he says. "I read until I think I get it." Of course, there are times when he has to hit the book just a bit harder. "I come up with a jacket, and if they don't like it, I keep reading."

Reflecting the linear, spare aesthetic of its subject, *NorCalMod* uses design techniques to enhance the subject matter while allowing the designer to make his presence felt.

Notes on Northern California Modernism

Introduction

My suggestion, which has the earmarks of a paradox, is that in order to look to the future with confidence it will be necessary to look to the past with understanding. In other words, I would like to re-examine that obscure concept, TRADITION. The paradox is of course superficial, for our idea of architecture itself is consciously and unconsciously formed from an experience of its past, and it will be difficult to decide where it is to go if we do not know where it has been.

James S. Ackerman,
California Monthly, 1954

80

DON'T BE A CRITIC

CARIN **GOLDBERG**

How you read is as important as how much you read. "It's important to not become a critic," says Carin Goldberg, "but to look at the book analytically, to look at what the writer had in mind and try and understand what he or she was trying to do as an artist, an academic, a historian." This is a fine balancing act because even though book designers need to think critically about what the writer is doing, they can't critique the book itself or the writer's level of artistic achievement. A designer must focus simply on expressing the vision the author already created, whether you like that vision or not. "You can't become critical. You have to remain objective," Goldberg explains. "It's an analytical, deconstructive way of looking at another person's creativity. You read the book the way you'd look at anything—architecture, art, a play. You analyze it formally and conceptually, and then try to interpret it visually."

She focuses on the design job she has to do, and just that job. "I'm not in the business of telling the reader the beginning, middle, and end, or who the main character is, or what she looks like," she explains. "Not only is that going to be too obvious or blatant, but it's irresponsible. As I'm reading, I switch on my visual process. I am reading with the pencil in my hand. I will look for clues, a voice, a temperament, and I will immediately make associations in my head on how I'll approach it visually, how I will take their art and translate it into visual art. My aesthetic will often be evident, but it's not about me."

***NorCalMod*, designed by Brett MacFadden**

81 LET DESIGN TELL A STORY

VICTOR **BURTON**

A book tells a narrative story; design must tell a visual story. "To design a book," says Victor Burton, "is to tell a story and allow the reader to receive this pleasure. Also, I always remember that the basic function of our job is to fascinate, and to bring in the reader to a particular book, which in turn needs to stand out from a sea of stories that overcrowd bookstores today." He explains how he achieves this singular quality in the books he designs. "What is important in creating a book is a visual, referential background that will allow the understanding of a period, place, and atmosphere." In other words, give browsers enough of a visual story on the cover that they can't wait to open the pages of the book and read the rest of it.

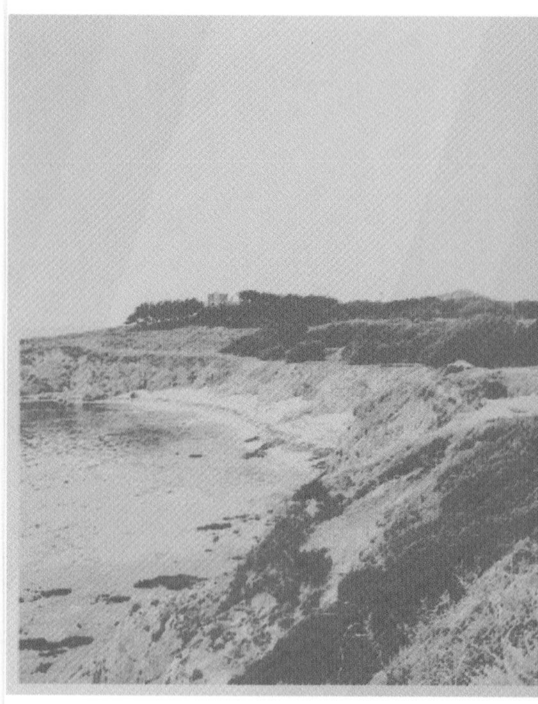

82 DESIGN A BLAD

MAYA **DROZDZ**

BLAD stands for "book layout art document," and it's another necessary tool to ensuring a book's design and commercial success. "On a technical level, after the cover has been designed and approved, I design a BLAD," says Maya Drozdz. "It's a promotional piece to presell the book. Typically it's eight pages, and gives you a front cover, table of contents, and sample of the content that will be inside the book." The BLAD is not used to sell the book to the public; it is a marketing tool to present the book to the legions of booksellers who are trying to decide what will appear on their shelves in the coming season. Drozdz notes that a BLAD also performs a very useful service for the designer. "The good thing about a BLAD is that it forces you to start making interior design decisions without having to contend with a book of 100 pages. It's like a practice run." The BLAD also gives the designer the opportunity to begin negotiating with the various elements that can occur in a complex book; by the time he has all the material for the complete book, the designer already has some experience with the component parts. "Once the manuscript is completely finished," Drozdz explains, "I get an annotated list of all the various instances of all the different kinds of elements inside the book. The editor will annotate sidebars that are shortest or longest, or the captions that are longest and shortest. I get a map of sorts, so I can think about what I want to develop and what limitations the design has to accommodate."

Voices of California Modernism

4

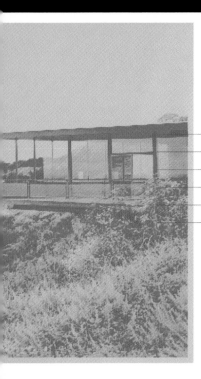

And I said to myself: "This is going nowhere." I was not comfortable. Some stuff is terrible, and they want to publish anyway simply because you had developed a Mickey Mouse reputation. It just bothered me, and I shut it down, I disappeared. I don't want any of this stuff.

Beverley (David) Thorne
Interview by the author, November 10, 2002

NorCalMod
112/113

10

10.11
Olympic Arena,
Squaw Valley;
William Corlett, architect;
Randal Partridge,
photographer, 1959

The selection of Squaw Valley for the Eighth Winter Olympic Games in 1960 generated state-of-the-art facilities for this well-known ski resort in the High Sierra. The Blyth Arena—built for Charles R. Blyth, then California Olympic Commission Chairman—was designed to shelter 8,500 spectators sitting on three sides with the fourth one open to the southern exposure. A hallmark of the scheme was the clear three-hundred-foot structural span covering the eighty-five-by-one-hundred-and-ninety-foot ice hockey rink. Sixteen tapered steel masts supported the roof, which was made of hollow cellular steel decking connected with steel bridge cables. The Olympic Arena received a 1960 A.I.A. national award. In 1984, the Olympic Arena collapsed due to compound in the waterproofing.

Chapter 3 Looking Sharp:
A Glimpse into Architectural Photography

11

NorCalMod, designed by Brett MacFadden

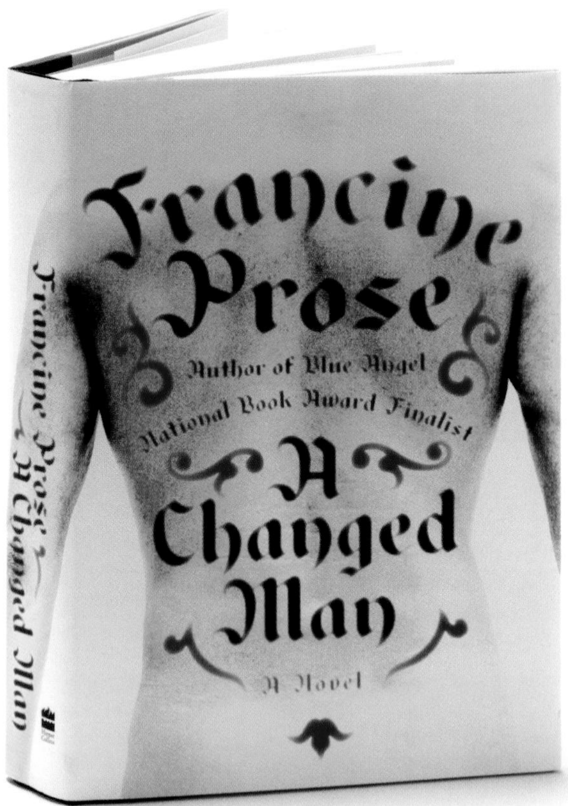

In these book covers, Roberto de Vicq combines illustration with type to create a singular, arresting image that "seduces" the casual browser as well as the well-read fan.

83

JASON **GODFREY**

COUNT THE WORDS

Books are about words; book designers make those words pleasing to read. "The most important thing you have to work with is how much text there is going to be, and working out how many words you're going to have per page," says Jason Godfrey. "A lot of books work around one spread per item, but I prefer the ones with running text, where you have to work out how many words per page, which tells you how dense it will be." The word count and the text density then give you a basis for creating the structure of the book. "Working from there and using the context of the book, you decide how you want to set up a grid, how many columns you'll have," he explains. Of course, within this system, the designer should also create opportunities for their creativity to show. "There's always this underlying thing," says Godfrey, "this ideal book you have in your mind, and you're trying to twist the structure in some kind of fashion to give it a bit of interest, to figure out when it's best to play your cards."

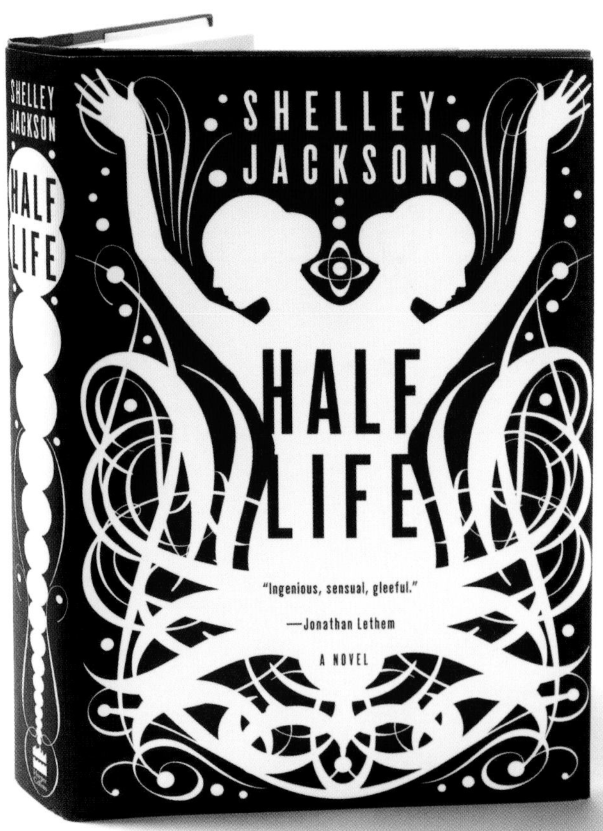

84

MAYA **DROZDZ**

FIND OUT IF IT WILL BE TRANSLATED

If a book will be translated, this will affect design in a variety of ways that must be considered and accounted for. "One of the logistical challenges we face is that in almost every case, we want our books to be easily translated and reprinted," says Maya Drozdz. "So if a title has any potential for translation, we have to face plate changes, which means type has to be black or gray. Plus, different languages take up different amounts of space, so this has certain effects," she explains. "Like we can't reverse out type and we have to consider if something becomes longer or shorter, and how that affects what's on the page. I can't just use typography willy-nilly or hand-draw letters or customize them in all the ways I'd like to because I have to consider production challenges." Looking down the long and sometimes dark production road in this way allows a designer to work up solutions before problems occur that could force a later—and more costly and disruptive—redesign.

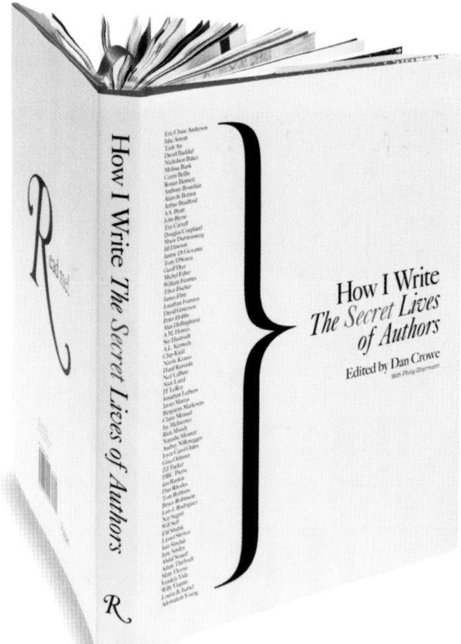

***How I Write*, designed by Frost Design, takes the simple form of an iconic punctuation mark and turns it into an elegant design device by using it as both artwork and type tool.**

85

RESPECT THE GIVENS

JASON **GODFREY**

Books, like other publications, generally follow a certain format, meeting reader expectation for a logical progression of information and the conventions of standard navigation. Whereas magazines may offer more leeway to confound these structures, books are usually more conservative in their adherence to form. "With books, there's a more formal process," says Jason Godfrey. "Books have the front matter and the chapters, and often, as a designer, you come to it after things have been worked out to a certain extent. And book work has a lot more things that are quite standard or necessary for each book, such as pagination and running heads and things like that. There are component parts that have to be in there. There is a different set of rules that you have to pay attention to."

Of course, this doesn't mean that a designer shouldn't try to do interesting things, where possible and where the unexpected might serve design requirements. "Some publishers have their own styles in terms of what they expect and in terms of what needs to be on there," says Godfrey. "And then there are some things you argue out." He describes a book he was designing that included a series of numbered items. "I was trying to make a case that we didn't need pagination, that the index at the back would refer to the item numbers, and the table of contents would tell the chapter contents, and therefore pagination was not necessary. I thought it was superfluous. But this is one of these bridges some people can't cross with books; people can't conceive of a book without page numbers."

While Godfrey didn't win this particular design argument, he doesn't let these kinds of constraints limit his creativity. "I like the conventions," he says. "I like that the design has this kind of history behind it. It's healthy in a way; it's evolved in this way because I think that it helps the reader. There's no harm in every now and again breaking from that, but I don't feel constrained because it's always quite interesting how you spend care and effort doing pagination and running heads. It can be an important part of the design."

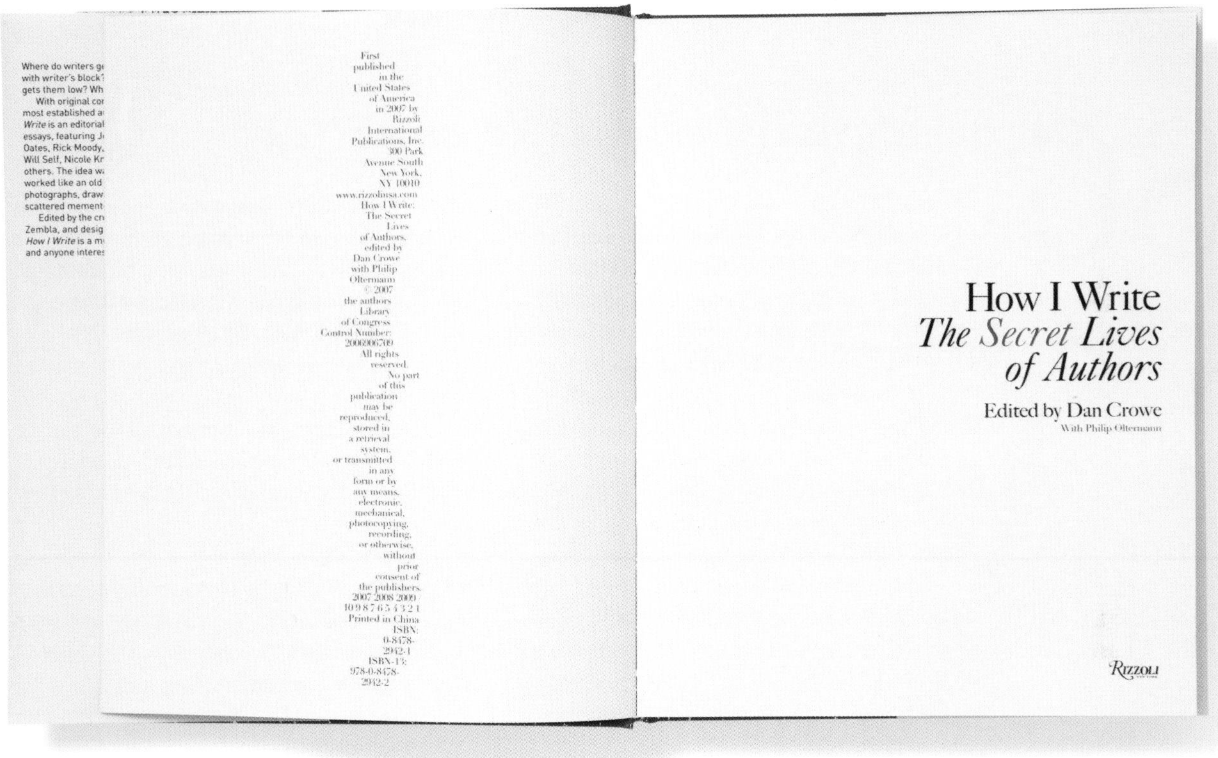

Where do writers ge
with writer's block?
gets them low? Wh
With original cor
most established a
Write is an editorial
essays, featuring J
Oates, Rick Moody,
Will Self, Nicole Kr
others. The idea w
worked like an old
photographs, draw
scattered memen
Edited by the cr
Zembla, and desig
How I Write is a m
and anyone interes

First published in the United States of America in 2007 by Rizzoli International Publications, Inc. 300 Park Avenue South New York, NY 10010 www.rizzoliusa.com How I Write: The Secret Lives of Authors, edited by Dan Crowe with Philip Oltermann

Library of Congress Control Number: 2006906709

2007 2008 2009 / 10 9 8 7 6 5 4 3 2 1
Printed in China
ISBN: 0-8478-2942-1
ISBN-13: 978-0-8478-2942-2

How I Write
The Secret Lives of Authors

Edited by Dan Crowe
With Philip Oltermann

Rizzoli

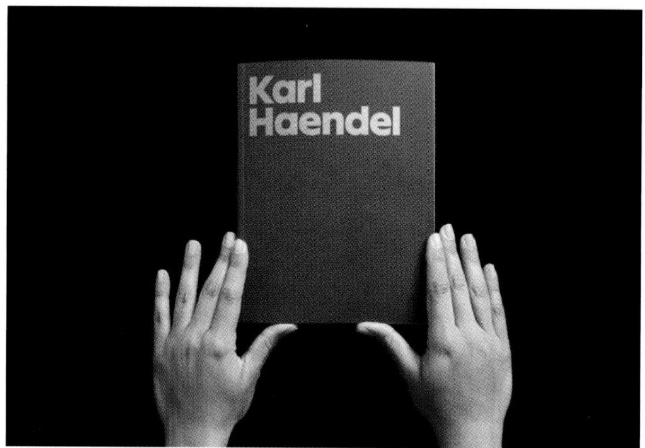

86

CONSIDER THE BOOK AS AN OBJECT

JASON **GODFREY**

VINCE **FROST**

BRETT **MACFADDEN**

The sheer physicality of the book as object has a dramatic effect on design. "Books are three-dimensional objects, and that's important," says Jason Godfrey. "As opposed to identity and things, you're dealing with quite an interactive object, with page turning and such. You have to be conscious about what's happening behind you and in front of you as you're doing it," he explains. And in this age of computerized everything, designers have to work a little harder to engage with the dimensionality of the book they're working on. "I started working two years before Macs came along," says Vince Frost. "I was familiar with typesetting. I continue to print out books at 100 percent and lay them out on the floor or the walls so we get the book out of the computer and make it a physical object as soon as possible."

Designers ignore this step of getting the book out of the computer at their own peril. "The scale of the computer and its ability to zoom in on details affects how the book actually looks," notes Brett MacFadden. "I was working on a 7 x 7-inch (17.8 x 17.8 cm) book, and on screen, the presence of the type seemed too big. But then, when I printed it out, it seemed too delicate. It's always useful to just vary your options," he suggests. "Try to make strong gestures in a variety of ways, try to scale things up, or make type more diminutive than you think will work, and then just print it out. It is important to look at it as a physical object."

Godfrey goes even one step further when working on cover designs. "When you're making a presentation, put the cover on a bit of foam or something to make it a three-dimensional object," he suggests. "It looks very different than on a flat bit of paper. You also have to look at how the cover reacts with the spine. Especially on bigger books, the spine can become quite important, and how it interacts with the front can be an important aspect of how you treat it."

Book designers never forget that a book is something that will be held in a human hand. "A book is a medium that's physical," says Frost. "I believe a book has an aura and people are drawn to it because it has this energy that comes out of it. You have to create an identity that's radiating out of the thing."

Karl Haendel's work involves a range of different scales, sizes, and interpretations, often of the same piece. "He's interested in the idea that there's no authoritative image of the work," says Michael Worthington. "We tried to find a way to demonstrate that in the book by using a bunch of different strategies, such as having things wrap over the edges, making some captions way too big, and using odd scale relationships."

Karl Haendel:
The things that I am
about to tell you are the
things that I have
come to regard as true
Gloria Sutton

87

JASON **GODFREY**

DON'T FORGET THE FUNDAMENTALS

Describing a book project where he was expecting to have stunning photography, only to find the pictures were "quite ordinary," Jason Godfrey reacquainted himself with the pleasures and satisfactions of old-fashioned design work. "Sometimes it's nice to create a standard, straight book that is anonymous in design and well put together," he observes. "You may have this idea of an idealized book, and you try to lay out things to give it a bit of fun, but sometimes it's good to do a straight-forward and honest-looking book that doesn't scream out that you're the designer of this book." This is not to say that a simple design is any easier than a complicated one—in fact, as Godfrey notes, it's quite the opposite. "People forget that it's not as easy as it looks to work in all the standard things you have to have for a book. It's quite hard work to get that type of look. You have to go through lots of galleys with different kinds of leading so it looks right. It can be hard to just say I'm going to do a fundamentally good book instead of always trying to push the envelope, but the danger is that in five or ten years that book may look dated, whereas a good book will have quite a long shelf life."

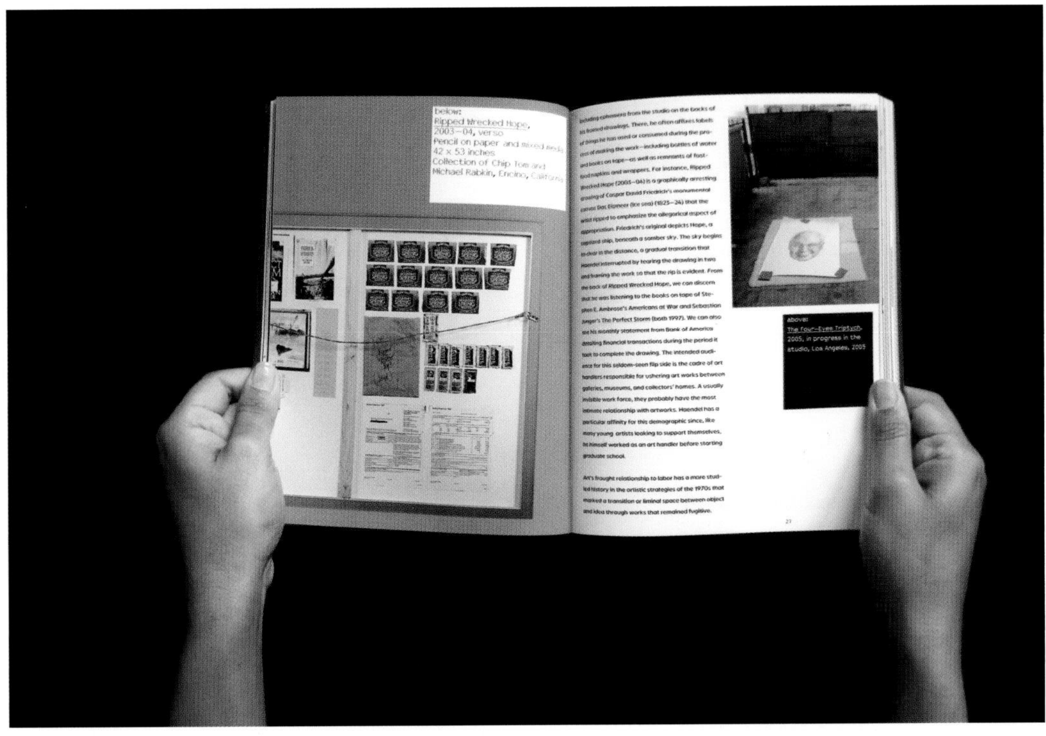

Karl Haendel, designed by Counterspace

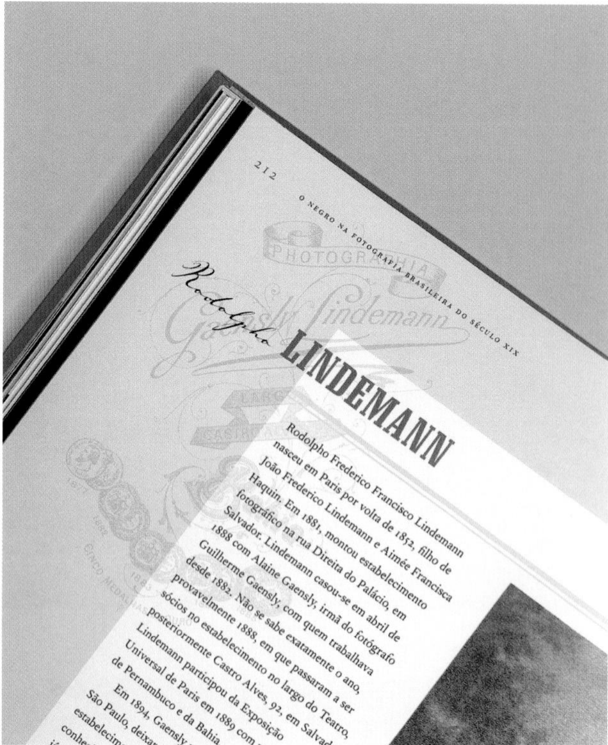

The book *O Negro* "tells, through nineteenth-century photography, part of the dramatic history of black people in Brazil," says Victor Burton. "The typographic eclecticism evokes nineteenth-century aesthetics by placing Egypcia Shadow, with its abrupt, almost violent strokes, as a principal actor. I also used gold to evoke the metallic materials used in developing photographs at that time."

88

MICHAEL **WORTHINGTON**

BRETT **MACFADDEN**

CREATE A SECONDARY NARRATIVE STREAM

Just because book designers work hard to let the content shine does not mean that they make design subservient or invisible. It's a matter of design and content working with one another. "We're creating a sympathetic graphic environment," says Michael Worthington. "You can't mess with or totally overshadow the artwork, so the design has to be a little more subtle, and that tends to involve strategies that might be considered as a secondary narrative stream."

Even the strongest visual content does not let designers off the hook. "In a philosophical sense, I've never been on board with the idea that the designer should stand back and let the art take center stage," says Brett MacFadden. "To me, that's shrinking from the greater challenge, which is trying to make design an active partner. I've always tried to create a typographic or visual language that rides along with the art."

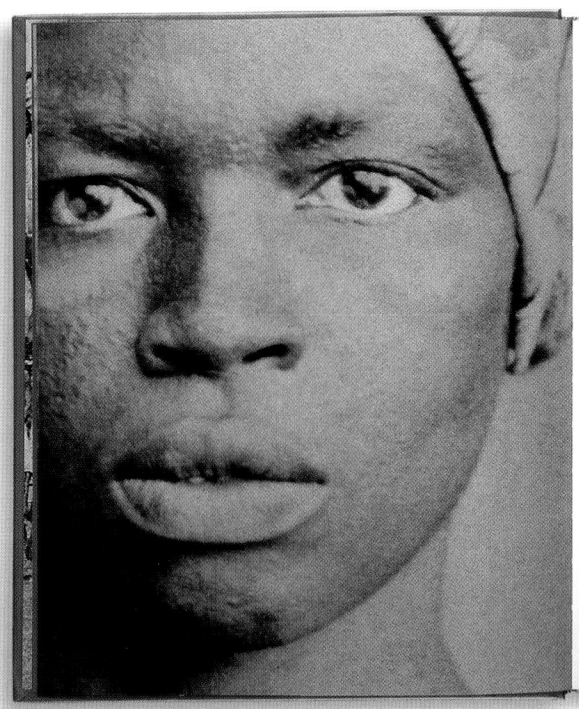

G.Ermakoff CASA EDITORIAL Rio de Janeiro 2004

George Ermakoff

O NEGRO NA FOTOGRAFIA BRASILEIRA DO SÉCULO XIX

40 O NEGRO NA FOTOGRAFIA BRASILEIRA DO SÉCULO XIX

Capítulo 2

SONHO DE LIBERDADE

POR TER A ESCRAVIDÃO PERDURADO quase quatro séculos, abrangido uma população de alguns milhões de cativos e estado presente em todas as províncias do Império, todo comentário sobre o dia-a-dia dessas pessoas é muito relativo, em razão da diversidade de opiniões deixadas por contemporâneos do regime, tanto escravocratas quanto abolicionistas. Alguns estudiosos posteriores ao regime escravista, embora tenham tido a oportunidade de examinar detidamente a documentação disponível, emitiram conceitos e opiniões que, em nenhum dos casos, podem ser considerados verdades absolutas.

Em seu memorável *Casa-grande e senzala*, Gilberto Freyre polemizou, ao afirmar:

Da energia africana ao seu serviço cedo aprenderam muitos dos grandes proprietários que, abusada ou esticada, rendia menos que bem conservada; daí passarem a explorar o escravo no objetivo do maior rendimento mas sem prejuízo da sua normalidade de eficiência. A eficiência estava no interesse do senhor conservar no negro — seu capital, sua máquina de trabalho — alguma coisa de si mesmo. De onde a alimentação farta e reparadora que Peckolt observou dispensarem os senhores aos escravos no Brasil.

SONHO DE LIBERDADE 41

A alimentação do negro nos engenhos brasileiros podia não ser nenhum primor de culinária, mas faltar nunca faltava. E sua abundância em milho, toucinho e feijão recomenda-a como regime apropriado ao duro esforço exigido do escravo agrícola.

O escravo negro no Brasil parece-nos ter sido, com todas as deficiências do seu regime alimentar, o elemento melhor nutrido em nossa sociedade patriarcal [...]. De modo que da antiga ordem econômica persiste a pior parte do ponto de vista do bem-estar geral e das classes trabalhadoras — desfeito em 88 o patriarcalismo que até então amparou os escravos alimentou-os com certa largueza, socorreu-lhes na velhice e na doença, proporcionou-lhes aos filhos oportunidades de acesso social. O escravo foi substituído pelo pária de usina; a senzala pelo mucambo; o senhor de engenho pelo usineiro ou pelo capitalista ausente. Muitas casas-grandes ficaram vazias, os capitalistas latifundiários rodando de automóvel pelas cidades, morando em chalés suíços e palacetes normandos, indo a Paris se divertir com as francesas de aluguel.

As afirmativas de Gilberto Freyre podem se aplicar a alguns casos, mas não podem ser generalizadas para todas as regiões do país, nem mesmo no Nordeste e talvez sequer nos engenhos da Província de Pernambuco.

Os negros se submeteram ao trabalho escravo e ao rigor do cativeiro pressionados pelos castigos corporais, mas nunca perderam o ideal de liberdade. Costumeiramente, esse ideal os levava à fuga, em busca de uma existência menos sofrida. As tentativas de fuga eram muito perigosas para os escravos porque, quando recapturados pelo "capitão do mato", o castigo vinha em dobro e não raro era fatal.

Um exemplo da busca da liberdade coletiva foi a formação dos quilombos, comunidades de negros fugidos que buscavam a vida em comum em segurança. Para eles, a segurança sempre foi muito relativa, pois eram alvos constantes das milícias armadas dos escravistas, que não lhes davam sossego. A força da união de quilombolas, entretanto, permitia a defesa de seus domínios, e assim o fizeram muitas vezes com êxito, à diferença das ações individuais, invariavelmente mais arriscadas.

A primeira concentração de escravos fugidos de que se tem notícia ocorreu entre Alagoas e Pernambuco e ficou conhecida como quilombo dos Palmares. Provavelmente, formou-se na passagem do século XVI para o século XVII, pois entre 1602 e 1608 já havia sido atacado por ordem do governador Diogo Botelho, que incumbira Bartolomeu Bezerra de formar uma expedição para aniquilá-lo.

Os escravos oriundos das fazendas pernambucanas de açúcar se aproveitaram da desorganização causada pela invasão holandesa para fugir em grande quantidade, incrementando a população dos quilombos.

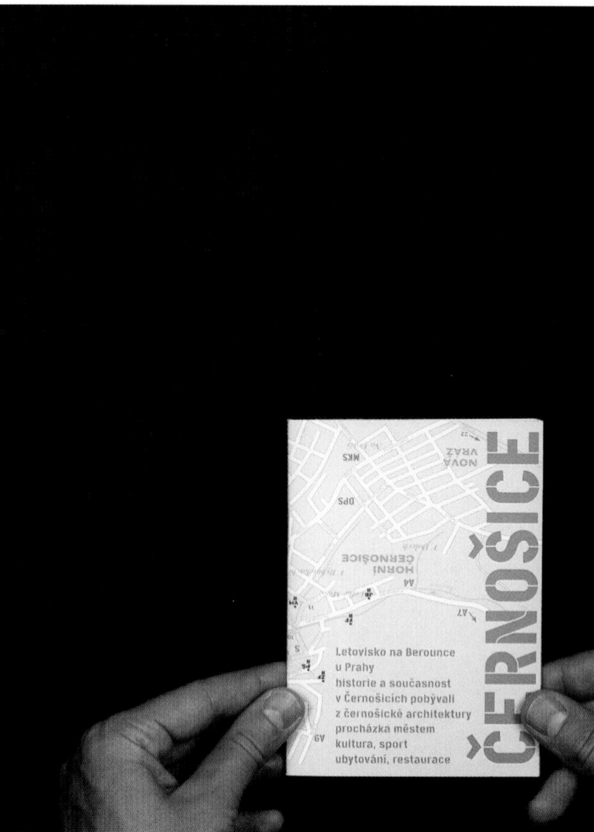

Černošice is a town in the central Bohemian region of the Czech Republic, just southwest of Prague. This publication, designed by Welcometo.as, combines a fold-out map bound with a booklet that gives historical and travel information, coded so everything is easy to find. The back of the map features a picturesque image of the village.

89

FIND A WAY IN TO THE MATERIAL

MAYA **DROZDZ**

MICHAEL **WORTHINGTON**

BRETT **MACFADDEN**

Sometimes the best way to balance content and design is to allow design to flow from the content itself. "A book is so complex and composed of so many parts that even something like meeting the author and liking him or her helps me find an 'in,'" says Maya Drozdz. Other opportunities come from the work instead of the words inside the book. For example, when designing an art book, Michael Worthington tries to pick up themes from the show itself. Drozdz tries to create connections between the material provided and her personal experiences. "I try and look out in the world for the common ground between the book and what's inspired me," she says. Brett MacFadden looks for "graphic cues," which may come from things he finds in the photographs that appear in a book. "I look for bits of typography or colors in the photos," he says. "A lot of times, I'm hunting for where the graphic design is within the imagery." He also looks within the tone established by the writer. "I look at the style of writing. If it's more academic and has footnotes and is scholarly, a lot of the design is logistical, in a sense. Other books are jaunty, so their design should also be open and fun. There's a tone you can interpret really quickly."

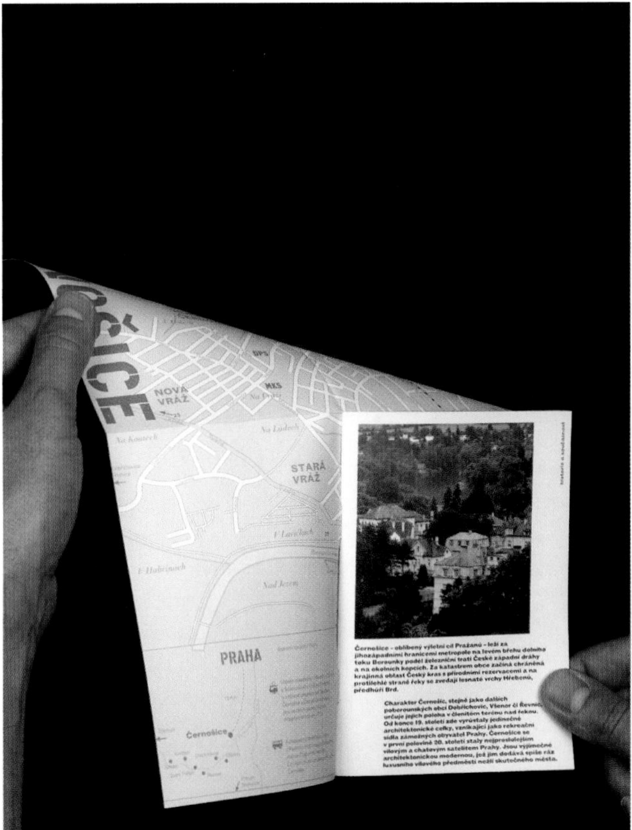

90

CARIN **GOLDBERG**

BRETT **MACFADDEN**

LOOK FOR INSPIRATION FROM HISTORY

Another way into the design and material of a book is to research the historical period the content reflects. "Years ago, I designed a nonfiction, historically referenced book titled *Soviet Power*," says Carin Goldberg. "It would be kind of dopey to not look at the posters of the period." However, this is not a recommendation to poach historical references indiscriminately. "I'm not trying to re-create or pillage history; I'm responding to it," she emphasizes. "This is where you find accurate visual connections and references. You have to go to the source, but also create a unique interpretation."

Brett MacFadden uses historical research to "look for things that will inspire a direction. I'll start by looking at stuff from that era—magazines, ads—trying to get a sense of the graphic tics of the time." Like Goldberg, he espouses using references in moderation. "A lot of times, it's not super strong gestures," MacFadden says. "It's a balance of the two eras—the time of the content and of the current offering. Even if I tried to ape an era perfectly, it would inevitably come off inexact. It's more like pulling some gestures of that era, some typographic fashions of that era, but otherwise, making sure the layout and use of imagery and printing feels current."

91 USE TYPOGRAPHY AS YOUR PRINCIPAL INSTRUMENT

VICTOR **BURTON**

MICHAEL **WORTHINGTON**

ROBERTO **DE VICQ**

"Typography is my principal instrument," says Victor Burton. "It is the only one that is specific to our profession alongside the architecture of the white page. A good project or book cover does not exist without good typography. And, the best image can be destroyed by wrong typography." Roberto De Vicq concurs. "Type is the only thing that is particular to graphic designers; you don't borrow it from the other arts."

So what makes good typography in a book? According to Michael Worthington, it's a combination of art and practicality, old and new. "We try to walk a fine line between things that are expressive and connotative of the theme of the show or the artist's work," he says. "And then the other side is purely about functionality: how well a typeface is drawn, how well it functions on the page. We try to do both things. One of the ways we do this is to use a combination of typefaces and unusual things that you haven't seen together before. Some of it is about discovering new typefaces and rediscovering old typefaces that have been overlooked. We'll try to work something that's traditional and known with something designed just this year."

92 ANYTHING BUT HELVETICA

MICHAEL **WORTHINGTON**

For Michael Worthington, as for many designers, books present a welcome opportunity to deeply consider the possibilities presented by a primarily typographical-based design solution. They're not about to waste this chance on any old typeface. "As a typographer, I get bored looking at the same typefaces," says Worthington. "When I see yet another book in Helvetica, it's just not that interesting to me. I know what it does, I know when it works well and when it doesn't; it's been examined pretty thoroughly." With all the fonts available, setting another book in Helvetica suggests, perhaps, nothing so much as design laziness and inattention.

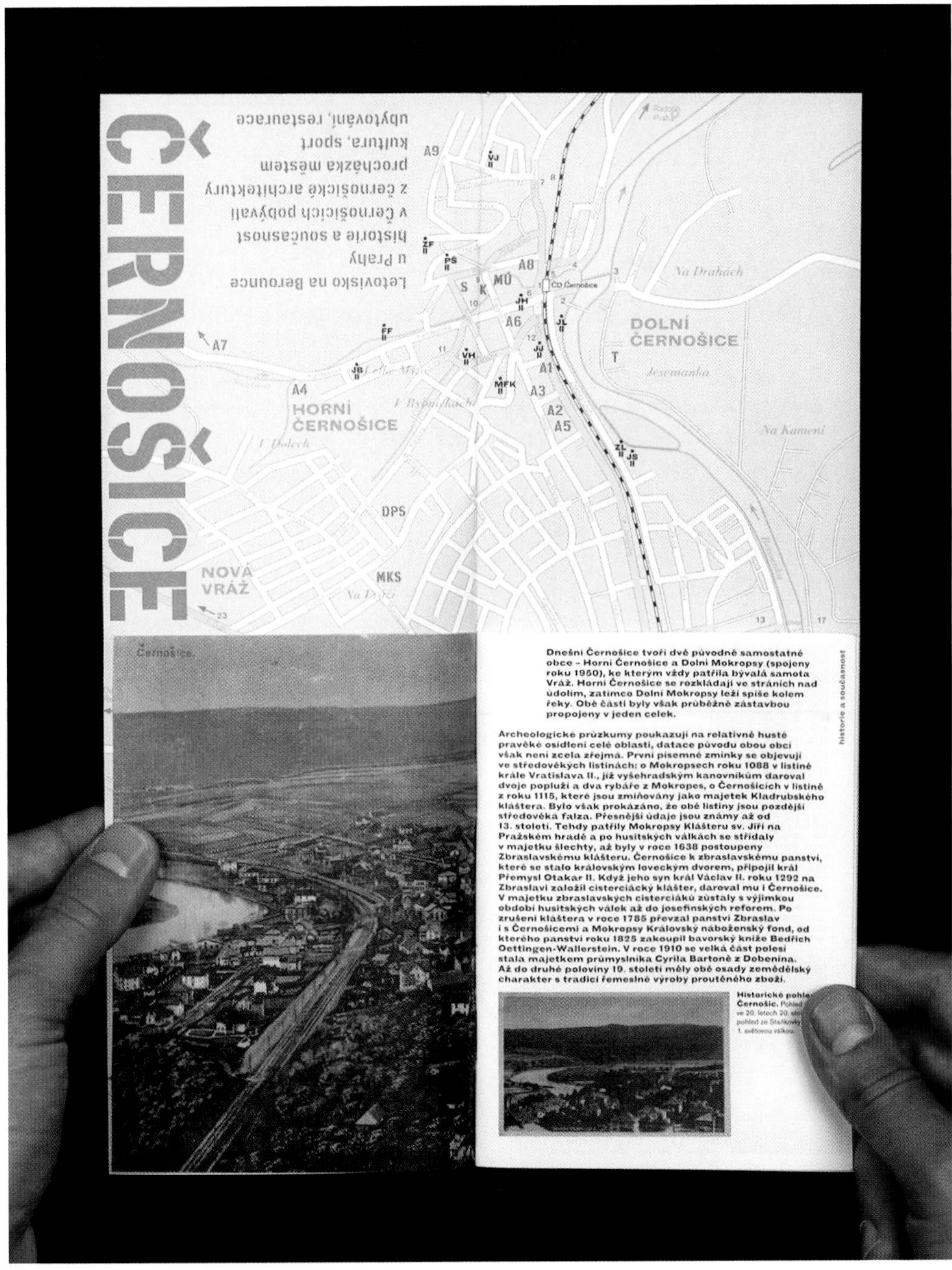

Černošice, designed by Welcometo.as

93

CARIN **GOLDBERG**

MAKE SOMETHING YOURSELF

Because almost everything is done on computers these days, especially in the design world, many designers seem to have forgotten the pleasures and satisfactions of low-tech solutions. "The budgets for book jackets were never very high, so very rarely did I have the option to hire a photographer or an illustrator," says Carin Goldberg. "So I made a lot of things out of what was at my fingertips." Not that this was a problem. "This is what I enjoy anyway. Half of my book jacket career was done without a computer, so a lot was done with a photocopier, cutting and pasting. I had a different way of approaching the work back then. Making things with my hands was more interesting than art directing." While she concedes that working on a computer helped her work in many ways for the good, she also feels, "My work got more mechanical and colder when I started working on a computer because of my limitations and knowledge of the applications." Personally making a completely customized piece of artwork for a book cover—whether out of necessity or preference—is also a way to enhance the dimensionality of the object while adding a welcome hint of humanity to the end result.

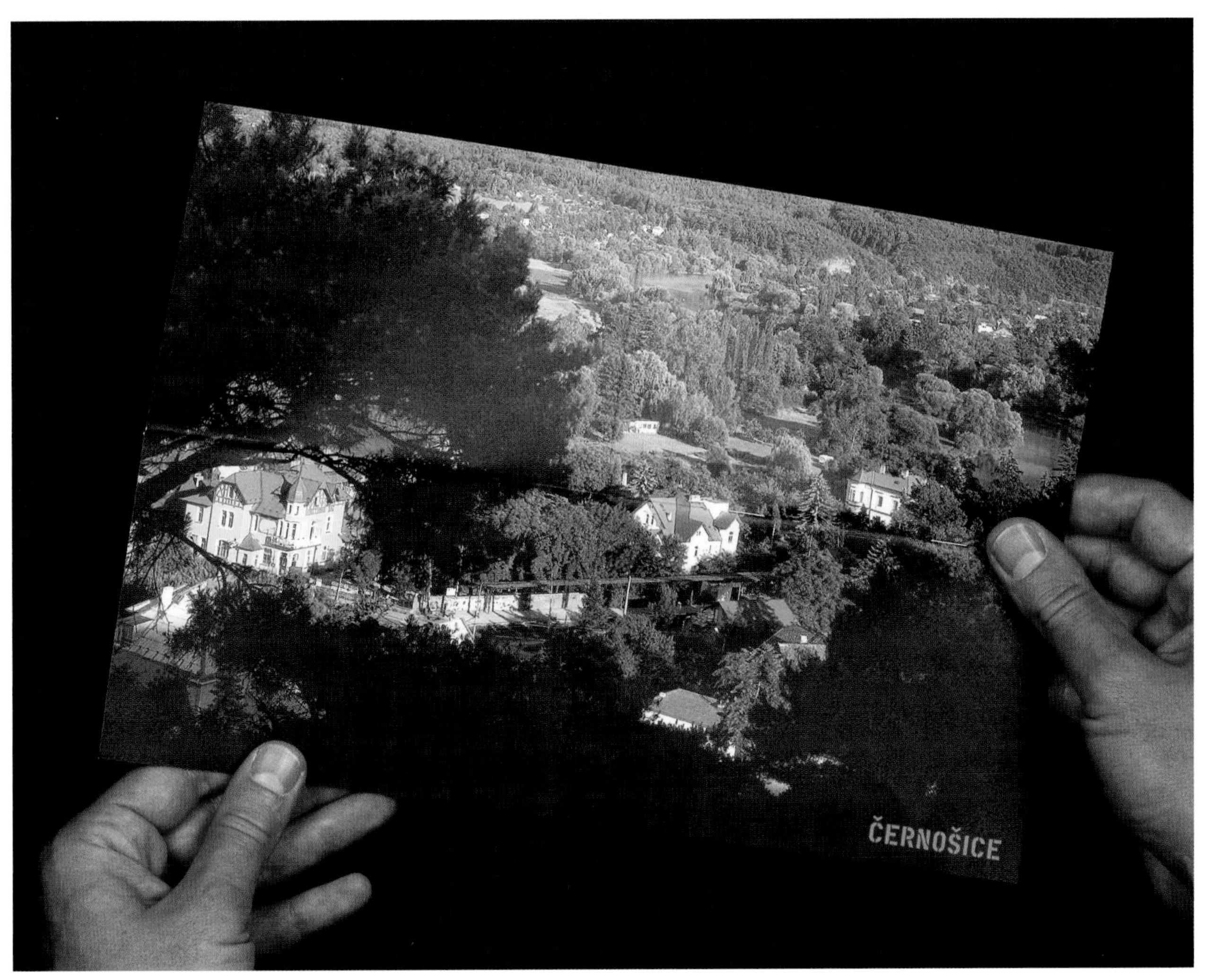

Černošice, designed by Welcometo.as

94

ROBERTO **DE VICQ**

USE YOUR "DRAWER OF WONDERS"

When describing how he finally found a book-cover-excuse to use an image he'd been admiring for years, Roberto de Vicq referred to his "drawer of wonders." "It's something Chip Kidd said," de Vicq recalls. "It means all those things you hold onto forever, waiting for the opportunity to use them." In other words, whether they get thrown into a drawer, bin, folder, or on your desktop, don't discard those pieces of inspiration, found images, or favorite ephemera—you never know when you'll find the perfect opportunity to use one of them.

In a book of thesis projects for an art school in Holland, "most of the artists tend to dislike graphic design and don't want design to interfere with their work," notes Arjen Noordeman. "We wanted to honor the wishes of the artists to have their work on a white page, but also wanted to impress people with our design. We solved this by inviting people to send us their sources of inspiration, which we made into a collage that wraps around the group, but within the book, all their work was displayed as if within a gallery."

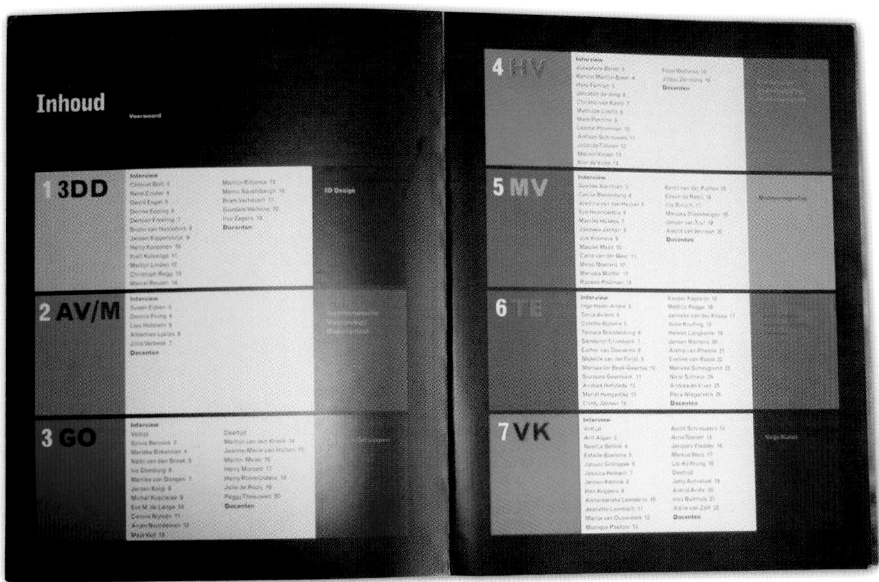

HKA, designed by Arjen Noordemann

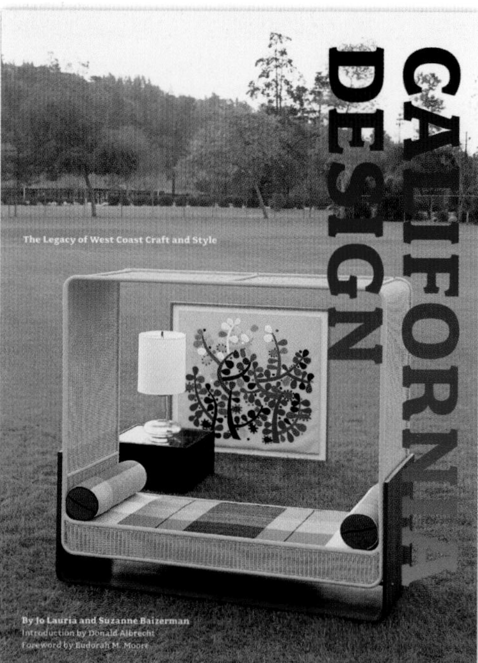

For a book on the craft and design innovations that took place in California during the boom years between the mid 1950s and mid 1970s, MacFadden took color cues from some of the highlighted products and interspersed the bold palate with the reprieve of black and white.

95

MICHAEL **WORTHINGTON**

BRETT **MACFADDEN**

PAY ATTENTION TO PACING

While a designer cannot completely control how a reader works his or her way through a book—especially an image-filled book on art, photography, or architecture—it is still incumbent upon the designer to try to direct the reader down a particular path and thereby create a specific kind of journey. "There's this idea of pacing in a book," says Michael Worthington. "People look at books in two ways: They pick them up and flip through them from back to front and they may stop at a page that catches their interest; the other way is to go from page 1 to 2 to 3, and so on. As the designer, you're trying to control a narrative and also create an overall mood with the design when the viewer is flipping through it."

Brett MacFadden tries to manage this mood by finding and enhancing the connections between images. "The author creates quite a bit of the pacing, but beyond that, you start out with this whole pile of imagery and you look for what sits well next to each other. The majority of the work in these image-heavy books is about dropping things in, resizing them, trying to work it until it holds as a spread." MacFadden consistently finds pacing mechanisms within the material itself. "Sometimes I look for lines in images that will connect them to other images; connecting horizon lines or connecting other elements within images will give me clues. I might match textures, colors, atmospheres. There can be a musical patterning, where you let things fall quiet, or bring them to a crescendo. Pacing is essential, and a lot of it is intuitive. Mostly, it's aesthetics and balance. You just go back and see what feels right or feels off."

Introduction DONALD ALBRECHT

"One does not need to share all the illusions of the boosters to believe, as I believe," historian Carey McWilliams wrote in 1946, "that the most fantastic city in the world will one day exist in this region: a city embracing the entire region from the mountains to the sea."[1] Although he was boasting about post–World War II Los Angeles, McWilliams's prophesy of growth and prosperity could also be applied to all of California. The state had been a major destination in the vast national migration of Americans who moved during the war in search of well-paid defense work. The whole West Coast, with its massive aircraft and shipbuilding facilities, witnessed remarkable changes, but it was California that profited most from $35 billion in wartime federal funding. After the war, Americans continued to be lured by the state's mild climate and expansive Cold War–related industries. By 1967, California's economy ranked sixth among nations in the world.[2]

These economic and demographic shifts permanently changed the nation's regional balance, giving California newfound status and independence from the East Coast. Benefiting from their exalted position, Californians boldly redefined the American Dream. They popularized then-radical ways of living, from patio houses to automobile-based cities, which were promoted through media such as magazines, movies, and music. High-profile postwar architecture and design initiatives helped raise California lifestyles and their accoutrements to national consciousness. In 1945 the avant-garde magazine *Arts + Architecture* launched the Case Study House Program, which sponsored the design and construction of a series of modern homes as prototypes for postwar housing. Equally ambitious—yet curiously less celebrated—were the *California Design* exhibitions, a series of thirteen shows featuring the applied arts and presented primarily at the Pasadena Art Museum between 1954 and 1976. Combining both handcrafted and mass-produced goods, the series sought to highlight and encourage new talent throughout California. New forms, materials, and technologies were showcased as the state's designers and artisans exploited revolutionary innovations in lightweight metals, molded plywood, reinforced concrete, and plastics. Prototypes of innovative furniture and accessories, persuasive harbingers of things to come, were featured in virtually every show. Ultimately, *California Design* put the Golden State on the national design map.[3]

opposite:
Figure 1.40
Svetozar Radakovitch in collaboration with Karl Eckburg; manufactured by Architectural Fiberglass;
Double Door;
fiberglass, polyurethane foam, wood.
1968 (*California Design 10*)

below:
Figure 1.41
Douglas Deeds for Architectural Fiberglass,
White Bench,
fiberglass.
Shown with La Gardo Tackett's *Ceramic Planter* for Architectural Pottery.
1965 (*California Design 9*)

Groundbreaking fiberglass forms for public places and garden spaces were designed for the company by Douglas Deeds and Elsie Crawford. Deeds's curvaceous, sculptural benches for streets, gardens, airports, and bus stops were exhibited in *CD 9* (1965), *CD 10* (1968), and *CD 11* (1971) (figs. 1.36, 1.37, 1.39, 1.41). Additionally, a Deeds-designed line of futuristic-looking contract furniture, composed of three chairs and two table-ottomans, was shown in *CD 10* (fig. 1.38). No less prolific was Elsie Crawford, whose highly imaginative, large-scale garden planters, planter benches, and gracefully fluid *Light Column* appeared in *CD 10* and *CD 11* (figs. 1.45, 1.46, 1.47). Designs by Donald Chadwick were also noted for their thoughtful exploitation of the material properties of plastic. Chadwick's prototype *Plastic Dining Chair* was a highly abstract shape of flowing lines and intersecting curves, whose monolithic construction and exaggerated volumes endowed it with great sculptural presence (fig. 1.42). Similarly, his prototype *Side Chair/Dining Chair* of bright red molded plastic wedded functional, economic, and ergonomic imperatives

49 Production Furniture

California Design, designed by Brett MacFadden

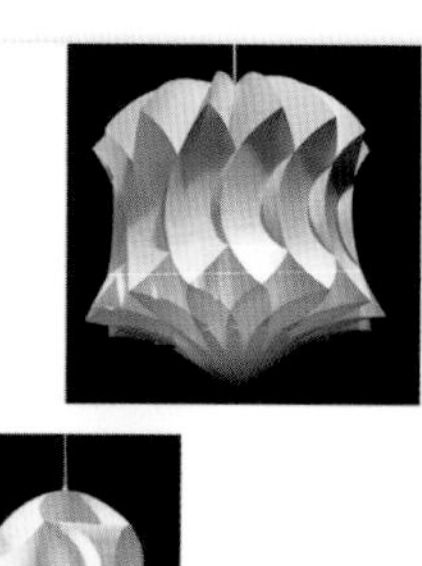

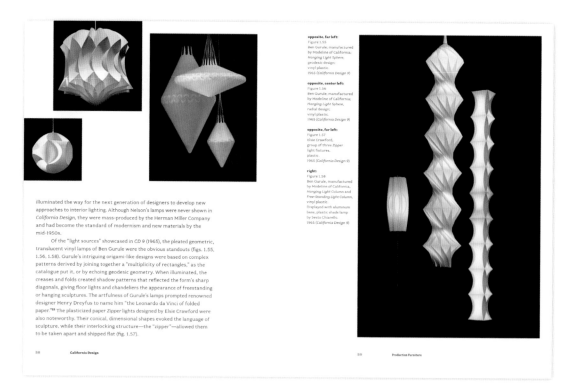

illuminated the way for the next generation of designers to develop new approaches to interior lighting. Although Nelson's lamps were never shown in *California Design*, they were mass-produced by the Herman Miller Company and had become the standard of modernism and new materials by the mid-1950s.

Of the "light sources" showcased in *CD 9* (1965), the pleated geometric, translucent vinyl lamps of Ben Gurule were the obvious standouts (figs. 1.55, 1.56, 1.58). Gurule's intriguing origami-like designs were based on complex patterns derived by joining together a "multiplicity of rectangles," as the catalogue put it, or by echoing geodesic geometry. When illuminated, the creases and folds created shadow patterns that reflected the form's sharp diagonals, giving floor lights and chandeliers the appearance of freestanding or hanging sculptures. The artfulness of Gurule's lamps prompted renowned designer Henry Dreyfus to name him "the Leonardo da Vinci of folded paper."[23] The plasticized paper *Zipper* lights designed by Elsie Crawford were also noteworthy. Their conical, dimensional shapes evoked the language of sculpture, while their interlocking structure—the "zipper"—allowed them to be taken apart and shipped flat (fig. 1.57).

58 **California Design**

opposite, far left:
Figure 1.55
Ben Gurule; manufactured by Modeline of California;
Hanging Light Sphere, geodesic design;
vinyl plastic.
1965 (*California Design 9*)

opposite, center left:
Figure 1.56
Ben Gurule; manufactured by Modeline of California;
Hanging Light Sphere, radial design;
vinyl plastic.
1965 (*California Design 9*)

opposite, far left:
Figure 1.57
Elsie Crawford, group of three *Zipper* light fixtures,
plastic.
1965 (*California Design 9*)

right:
Figure 1.58
Ben Gurule, manufactured by Modeline of California,
Hanging Light Column and *Free-Standing Light Column*,
vinyl plastic.
Displayed with aluminum base, plastic shade lamp by Sesto Chiarello.
1965 (*California Design 9*)

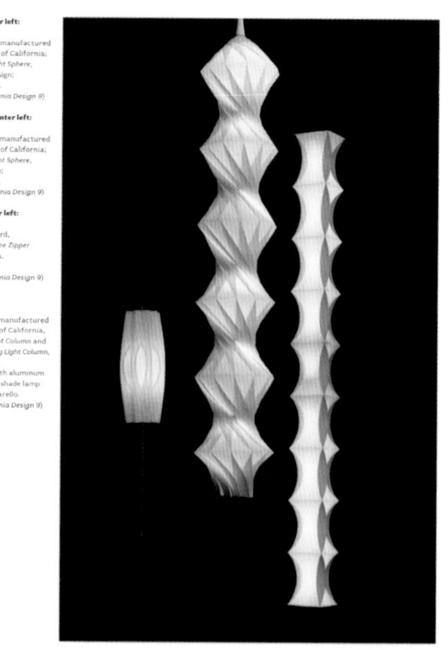

59 **Production Furniture**

96

ENJOY THE LENGTH OF THE PROCESS

DAVID **ALBERTSON**

JASON **GODFREY**

"Book design is very civilized," says David Albertson. "It's on a much longer timeline, it tends to require fewer variations in your templating, and you tend to be designing more in a linear way than a multidimensional way." All of which can add up to pleasures akin to planting seeds and having to wait until the spring to see exactly how they'll bloom. "Often you design a book and it's at least six months from when you hand over the files to when you have a book in your hand," Jason Godfrey points out. "In the amount of time that it takes to produce a book, you could have built a house. It's amazing that that's the case. And with book designs, you don't get to see it working until you see the final piece," he notes. "You're never quite sure how it will work out. It can surprise you at the end of the day, because of that translation from layout to having the pages you're flipping through. I enjoy that part of the process, that lag and the not quite knowing. I think that's quite a unique experience when you finally get the books in your hand. It feels so great."

***California Design*, designed by Brett MacFadden**

WHAT A COVER NEEDS TO DO

MARCUS **PIPER**, NICKI **KALISH**,
AREM **DUPLESSIS**, ROBERTO **DE VICQ**

A cover is the face a magazine or book presents to the public. Of course, it has to provide some sense of what's inside, but this is a job full of nuance, portent, and gentle coaxing. "What a cover has to do depends upon the magazine," says Marcus Piper. "But in general, it has to invite people to pick it up." However, the cover can't promise more than what's provided on the inside. "It comes down to perceived value," Piper notes. "If you put a beautiful image on the cover, someone might leave the magazine on the coffee table, as opposed to someone who reads a gossip magazine on the train and then leaves it behind." Whatever the content, designers should be looking for some way to get the reader to first, take a look, and second, take a read. "When I find out what the lead story is," says Nicki Kalish, "I want it to carry the page. So I design something that immediately conveys the essence of what the article is about, in a way that's not been done too many times. I want to find a new or fresh approach."

Magazines that do not have to compete on the newsstand—such as airline magazines, subscription-only publications, or Sunday newspaper magazines—can generally be less concerned with trite, attention-grabbing, commercial appeal on their covers. "We have the luxury of taking more risks with our covers," says Arem Duplessis about the *New York Times Magazine*. "There are not too many magazines that can conceptualize a cover with a fine artist and actually run it. It wouldn't sell. The commercialism factor is just not as much of an issue for us. This fact helps us avoid putting obscure numbers on our covers, like '43 Ways to a Healthy You.'"

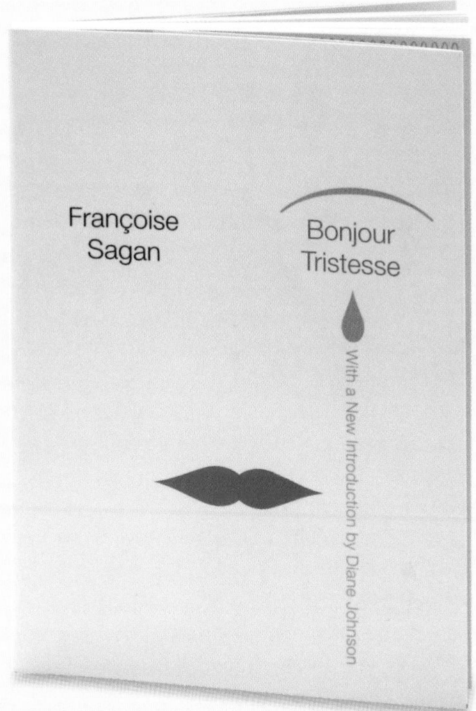

ROBERTO DE VICQ

Books jackets face a different challenge in that they generally have to do more, over a longer time period. They must also convey, or at least hint at, the much more comprehensive and singular story line contained between the front and back covers. "The function of a jacket is this: If you read the review and you see a little photo in the newspaper, it makes an impression, and then the next time you go to the bookstore, you'll be reminded of the book," notes Roberto de Vicq. "Also when you're walking through the store, the jacket attracts you to pick up the book and after that, it's the quality of the writing, the blurbs, the jacket copy that gets your attention. The function of the design is to create a bridge between a customer and a product." De Vicq actually minimizes the commercial aspects of book jacket design, as well. "The job of a jacket is not to sell the product," he says. "It's to relate to the audience. After that, it's the quality of product that will sell." This limiting of the role of a book cover helps him home in on suitable design solutions. "You have to have one central idea that is good," de Vicq says. "You try to be as minimal as possible and solve as much as possible simply because you have a very small canvas. It's only 6 x 9 inches (15.2 x 22.9 cm)."

NICOLE DUDKA

THE HARTFORD COURANT | JULY 20 -26, 2006

fiona apple

The eccentric songwriter steps out of her head and back into music. Page 8

caL

C M Y K YTxx,2007-05-02,D,001,Bs-4C,E1

YT D1

Dining In

The New York Times

WEDNESDAY, MAY 2, 2007

Questions Linger For Beard Foundation

By NICK FOX

ON Monday the year's biggest gathering of chefs, food journalists, and other culinary professionals and amateurs will convene at one of the grander locales in New York, Avery Fisher Hall at Lincoln Center, for the James Beard Foundation Awards.

It will be quite a step up from the ballroom at the Marriott Marquis, the longtime venue for the food world's most prestigious awards.

After cleaning up an embezzlement scandal that led to the imprisonment of the foundation's former president, the current president, Susan Ungaro, said it was time for the organization to show some pride and have some fun.

"The foundation needed to take its rightful place as a place of excitement, and a place of intelligent planning," Ms. Ungaro said, "after a few years of hard knocks."

But the hard knocks continue more than two years after the former president, Leonard F. Pickell Jr., and later the entire board of directors, resigned. While it is being run more professionally and openly, the organization is in worse shape financially. And questions about its mission that were raised by the scandal have not all been resolved.

After being robbed by a president who worked for years without pay, and few fiscal controls, the foundation now has a salaried president (who earns $225,000) and chief financial officer, auditors and a bigger professional staff.

Ms. Ungaro says that the fiscal year that ended on March 31 will show a big improvement over last year's bottom line. But the foundation will still be in the red, for the fifth year in a row.

In that time the foundation, which has been spending about $5 million each year, has run up almost $3 million in deficits, mostly since Mr. Pickell left, according to its financial statements.

The losses began with about $1 million in unsubstantiated expenses under Mr. Pickell. It then cost about $750,000 for lawyers and accountants to help clean up the mess. After the scandal broke, annual revenues from sponsorships, donations and events

Continued on Page 10

INSIDE

GINS OF THE TIMES

No, Really, It Was Tough: 4 People, 80 Martinis

By ERIC ASIMOV

HAVE I told you about my 80-martini lunch?

I exaggerate. Actually, four of us shared 80 martinis, so it was really a 20-martini lunch.

Frankly, once you get past the first 12 martinis, it might as well be 80. But it was worth it.

The occasion was the spirits panel's martini tasting. Florence Fabricant and I were joined by Audrey Saunders, bartender extraordinaire and an owner of the Pegu Club on West Houston Street, and Pete Wells, editor of the Dining section, who has written extensively about drinks.

The subject was supposed to be solely gin. But because gin is often consumed in a martini, we decided to taste the gin as expressed through the world's most famous (and perhaps least understood) cocktail. We discovered that while great martinis require great gins, great gins don't necessarily make great martinis.

The gin category has exploded in the last decade, with distillers offering unusual riffs on the classic theme. Some of these make for striking gins, although they struck out as martinis. Our task was to sort out which gins produced classic martinis, which added welcome nuances and which really ought to seek another line of cocktail.

Before we discuss the findings, though, we need to clear up a little matter. It's come to my attention that some people believe martinis are made with vodka. I hate to get snobbish about it, but a martini should be made with gin or it's not a martini. Call it a vodkatini if you must, but not a martini. Gin and vodka have as much in common hi-

Continued on Page 8

The Matriarchs Of Mexican Flavor

Adriana Zehbrauskas for The New York Times

CLASSICIST Carmen Ramírez Degollado owns and runs El Bajío in Mexico City.

By MARK BITTMAN

MEXICO CITY

TO the casual observer, and even to a slightly more diligent one, the two women have more in common than not. They are roughly the same age (let's say over 50), their roots are in Veracruz — their food shows it — and they learned to cook at home from their mothers and grandmothers. After leaving home, they were essentially self-taught, came to the restaurant business more or less by accident and became symbols of strong, independent women in an industry long dominated by men.

Most important, they run two of the best and most distinctive restaurants in Mexico City. Which is another way of saying they run two of the best and most distinctive Mexican restaurants in the world.

They are Carmen (Titita) Ramírez Degollado and Patricia Quintana, and after three visits to each of their restaurants over the last few years I was surprised to find myself concluding that despite their similarities, the food they cook is as different as food from the same region and genre can be.

THE CHEFS: CARMEN RAMÍREZ DEGOLLADO AND PATRICIA QUINTANA

Ms. Quintana's, as served at Izote, her restaurant in the swank Polanco neighborhood, is refined, sometimes bordering on experimental. She remains true to the origins of Mexican cooking, but this allegiance includes bringing in the Spanish influences that launched it as one of the world's original fusion cuisines. She argues quite persuasively, for example, that olive oil is an integral, or at least sensible, part of the Mexican larder.

Ms. Ramírez's more rustic, almost devotional cooking is equally celebrated. Her career began about 35 years ago, at a restaurant called El Bajío, founded by her husband, Raúl, in the industrial neighborhood Azcapotzalco. When he died of cancer 29 years ago, Ms. Ramírez stepped in. She has been running the place ever since.

"El Bajío, without any doubt, is the best restaurant of Mexican cuisine that I have been in in my life," Ferran Adrià of El Bulli in Spain, one of the world's most influential chefs, wrote in an e-mail message translated from Spanish.

The restaurant is colorful, brilliant in its deep blue and bright orange scheme, and

Continued on Page 6

VICTOR BURTON

ROBERTO DE VICQ

CARIN GOLDBERG

CARIN GOLDBERG

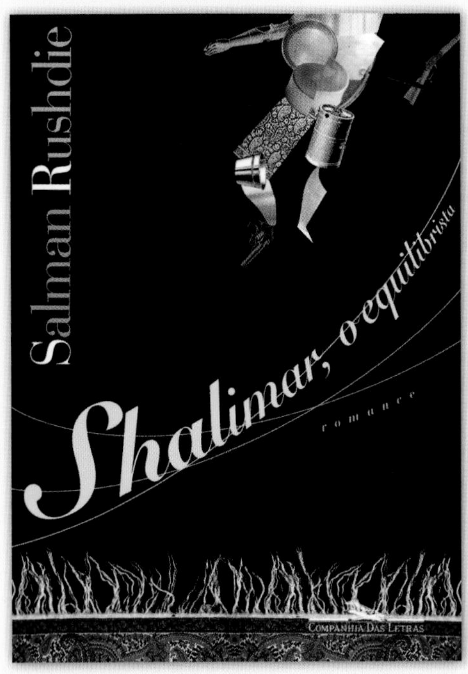

VICTOR BURTON

CARIN GOLDBERG

Chapter Five:

WHERE ARE MAGAZINES HEADED?

97

JEREMY **LESLIE**

ARTHUR **HOCHSTEIN**

MARCUS **PIPER**

ACCEPT THE INFLUENCE OF THE WEB

With almost every publication now appearing online as well as in print, the designer must consider both media, often simultaneously. And because consumers are getting so much information from the Internet, it is inevitable that the habits and devices used in interactive design are bleeding onto the printed page. "The Web has had a very specific effect on page design," says Jeremy Leslie. "It's accelerated a process that was happening anyway, with the bite size chunk of information getting smaller and smaller. You have to have pictures and pull quotes and sells and as many devices as possible." This is the result of the changing nature of our culture. "All magazines looked like the *New Yorker* seventy years ago," he says, "but now, a new magazine couldn't hope to have a successful launch looking like that. It's just a matter of degree, of how much you're going to cede ground to this process."

The Web has not only influenced how print looks, it's also changed the kind of information people gather from different resources. For example, people are increasingly going to the Web for quick hits of fast-breaking and changing news. This has forced news magazines especially to rethink the kind of information they present in order to stay relevant and compete on their own ground. "For a while," Arthur Hochstein notes, "print was trying to emulate the Internet, and now there's a backlash, which is smart, because print is print and electronics is electronics and each should do what it does well." In the case of *Time*, this includes focusing less on breaking news and more on analysis and opinion, using columnists and features to help readers interpret and understand the information they've been gathering all week from their desktop.

By working together, the two media actually support and reinforce one another. "The Web is not an enemy," says Hochstein. "We encourage our reporters to contribute to both our online and print versions. They're increasingly seen as one entity, but the magazine doesn't need to and shouldn't need to keep up with the Internet. News magazines have been on everyone's hit list for twenty years, but the more likely scenario is simply a retrenching, a redefinition." Marcus Piper agrees: "The Internet has changed the way people interact with things, their attention spans, and how they receive information. People want snippets, and they need to be grabbed and told to read something. Creatively, the dominance of the Internet as a source of information is a great thing because magazines are forced to be better. Things like tactility are now key for publication designers. It's an opportunity to make magazines work harder and be better, and that is exciting."

contents

July/August 2004
special art issue

features

cover: The living room of a Tiburon, California, residence by Gary Hutton for collector Chara Schreyer. Photography by Cesar Rubio. See page 92. **above**: Donald Judd's untitled works in concrete, 1980–84, at The Chinati Foundation in Marfa, Texas. Photography by Hester + Hardaway. See page 120. **below**: The garden of artist John Baldessari's Santa Monica, California, residence. Photography by Tim Street-Porter. See page 110.

letters to the editor:
5410 Wilshire Blvd.,
Suite 200 West
Los Angeles, CA 90036
editorial@westernid.com

for subscriptions call:
1.800.477.5988 in US
1.850.682.7644 in Canada
and all other countries

visit our web site:
www.westernid.com

photography by Hester + Hardaway / text by Laura Mauk

DONALD JUDD'S MARFA

THE LANDSCAPES OF WEST TEXAS INFORMED THE SEMINAL AMERICAN ARTIST'S INVESTIGATIONS OF SPACE AND COLOR. SINCE HIS DEATH, THE COMPLEX OF BUILDINGS HE BOUGHT IN MARFA HAS BECOME AN INTERNATIONAL MECCA FOR THE CONTEMPORARY ART WORLD, WHICH IS STILL COMING TO TERMS WITH HIS POTENT LEGACY.

Donald Judd (1928–1994) left New York for Marfa, Texas, in 1977 to develop large-scale art in the desert landscape. His untitled fifteen works in concrete (left), 1980–84, are permanently installed at The Chinati Foundation, a military base he converted into a contemporary art museum. **top**: Judd's downtown Marfa ranch office. **above**: The artist outfitted The Block (or La Mansana de Chinati), his compoundlike living space, with a Gustav Stickley table and chairs and his 1963 "harp piece."

121

98

EMBRACE THE DIFFERENCES BETWEEN PRINT AND THE WEB

ARTHUR **HOCHSTEIN**

CASEY **CAPLOWE**

JASON **GODFREY**

By focusing on the strengths—and pleasures—of print, publications can and will remain relevant. After all, while legions of people indulge in the guilty pleasure of checking the latest Hollywood gossip online before the boss gets in, it's the print version of *People* magazine that gets stuffed into the beach bag. Arthur Hochstein thinks of print as "more of a niche experience, but also a more satisfying experience, like the 'slow foods' movement. You have to focus on what you do well, like presenting photography and having discursive stories that are more pleasurable than utilitarian." Casey Caplowe agrees. "Certainly you consider how things will work online when you're designing the magazine, so there's that interplay. But it's important to make a good magazine first. You have opportunities to do things in print that you can't do online, such as big pictures and illustrative headlines. The interplay of text and images is way more interesting in print than online." After all, there's something deeply gratifying about the experience of turning pages. As Jason Godfrey notes, "I don't see the Internet as a replacement for books. Books are the most interactive stuff that we have, actually."

The open feel of page layout and type choices in *Western Interiors and Design* magazine are as crisp and clear as the light and landscape where the images were taken.

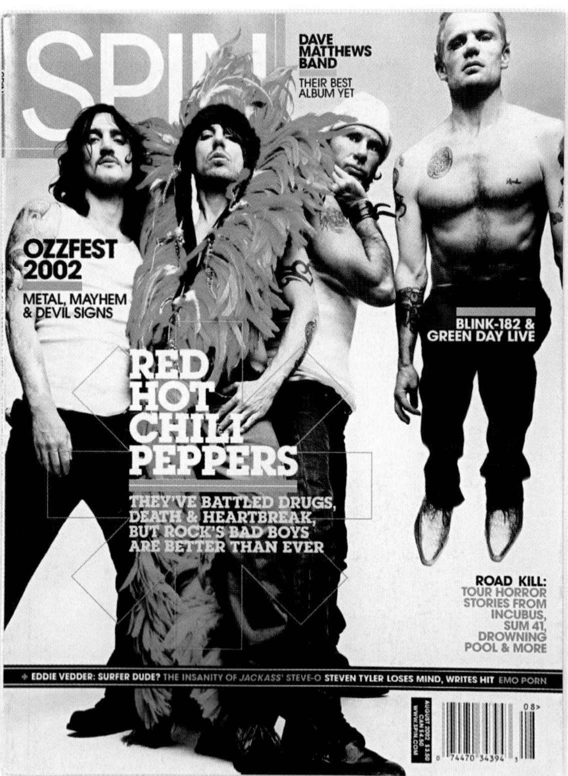

Spin magazine, art directed by Arem Duplessis, combines photographs that reveal character and type that tells a story before you even read the words. The ambience on the printed page captures the essential vibe of the subject matter at hand.

99

HURRY UP

VINCE **FROST**

"If you're into making books, hurry up before there are no more books being published," says Vince Frost. "I think there's going to be a migration to people producing things online." Frost sees printing books as an outdated mode of communication. "It's quite an antiquated thing to produce a book," he says. "Publishers are buying digital companies and things are changing." Certainly, with the advent of digital book readers, self-publishing, on-demand publishing, and authors serializing their books online, there are changing opportunities for people who want to be read, beyond the more standard channels of traditional book publishing. "It's going to be far more fluid than it is now," Frost predicts. "It's very exciting." He also points out that the digital world can certainly help address some of our pressing global concerns. "There are serious environmental issues here," he notes. "We're using up all the world's resources, and now the digital world is taking off."

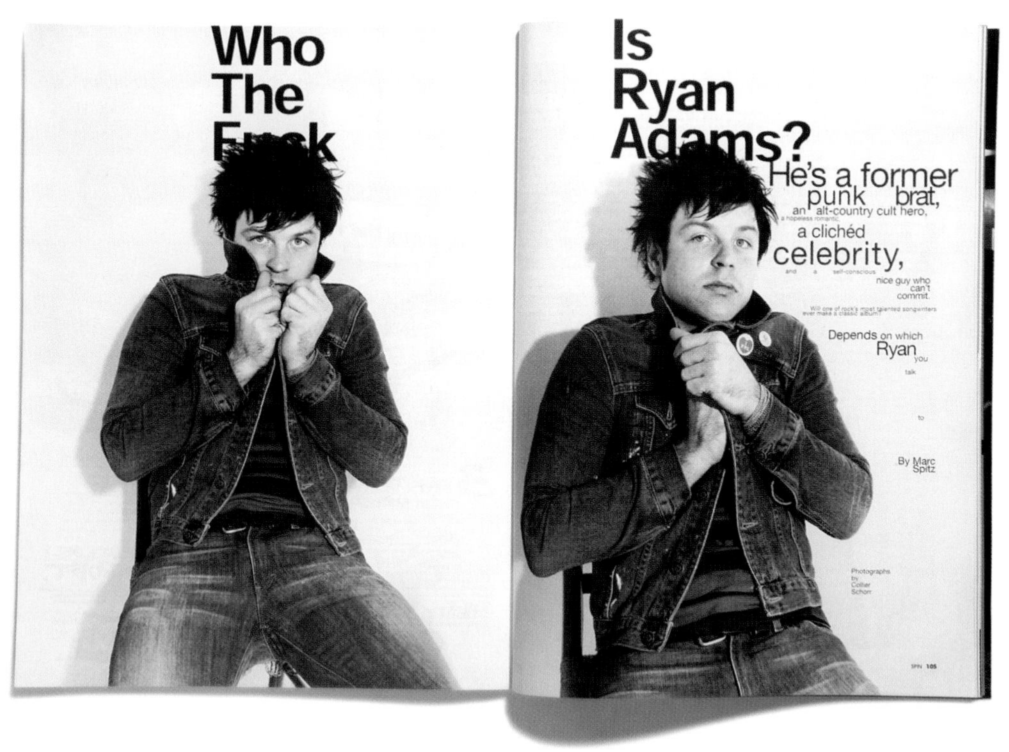

Who The Fuck Is Ryan Adams?

He's a former punk brat, an alt-country cult hero, a hopeless romantic, a clichéd celebrity, and a self-conscious nice guy who can't commit. Will one of rock's most talented songwriters ever make a classic album? Depends on which Ryan you talk to

By Marc Spitz

Photographs by Collier Schorr

SPIN 105

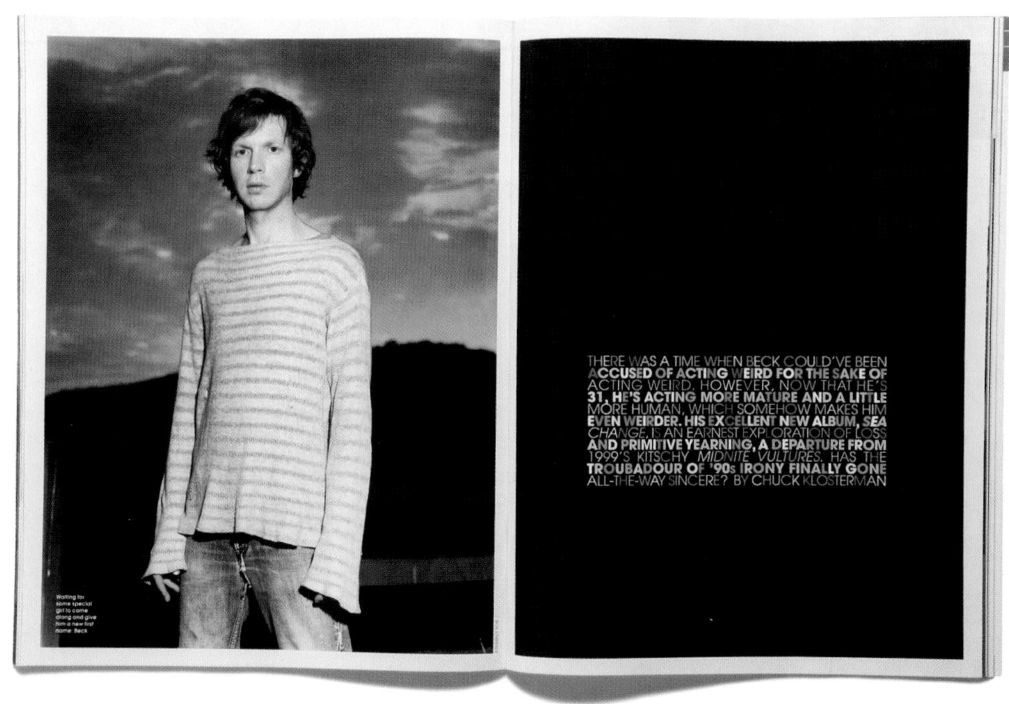

Waiting for some special girl to come along and give him a new first name: Beck

THERE WAS A TIME WHEN BECK COULD'VE BEEN ACCUSED OF ACTING WEIRD FOR THE SAKE OF ACTING WEIRD. HOWEVER, NOW THAT HE'S 31, HE'S ACTING MORE MATURE AND A LITTLE MORE HUMAN, WHICH SOMEHOW MAKES HIM EVEN WEIRDER. HIS EXCELLENT NEW ALBUM, *SEA CHANGE*, IS AN EARNEST EXPLORATION OF LOSS AND PRIMITIVE YEARNING, A DEPARTURE FROM 1999'S KITSCHY *MIDNITE VULTURES*. HAS THE TROUBADOUR OF '90s IRONY FINALLY GONE ALL-THE-WAY SINCERE? BY CHUCK KLOSTERMAN

100

KALLE **LASN**

CASEY **CAPLOWE**

JEREMY **LESLIE**

TODD **SIMMONS**

WHEN IN DOUBT, MAKE YOUR OWN

When clients, deadlines, and conventions begin to chafe, or there's no apparent place to speak with an alternative voice, there's nothing quite like starting your own publication for the like-minded. *Adbusters* was the concrete result of just this dilemma. Formerly a documentary filmmaker, Kalle Lasn got involved in Pacific Northwest political issues and set out to use his film skills to make and air television spots. "I was interested in getting people together and airing these spots to get some provocative stuff on the television," he recalls. "But none of these stations would give me any airtime." Instead of being stymied by the available media, he simply made his own, starting first with a 'zine, which became a newsletter, which became a magazine, which now has a circulation of 120,000 worldwide. "I got into it because of a passion for what I was doing, and I learned my lessons along the way," he says.

The advent of *GOOD* magazine followed a similar trajectory from film to page. "The founder, Ben Goldhirsh, wanted to be involved in creating media that mattered and could reach a lot of people," notes Casey Caplowe. He started a film company with a mission to make films "around socially relevant topics that would put people in seats, but have a socially redeeming value." Then he and his cohorts realized they were not alone. "We started to realize that there was this burgeoning movement of people who wanted to live well and do good in a new way that's not just pure idealism but sees the system as part of the solution." *GOOD* magazine became their means of collecting and providing communication opportunities to and for this group of similarly inclined people: "a publication that would celebrate, inspire, and catalyze this movement."

Even if your aspirations are less grand or socially redeeming, creating your own publication is a great means to meet people, share ideas, and learn how to use financial and production limitations to inventive and fruitful design ends. "When I was in university," Jeremy Leslie recalls, "we published our own music fan 'zines. They were just black-and-white copies with staples, which was the correct aesthetic of the time, but that wasn't through choice; it was the only aesthetic available to us." The advent of cheap computers, printers, and the Internet has made much more possible. "What is available now with digital technology," he notes, "is that it's relatively cheap and easy to produce a few thousand copies of your own magazine—subject to your and your friends' skills and abilities. The only way I could sell my magazine was go to concerts and stand out there and try to get someone to buy it. Now I can print 5,000 copies of something, and if it's all right, I know I can sell 500 in London, 500 in Paris, 500 in Berlin, New York, Tokyo, Sydney, etc., through the Internet. The logistics are far easier, and so there are a lot of really good independent magazines out there; there are plenty of poor ones as well, but that's not the point. There's an audience out there that is hungry to buy international magazines that are cool." This means there's no reason for any creative, inventive, and enterprising publication designer to limit him or herself to conventions of commercial magazines, alone. If you want to see your designs hit the page, create the page as well as the design. As Jason Godfrey notes, "Self-publishing will not dumb down design. If anything, it allows people to do what they want and create quite personal things, and I think that's a good thing."

ANTICRAFT
KNITTING
BEADING
AND STITCHING
FOR THE
SLIGHTLY
SINISTER
RENÉE RIGDON AND ZABET STEWART

BELLADONNA SL

BY ERSSIE

This project was inspired by the Belladonna plant. Large bobbles glisten wickedly like the dark cherry-like fruit of this poisonous herb also known as Deadly Nightshade and the sleeves gently flare like the small purple fluted flowers. As well as providing an atropine for Venetian ladies to dilate their pupils, the poison has been combined with other fatal herbs to make a flying ointment that could put witches into a trance state close to death just by rubbing ointment onto their temples. It has been well recorded that on these occasions, a body can become uncommonly cold whilst the spirit is absent in another dimension and a lady has to have something in her handbag she can slip on her arms whilst in a strappy evening dress. The sleeves can also be worn under a T-shirt and are easily folded like gloves to pop in your bag for an evening out when a cardigan is just too bulky.

MOOD ENHANCERS:
"Belladonna," *Hyaena* by Siouxsie and the Banshees

SKILLS USED:
Basic knitting (see page 131)
Bobble (as explained in project instructions)

MATERIALS AND TOOLS:
2 balls (227 yards or 204 meters ea) Rowan Kidsilk Night kid mohair/silk/polyester/nylon blend yarn in color 614 Macbeth (Yarn A)
2 (3, 3) balls (103 yards or 93 meters ea) Rooster Almerino Aran baby alpaca/merino wool blend yarn in color 308 Spiced Plum (Yarn B)
1 reel (208 yards or 187 meters) of black knitting elastic for ribbing on upper arm (optional)
1 set 7mm double-point needles, or size needed to obtain gauge (the closest equivalent US size is US #10 [6mm])
1 set 7.5mm double-point needles, or size .5mm larger than smallest needles (the closest equivalent US size is US #10.5 [6.5mm])
1 set US #13 (9mm) double-point needles (or size 2mm larger than smallest needles)
Tapestry needle

GAUGE:
12.5 sts × 17 rows = 4"
on smallest needles, using
held together.

FINISHED SIZE:
Size: Small (Medium, Larg
Sleeve length: 17 (18, 18
Wrist to upper ribbing len
[33, 33]cm)
Upper ribbing length: 3½
10cm)
Wrist circumference: 6 (6
19]cm)
See *Resizing* at the end of
learn how to calculate a c

SPECIAL STITCHES:
Make Bobble (MB)
Row 1: K1, Yo, K1, Yo, K1
the same st. Turn work.
Row 2: P5. Turn work.
Row 3: K5. Turn work.
Row 4: P2tog, P1, P2tog.
Row 5: Sl1 Kwise, K2tog,

NOTES:
Due to the large gauge c
increased at the end of th
the arm, instead of the t
round. All increased stitc
into the established ribb
cating the pattern, some
are made in order to sh
of the ribbing for the wi

For S–M:
*(Ch 4, dc) in next 2 ch 4 sp on back side RS facing, (ch 4, dc in ch 4 sp) on palm side WS facing directly behind next st. Repeat from * twice more. Do not sk sts on backside; only sk sts on palm side. Do not break off but continue to shape pinky finger.
For L–XL:
*(Ch 4, dc) in next 2 ch 4 sp on back side RS facing, (ch 4, dc in ch 4 sp) on palm side WS facing directly behind next st, sk next back side sp. Repeat from * twice more. Do not break off but continue to shape pinky finger.

Right hand finger shaping:
For S–M:
*(Ch 4, dc) in next 2 ch 4 sp on palm side RS facing, (ch 4, dc in ch 4 sp) on back side WS facing directly behind next st. Repeat from * twice more. Do not sk sts on palm side; only sk sts on back side. Do not break off but continue to shape pinky finger.
For L–XL:
*(Ch 4, dc) in next 2 ch 4 sp on palm side RS facing, (ch 4, dc in ch 4 sp) on back side WS facing directly behind next st, sk next palm side sp. Repeat from * twice more. Do not break off but continue to shape pinky finger.

Pinky finger:
(Ch 4, dc) in next 2 st. (ch 4, dc) around to next palm side sp. Work (ch 4, dc) around until next worked space; sk previously worked sp. (Ch 4, dc) evenly in a spiral around in each sp until desired length, ending between the fingers. Sc around in each space to close opening and fasten off. Weave in end to close the opening.

Ring, middle and index fingers:
Join with sl st between fingers. (Ch 6, dc) in next sp. Work (ch 4, dc) evenly in a spiral around in each sp until desired length, ending between the fingers. Sc around in each space to close opening and fasten off. Weave in ends to close the openings. Repeat for each finger.

Open edge:
Join thread at base of index finger and evenly sl st the back and palm sides together, until approximately half-way down the open edge, or until the edge meets the thumb. Fasten off.

Gusset and thumb:
Join with sl st in bottom edge corner and sl st together the open edge for one inch. (Ch 6, dc) in next edge sp. *(Ch 4, dc) around until sp before open edge seam and (ch 4, dc) around. Repeat * once. (Ch 4, dc) around as in other fingers until desired length. Fasten off.

Cuff:
The cuff is worked with the bottom edge upward-facing.
Foundation row: Join thread with sl st in the bottom edge, at the outside (pinky side) of the hand. Ch 8, dc in next sp. *Ch 4, dc in next ch 4 sp. Repeat from * across the bottom edge, ending with dc in the same sp as beginning ch 8. Do not join.
Row 1: Turn. Ch 8, dc in next sp. *Ch 4, dc in next ch 4 sp. Repeat from * across to end of row.
Repeat Row 1 until cuff is desired length, ending with a WS row.
Next Row: Turn. Ch 1. *(3 sc, ch 3, 3 sc) in next ch 4 sp. Repeat from * across to end of the row.
Next Row: Sc around the cuff row edges. Fasten off.

Finishing:
Attach button. Join thread opposite button with sl st and ch short chain for button loop.

Designer bio:
Kathryn Miller lives in Toronto, Ontario, Canada, with her husband and cat. She is an avid crocheter from a long line of needleworkers and can be found at www.dainty-kate.livejournal.com.

58

Tap into the Dark Side

Get ready for a night of candlelit introspection:

1. Put on our favorite song from The Smiths, "Asleep." Set your player to infinite repeat.
2. Turn off all the lights in the house.
3. Stumble blindly around looking for matches and candles.
4. Turn the lights back on.
5. Arrange and light candles.
6. Don't forget to turn the lights back off!
7. Welcome in the darkness. If you aren't suitably depressed by the fifth repeat of the song, you may want to consider joining another crafting subculture.

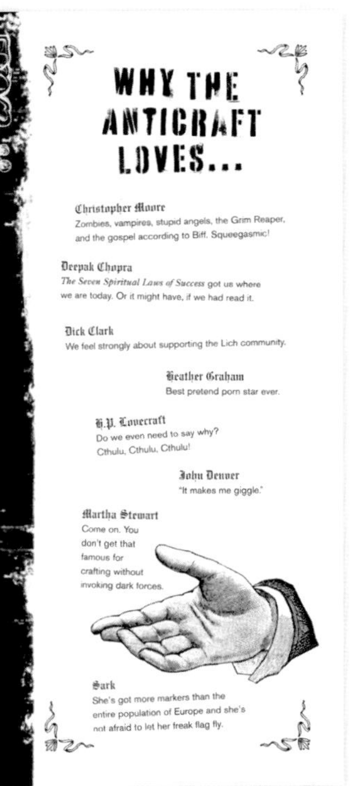

WHY THE ANTICRAFT LOVES...

Christopher Moore
Zombies, vampires, stupid angels, the Grim Reaper, and the gospel according to Biff. Squeegasmic!

Deepak Chopra
The Seven Spiritual Laws of Success got us where we are today. Or it might have, if we had read it.

Dick Clark
We feel strongly about supporting the Lich community.

Heather Graham
Best pretend porn star ever.

H.P. Lovecraft
Do we even need to say why? Cthulu, Cthulu, Cthulu!

John Denver
"It makes me giggle."

Martha Stewart
Come on. You don't get that famous for crafting without invoking dark forces.

Sark
She's got more markers than the entire population of Europe and she's not afraid to let her freak flag fly.

In yet another sign that everything old becomes new again, *Anticraft*, designed by Maya Drozdz, shows a younger generation how to repurpose and reinvent grandma's skills to suit their own, totally modern, somewhat twisted aesthetic.

THE FUTURE OF MAGAZINES

GRIM **REAPER**, MARCUS **PIPER**

Grim Reaper is the nom-de-online-plume of an unwilling-to-be-identified person who runs the blog and website *Magazine Death Pool.* Grim is convinced that, in the future, "We will be seeing fewer magazine launches (we are already) because the risks are just getting too high and nobody wants to invest with those kinds of odds." For Grim, the future belongs to the super glossies. "The magazines that will last the longest and be less susceptible to the Web will be the ones people read for the ads. Big luxury and fashion titles are really the ones we're talking about here," Grim continues. "You can't read *Vogue* online. It's missing the point of taking in those big beautiful ads."

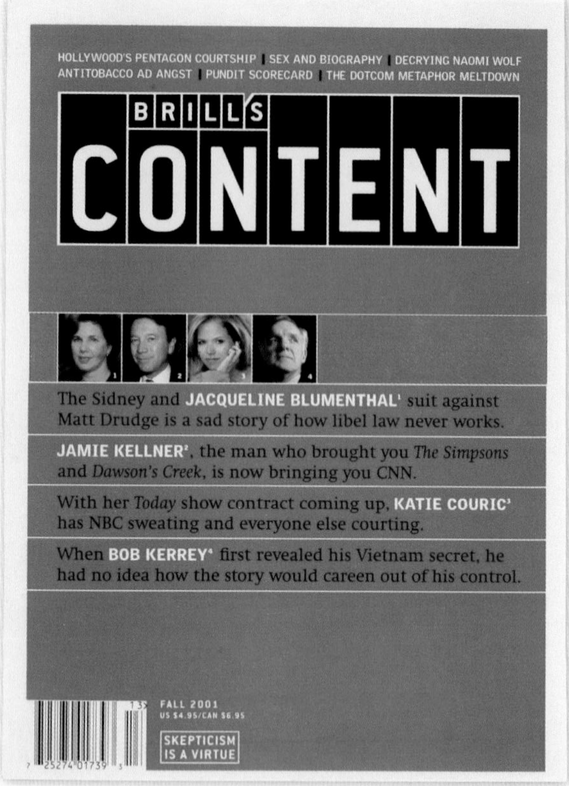

Even though it got good reviews, had in-depth content from great writers, and the best in editorial design, *Brill's Content*, designed by Luke Hayman, lasted only four years. A series of mergers, acquisitions, and other business dealings closed the magazine.

By George Ventura

I was arrested on September 17, 1998. That was the day my world changed forever. I was scheduled to participate in a deposition in Salt Lake City. Chiquita Brands International, Inc., my former employer, had issued a subpoena requesting that I be a witness in a civil suit the company had brought against Cincinnati Enquirer reporter Michael Gallagher, who had coauthored an extensive investigative report published that May about Chiquita's activities in Latin America.

At the time, my career was riding high. I had just been made a shareholder of the largest law firm in Utah, and I was living in Lima, Peru, on an assignment involving an enormous amount of responsibility and trust for one of the firm's biggest clients. I felt as if I were the golden boy, the guy who could pull together intricate deals in chaotic Latin American countries.

I had flown from Lima to Salt Lake City for the deposition at my own expense. I tried to be accommodating and even arranged to have Patrick Anderson, my former roommate at the University of Utah College of Law, accept the subpoena on my behalf. I had not been named or identified in any way in the Enquirer stories, but the subpoena asked that I provide details of any communications I may have had with Gallagher or any other Enquirer employee. Waiting for the court reporter to arrive so the deposition could begin, I joked around with Patrick and his partners, Ken Brown and Mark Moffat. We did know that there was some sort of criminal investigation surrounding the Enquirer stories; a man named Perry

EDITOR'S NOTE

Like most of us, George Ventura is no saint. He had a nice life as a lawyer, corporate executive, husband, and father. In 1996, he left his employer, Cincinnati-based Chiquita Brands International, in part over a compensation dispute.

Disgruntled former employees are among the richest ore for hard-digging reporters to mine, so when *Cincinnati Enquirer* reporters Michael Gallagher and Cameron McWhirter looked into the alleged dark dealings of Chiquita in Latin America, Ventura served as a willing confidential source.

Perhaps foolishly, this attorney, who thought himself savvy and world-wise, entrusted reporters he had never met with information that could destroy his life if his identity as a source were revealed. As do many confidential sources, Ventura told the reporters things he shouldn't have. Usually, no one finds out about such indiscretions, because such confidentiality agreements are honored. That we know Ventura's name at all means that something went very, very wrong.

The Enquirer stories, published on

(CONTINUED ON PAGE 86)

84 FEBRUARY 2000

Former corporate attorney George Ventura never wanted you to know his name.

Public to Press:
Cool It
yes 49% no 36%
DOES THE PRESS GO TOO FAR IN PURSUING THE TRUTH?
America may have a uniquely free press, but a surprising number of Americans don't like the results. In a ground-breaking poll, the people weigh in on curbing the media, the outlets we most trust, and our conflicted feelings about sensationalism. The chief pollster explains.
By Frank Luntz
OVERALL, WHAT IS YOUR OPINION OF THE NEWS MEDIA?
FAVORABLE 45.5%
very favorable 8.6%
somewhat favorable 36.9%
UNFAVORABLE 44.6%
somewhat unfavorable 29.1%
very unfavorable 15.4%
OTHER 10%
don't know/declined 10%
74 MARCH 2000
no 74% yes 22%
HOSTAGE AT GUNPOINT ON LIVE TV: SHOULD A STATION BROADCAST?
yes 59% no 38%
WOULD YOU WATCH?
no 91%
SHOULD THE MEDIA HAVE USED EXTRA-POWERFUL LENSES TO PHOTOGRAPH JFK JR.'S GRIEVING FAMILY?
no 82% yes 15%
WOULD YOU HAVE WATCHED FOOTAGE OF THE BODIES INSIDE THE PLANE WRECKAGE?
no 76% yes 20%
SHOULD EXECUTIONS BE SHOWN LIVE ON TELEVISION?
no 75% yes 21%
WOULD YOU WATCH?
BRILL'S CONTENT 75

FOCUS

For the magazine of the future to be successful, Grim Reaper offers a few tips, along with directions for those destined to take quick trip across the river Styx.

SUCCESS:

1. There is a genuine audience that is big enough to sustain the magazine.
2. There is a sensible digital strategy for making money. It helps to be a magazine that is less susceptible to prime Web audiences (e.g., young men and women, personal finance, recipes, etc).
3. There is some originality in the concept, delivering something that isn't out there yet.

THE DEATH KNELL:

1. Catering to advertisers before genuine readers
2. Copying another, more successful, magazine's concept
3. Desperate attempts to win an audience, whether it be trying different kinds of covers with regular frequency and/or shifting editorial direction
4. Producing a magazine that nobody really wants, except perhaps in the nail place (as I like to call it)
5. Getting rid of vital advertising and editorial staff
6. Going head to head with popular Web topics
7. No sound digital strategy

THE NEWSSTAND

Long-term success

With more new mags hitting the shelves than ever before, how do you make a new title stick – or keep an established brand at the top? *Julie Tomlin* investigates

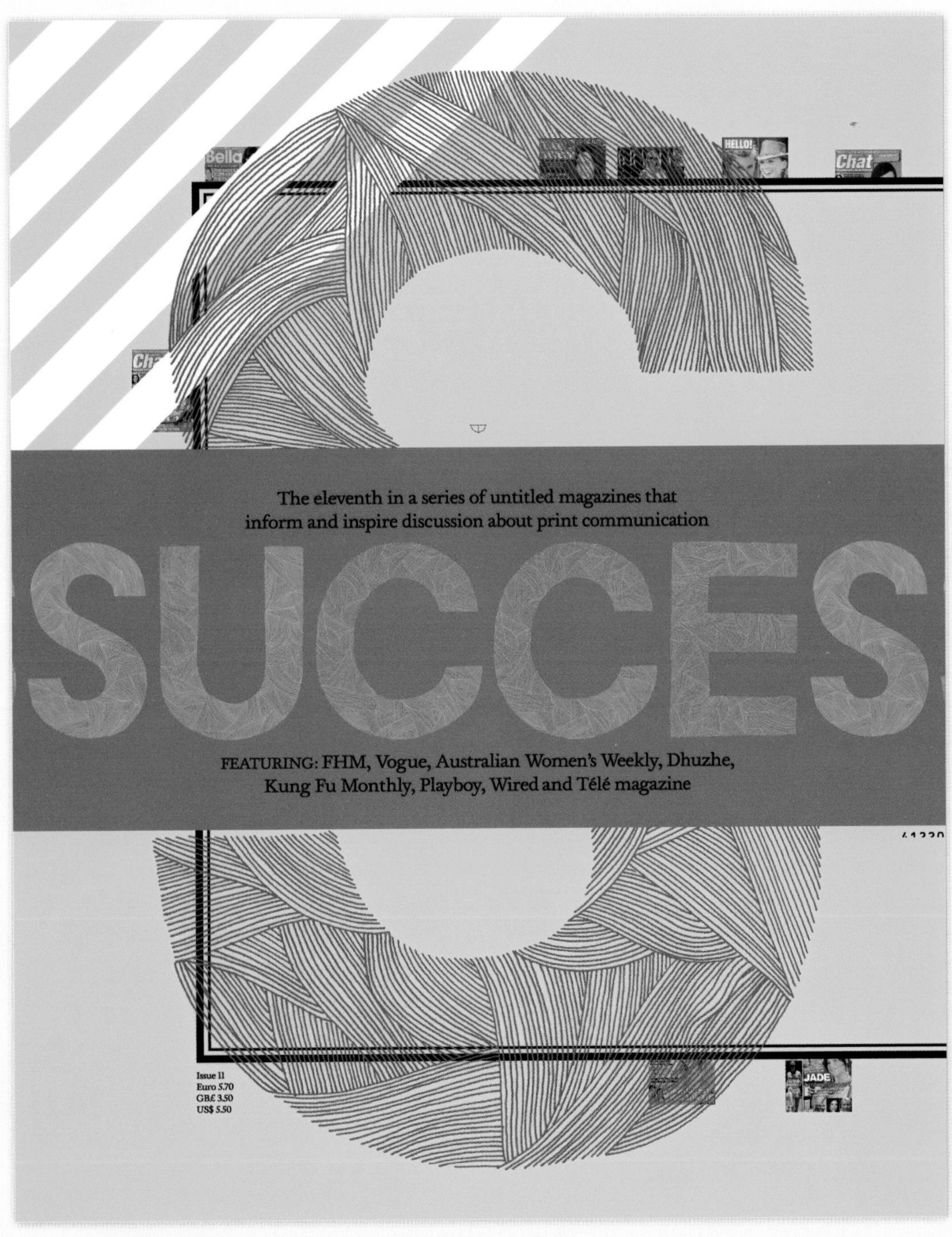

The eleventh in a series of untitled magazines that
inform and inspire discussion about print communication
SUCCES
FEATURING: FHM, Vogue, Australian Women's Weekly, Dhuzhe,
Kung Fu Monthly, Playboy, Wired and Télé magazine
Issue 11
Euro 5.70
GB£ 3.50
US$ 5.50

M-real Galerie Papers, designed by Jeremy Leslie, is the ultimate meta-magazine, a publication about publications.

For his part, Marcus Piper feels that magazines should aspire to even more than simply staying out of Charon's ferryboat; they should try to be relevant, not just profitable. And to do this, they need to be more than something that is flipped through for the pretty pictures or read for the scintillating content. "Magazines are going in two very distinct directions," he says. "There's the ones you pick up to read on the train ride home and then throw away, and the ones you buy almost like you would a book, as something to keep and collect. But to be successful, magazines have to think outside of the pages and get into running events: for example, running awards programs, having an online presence, or selling products," he says.

For many publications, this future is already here and goes beyond the ubiquitous awards programs offered by most design magazines. *Good* holds regular events to help create and coalesce its community of readers and "people who give a damn." *Adbusters* created the now internationally recognized "Buy Nothing Day" and "TV Turnoff Week." Wolverine Farm Publishing, publishers of *Matter*, also publishes books, runs an all-volunteer used bookstore and coffee house, and hosts a variety of events that combine bicycles, microbrews, and "literary antics." *IdN* publishes books, creates events, and includes a DVD of multimedia graphics with every issue of the magazine.

These extras are not beyond the purview of graphic designers, who should be "thinking beyond the page," as Piper says, "by making the magazine more of an experience, more alive and exciting and creating dimension. We have to get back to what was beautiful about magazines in the beginning: You can touch it and smell it and varnish it and cut holes in it, and you can't do that on the screen. Pushing the boundaries is what will keep magazines alive."

***M-real Galerie Papers*, designed by Jeremy Leslie**

MAGAZINES AND BOOKS

RESOURCES

American Institute of Graphic Art (AIGA), www.aiga.org

The Association of Magazine Editors (ASME), www.asme.magazine.org

Magazine Publishers of America (MPA), www.magazine.org

The Society of Publication Designers (SPD), www.spd.org

There are many blogs and websites dedicated to magazine and book design. A few are listed below, and on each of these sites there are multiple links to other, related blogs and sites.

www.blogmagazine.com

www.covers.fwis.com

www.designingmagazines.com

www.magazinedeathpool.com

www.magculture.com

www.mediabistro.com

www.mrmagazine.com

www.nytimesbooks.blogspot.com

ACKNOWLEDGMENTS

My deepest thanks go to the art directors, designers, editors, illustrators, and others who so generously shared their insights and experiences with me, and thereby, with our readers. It is your hard-won wisdom that made this book possible.

Many thanks to Winnie Prentiss, Emily Potts, Betsy Gammons, Regina Grenier, and the rest of the team at Rockport who helped to make this book come true.

And, as always, my love and thanks to JEL for everything else.

ABOUT THE AUTHOR

Laurel Saville writes books, articles, essays, short stories, and corporate communications from her home in Albany, New York. Her work has been published in several magazines, journals, and newspapers, including *Adbusters*, *STEP Inside Design*, and *Dynamic Graphics*. This is her third book for Rockport Publishers; previous titles include *Design Secrets: Furniture* and *Outdoor Stonework*. She is also a contributing author to the forthcoming, *100 Habits of Successful Freelance Designers*.